High/Scope K–3 Curriculum Series

Language & Literacy

Related High/Scope K–3 Curriculum Materials

K–3 Curriculum Guides (now available):

Science
Mathematics

K–3 Curriculum Videotapes:

Active Learning
Classroom Environment
Language & Literacy
Mathematics

Related Publications of the High/Scope Press:

Young Children & Computers
High/Scope Survey of Early Childhood Software—1991
A School Administrator's Guide to Early Childhood Programs

Available from
The High/Scope Press
600 North River Street, Ypsilanti, Michigan 48198
313/485-2000, FAX 313/485-0704

High/Scope K–3 Curriculum Series

Language & Literacy

Field Test Edition

by

Jane M. Maehr

Series Consultant: Frank F. Blackwell

The High/Scope Press
Ypsilanti, Michigan

Published by the High/Scope® Press
A division of the
High/Scope Educational Research Foundation
600 North River Street
Ypsilanti, Michigan 48198
313/485-2000, FAX 313/485-0704

Editors: Lynn Taylor, Mary Vardigan

Library of Congress Catalog-in-Publication Data Number: 90-22885

ISBN 0-929816-23-4

Printed in the United States of America

10 9 8 7 6 5 4 3 2

Contents

Part 2: Key Experiences, Activities, & Assessment

Acknowledgments

We appreciate the assistance of teachers and students in the many classrooms we visited to gather information for this guide, collect examples of children's writing, and photograph children in active learning situations. We especially thank Follow Through Director Dianne Watkins of the Richmond, Virginia, Public Schools; the staff of Fairfield Court Elementary School in Richmond, Virginia: Ernestine Bennett, Dolores Brunson, Deborah Carter, Daisy Howard-Douglas, Sandra Hurt, Greg Neylan, Bessie Royster, Louise Smith, Joan Wilson, and Elizabeth York, Principal; and the students in their classes. We also thank Cindy Williams and her students at St. Isidore School in Grand Rapids, Michigan.

▼

Part 1

A Framework for K–3 Language & Literacy

1
▼

Language & Literacy: Getting Started

Planning a journey poses many exciting questions: Where will you go? Where have you been before? When will you start? Can you take more than one route to get there? Will you enjoy the trip? What will you do along the way? How will you judge your progress as you travel? What will you do when you arrive at your destination? Our approach to the subject of language and literacy in this High/Scope K–3 curriculum guide is in many ways analogous to planning and taking a journey. On our trip we explore children's **language**—the expression of ideas in oral form—and the ways children move toward **literacy**—the mastery of language in written forms. We map out a destination: helping children achieve fluency in both oral and written language. We review historical as well as current perspectives on the acquisition of language skills. We lay out some instructional paths, so we can facilitate language development in young children through the use of techniques that are appropriate, enjoyable, functional, and educationally sound. Finally, we suggest ways to assess our progress as we help children become effective communicators in both oral and written language.

To assure a successful start, we define in the next section the terminology that will be used frequently throughout this book, and we introduce some of the philosophical underpinnings of the High/Scope approach to language. Following that, we look at how children acquire language and enter into the world of literacy.

And it wasn't just a word.
It was a whole sentence.
And that sentence was...
"I made it!"

— In *Leo the Late Bloomer*
by Robert Kraus

Some Definitions

Embarking on the "language and literacy journey" becomes even more exciting when we realize that recent research and scholarship relating to language have brought new and broadened perspectives on the topic. These fresh perspectives demand that we reexamine our approach to language and literacy and that we alter the way we define our terms.

Textbook titles provide examples of this recent shift in terminology. Respected textbooks of the 1970s carried such titles as *Teaching Young Children to Read* (Durkin, 1972) and *The Development of Language and Reading in Young Children* (Pflaum, 1978). Yet the 1986 edition of Pflaum's book is titled *The Development of Language and Literacy in Young Children*. Other titles of the 1980s—*Literacy Learning in the Early Years: Through Children's Eyes* (Gibson, 1989), *The Emergence of Literacy* (Hall, 1987), and *Emergent Literacy: Writing and Reading* (Teale & Sulzby, 1986)—point to further changes in the field. We are redefining our approach to oral language, reading, and writing to reflect an inclusive view, i.e., one in which oral and written language are bound into a system that is useful and has meaning.

This holistic perspective toward language also encourages the use of the term **literacy** in a wider sense as a way of incorporating all print forms of language into a unified expression. When he uses the term literacy, Nigel Hall (1987) expands the sense of the word by pointing to relationships that exist between oral language and learning about written language. Pflaum (1986) urges that all the information about print forms, e.g., letter names and letter-sound relationships, not be isolated from the main premise of language use—which is that language, whether spoken or written, communicates meaning.

In this book we necessarily at times discuss the different spoken and written forms of language separately; we isolate "speaking," "listening," "reading," and "writing" to describe accurately the strategies involved with the development of each of these discrete skills. But we attempt whenever possible to communicate the view that all forms of language exist in relationship to one another. That the spoken and written forms of language are interconnected is of special concern during the years when young children are gaining control over modes of expression. Arbitrarily separating out the different forms can hinder or obstruct a full understanding of the nature of language development and mastery.

Another term that has only recently appeared in language textbooks is **emergent literacy.** Sulzby (1986) defines emergent literacy as early, unconventional forms of writing and reading that precede conventional writing and reading. As we explain in the next chapter, the idea that literacy develops gradually is representative of the newer view. Those espousing this view believe that literacy develops in all normal children who possess the genetically determined capacity for language present at birth. From this "language capacity," literacy emerges over time in an environment where adults accept and support children's early forms of symbolization and encourage their further attempts to understand and to master the process.

Goodman (in Manning, 1987) uses the term **whole language** to describe "curricula that keep language whole and in the context of its thoughtful use in real situations." Reflecting this focus, the High/Scope K–3 Curriculum views holistically and integrates naturally the skills of listening, speaking, writing, and reading language. In addition, the High/Scope approach to language embraces the concept of *process*: we see the emergence of language and literacy in children as a dynamic, ongoing process of discovery involving both children and adults during the early elementary years. In this spirit of discovery, we begin our journey, seeking to translate theory into effective practice. The journey results in decisions about methodology, scheduling, and materials—all made within a context of sound research about how children learn and how teachers teach.

A Look at Children and Language

How do children acquire language and how is language acquisition related to the social context of the home? In recent years many scholars and researchers have addressed these questions, and their studies have resulted in new theories that have revolutionized the field. Until the early 1970s linguists and psychologists were primarily concerned with how children learn to generate the phonological and grammatical units of language. Consequently,

...Without looking to left or right, Jamie hurried up the aisle. Father and Saro followed him. Beside the pallet he dropped to his knees.

"Here's a Christmas gift for the Child," he said, clear and strong.

"Father!" gasped Saro. "Father, listen to Jamie!"

The woman turned back the covers from the baby's face. Jamie gently laid the orange beside the baby's tiny hand.

"And here's a Christmas gift for the Mother," Jamie said to the woman.

He put a dime in her hand...

In the hush that followed, Christmas in all its joy and majesty came to Hurricane Gap. And it wasn't so long ago at that.

— In *A Certain Small Shepherd* by Rebecca Caudill

studies of infant sounds and attempts to isolate just how sounds are produced were important research areas.

More recently, however, research on language has shifted its focus, researchers have begun to approach language from the perspective of its primary function—communication between humans. Hall (1987) quotes Michael Halliday, the British linguist, as saying, "Learning one's mother tongue is learning the use of language, and the meanings, or rather the meaning potential, associated with them . . . The child is surrounded by language, but not in the form of grammars and dictionaries, or of randomly chosen words and sentences, or of undirected monologue. What he encounters is 'text,' or language in use: sequences of language articulated each within itself and within the situation in which it occurs. Such sequences are purposive—though very varied in purpose—and have an evident social significance" (pp. 12–13).

Language within a cultural context, Hall (1987) suggests, enables children to understand words in spoken sentences (continuous speech) and to use words to "regulate many aspects of their lives and in turn understand the regulation of their lives by others" (p. 15). Thus Hall sees language acquisition as an "interactionary" process rather than as an innate skill or a learned behavior resulting from imitation of adults. Language acquisition, then, is a vital "collaboration" between children's genetic predispositions and their environments.

Children attend to language because it enables them to make sense of the life they are living. The mechanical aspects of language (grammatical constructions and phonological characteristics) are important only insofar as they support or impede children's understanding of and ability to function in the world. For example, consider the early interactions between parents and infants. The structure of language is present as parents "converse" with their infants, but this early conversation is of secondary importance to the primary purpose of the exchange, which is to communicate and to connect. Hall (1987) suggests that "the child looks through language and sees the social function of the interaction. It is for this reason that children become users, indeed proficient users of language, without achieving what has come to be called linguistic awareness, i.e., an understanding of what language is, rather than an understanding of how it is used." (p. 13). In other words, children learn how to make language work for them.

This interactive view of language establishes important roles for both parents and children in the acquisition process. As parents communicate with infants in simple, clearly enunciated speech, that is frequently redundant and characterized by "motherese" or "baby-talk," parent and child begin to build a "scaffold" that expands as parents gradually convey to infants the purpose of language or speech.

This early interactive process generally does not include any kind of formal instruction or extensive error correction, however. While at times the parent-child language interaction may provide instruction or information, it is usually the child who initiates these interactions and terminates the involvement. More frequently, early language interchanges between parent and child are characterized by intuitive actions and reactions that permit the active participation of both parties and provide additional opportunities for language use.

Just as important as the informal, "natural" quality of these early exchanges is the fact that the experiences are embedded in pleasurable situations. The spontaneous conversations that occur in connection with enjoyable activities—eating, playing games, and other situations involving gratification—are likely to lead to pleasurable associations and to the desire to recreate the experiences.

A Look at Literacy

Both print forms and oral forms of language aid communication. The difference is that literacy, even in the early stages, offers the potential for communication to extend to individuals or groups beyond the range of hearing. Speaking, reading, and writing are explicitly social actions; and these actions seek to achieve some useful purpose within a community. We call these actions—i.e., actions that bring about speech, reading, and writing—**literacy events**. The understanding and knowledge that accrue from them is **literacy learning.**

Today's children are growing up in a literacy-oriented world. Print abounds in homes, schools, and businesses. Life today is quite different than life on the American frontier of the 1700s or 1800s, where newspapers were scarce and books were the possessions of a wealthy few. Today, millions of newspapers are printed across the country

...Owl lived at The Chestnuts, an old world residence of great charm, which was grander than anybody else's, or seemed so to Bear, because it had both a knocker and a bell-pull. Underneath the knocker there was a notice which said:

PLES RING IF AN RNSER IS REQIRD.

Underneath the bell-pull there was a notice which said:

PLEZ CNOKE IF AN RNSR IS NOT REQID.

These notices had been written by Christopher Robin, who was the only one in the forest who could spell; for Owl, wise though he was in many ways, able to read and write and spell his own name WOL, yet somehow went all to pieces over delicate words like MEASLES and BUTTERED TOAST ... .

— In *Winnie-the-Pooh* by A. A. Milne

once or twice a day, and books and magazines fill shelves in libraries, grocery stores, and many homes. Indeed, printed material surrounds us. As children strive to understand all of this printed matter in the context of their own lives, they see print wrapping McDonald's™ hamburgers and covering the Domino's Pizza™ box. They see print on signs indicating where cars should stop on the street and print defining which interstate highways lead to their city. Print identifies the "start" button on the microwave oven, accompanies commercials on television, distinguishes "Sesame Street" from other programs, and even decorates infant T-shirts.

In environments rich in print, parents or caregivers must interact with children to bring some sort of sense to the situation. Most often, the adult plays the role of facilitator, rather than instructor. Adults answer questions and provide names; they warn of obvious dangers such as hot stoves and open stairs; they look up phone numbers, read and react to salary checks, clip coupons, and write up grocery lists. Through their exchanges with adults, children pick up information that augments their knowledge and adds new layers of meaning to what they experience.

Both oral language facility and literacy emerge in early childhood—not so much as a result of "direct instruction" but as a result of children's instinctive desires to acquire understanding and give meaning to the world and the people around them. In such a social context, language and literacy develop holistically in relation to everyday routines and associations.

Now that we have looked at the way children acquire facility with language and begin to make sense of the symbolization of language, we will examine how adults have viewed the reading and writing process through the years and how children actually *do* learn to be literate users of language.

2
▼

Learning to Read & Write

Attitudes toward learning to read and write have changed dramatically over the years. Past generations' reasons for pursuing literacy and the method they used to teach reading and writing seem puzzling to us today as we explore our own views on learning about oral and written language. In this chapter we summarize historical approaches toward literacy and compare them with the emerging view—a view that is currently redefining how children learn to read and write.

Tell me a story, Mama,
About when you were little.

What kind of story, baby?

— In *Tell Me a Story, Mama,* by Angela Johnson

The Historical View

Encouraging children to read for pleasure or to express themselves in oral or printed language were foreign concepts to early Americans. But, these people did attach great importance to literacy as a means to other ends: early New Englanders valued literacy because it enabled their children to read the lessons of Scripture and to be instructed in leading the moral life.

Early reading materials reflected these widely held goals. The few books that were available to children featured verses from the Bible, homilies on how to use valuable time, and admonitions about honesty and thrift. Early texts bore little resemblance to today's colorful readers and trade books, but they did reveal Puritan settlers' sense of urgency about developing a literate population in the New World.

As the 13 colonies joined together to become the United States, reasons other than religious or moral ones argued for encouraging people to read and write. The population grew and the settlements spread; information could not always travel by word of mouth. A developing republican form of government emphasized the notion of a citizenry informed about issues. At the very least, citizens needed to be able to read announcements about new taxes or to know where to meet when the militia was drilling.

Commerce also contributed to the growing need for literacy in the 1800s. Opportunities to develop businesses and to manufacture industrial products opened up for those who had the ability to read and write coupled with sound business acumen.

As the United States continued to expand rapidly, other utilitarian reasons for emphasizing literacy in children came to the fore. To assimilate numerous foreign-born immigrants into young America's melting pot, information of various kinds, including patriotic messages and information about reasonable hygiene, had to reach the new populations. One way this could be accomplished was by ensuring that all children spoke the same language and that they learned to read and write the language as well.

Just as there were several different reasons for teaching children to read and write, there were several different methods for accomplishing the task. In fact, the methods of reading and writing instruction popular at one time or another were many, and frequently they represented only the bias of one author. In general, the methods did not incorporate pedagogical principles or any specific knowledge about the physical, emotional, and cognitive development of children.

Some methods of reading and writing instruction stressed identifying words but paid little attention to their meanings. Some spelling techniques emphasized naming and spelling letters and nonsense syllables as preparation for spelling lists of words. This spelling method became a popular one, as the following example from a "loud school" in Georgia during the 1800s demonstrates:

> The teacher had an odd contrivance nailed to a post set up in the middle of the room. It was known as a "spelling board." When he pulled the string to which the board was fastened, the students gave attention. If he let the board halfway down, the scholars could spell out words in moderate tones. If he pulled the

board up tight, everybody "spelled to themselves."
When he gave the cord a pull until the plank
dropped down, the hubbub began. Everything went
with a roar. Just as loud as you pleased, you could
spell anything. People along the road were happy to
know the children were having their lessons (in Goodman, Shannon, Freeman, & Murphy, 1988, p. 6).

Leigh McGuffey published the *New Eclectic Primer in
Pronouncing Orthography* in 1868 with a modified alphabet designed to overcome the lack of symbol-sound correspondence in English and to make phonics instruction
more effective. In reporting on a form of mechanical instruction used in Chicago in the late 1890s, Joseph
Mayer Rice documented yet another strange practice:

> After entering the room containing the youngest
> pupils, the principal said to the teacher, "Begin with
> the mouth movements and go right straight through"
> ... . About fifty pupils now began in concert to give
> utterance to the sounds of a, e, and oo varying their
> order, thus: a, e, oo, a, e, oo; e, a, oo, etc. ... When
> some time had been spent in thus maneuvering the
> jaw, the teacher remarked, "Your tongues are not
> loose." Fifty pupils now put out their tongues and
> wagged them in all directions. The principal compli-
> mented the children highly on their wagging (in Good-
> man et al., 1988, p. 8).

Commonly Held Assumptions

Commonly held assumptions and beliefs formed the basis
for most of the early instructional methodologies. These
assumptions about teaching literacy skills remained popular and relatively consistent throughout the 19th century
and well into the 20th century. Nigel Hall (1987) identifies
six:

■ Reading and writing are primarily visual-perceptual
processes involving printed unit/sound relationships.

■ Children are not ready to learn to read and write
until they are five or six years old.

■ Children have to be taught to be literate.

■ The teaching of literacy must be systematic and sequential in operation.

■ Proficiency in the "basic" skills has to be acquired before one can act in a literate way.

■ Teaching the "basic" skills of literacy is a neutral, value-free activity (p. 2).

Despite agreement among educators of the time about the value of these assumptions, educators and researchers continued to search for the "one best way" to teach children to read and write. Nevertheless, as a result of these beliefs, educators of the time came to define literacy skills as mechanical processes and to view these mechanical processes as more important than thinking and reasoning. Thinking about the meaning of the printed text was considered to be a high-level skill that emerged long after children had practiced decoding—or unpuzzling—the features of the print. The underlying assumptions about how children learn to read and write divorced the teaching of literacy skills from any learning experience that occurred at home. In fact, the assumptions failed to connect any learning that children might have gained *before* coming to school with any that would occur *during* school.

The prevailing assumptions and beliefs about teaching literacy skills also defined the role of the teacher. According to the accepted theory, responsibility for determining the "when" and "how" of instruction lay solely with the teacher. The teacher was viewed as a specialist who carried out a task considered to be so specialized that it could not be accomplished by anyone who had not learned its inner secrets. The teacher instructed students in this systematic, sequential, and somewhat mysterious "rite of passage" within the confines of the school. This physical location emphasized the separation of school language learning from the social context of home, community, and early learning experience.

The growing interest in investigation and experimentation of the early 1900s produced a climate in which some of the commonly held assumptions about teaching children to read and write were challenged and reexamined. This reexamination occurred partly as a result of the recognition that little attempt had been made to organize instruction around pedagogical principles.

Moreover, as Goodman et al. (1988) point out, the turn of the century was a time when business and industry found it both fashionable and profitable to analyze the discrete movements and actions of workers to determine exactly how tasks might be streamlined and made more efficient. This national interest in productivity and scientific management formed a natural backdrop for the work of psychologists such as Edward L. Thorndike and James Watson.

Thorndike conducted experiments on animals that led to descriptions of how knowledge was acquired and how teachers could best organize the environment in which learning would occur. Goodman et al. (1988) summarize the important contributions of Thorndike:

1. From associationist psychologists, he took the notion that learning is ordered, that efficient learning follows one best sequence—*The Law of Readiness.*

2. From James Watson, Thorndike accepted the idea that practice strengthens the bond between a stimulus and a response—*The Law of Exercise.*

3. From his own experiments, he concluded that rewards influenced the stimulus-response connection—*The Law of Effect.*

4. And from later work, Thorndike developed the idea that the learning of a particular stimulus-response connection should be tested separately and under the same conditions in which it was learned—*The Law of Identical Elements* (p. 12).

The basis for much of modern reading instruction arose largely as an outgrowth of these attempts to generate theories about the acquisition of knowledge and about effective learning environments, although the new theories were positioned against the familiar background of the earlier assumptions about literacy. Thorndike's "Laws of Learning" recommended analyzing methodology, measuring the results of methodology with tests, and adopting the most efficient methods. These new procedures, along with other results, influenced the report of the National Society for the Study of Education in 1919. William S. Gray, the principal spokesman for the Society, published the *Principles of Method in Teaching Reading, as Derived from Scientific Investigation*; in these 48 maxims developed from summaries of scientific investigation of reading, he formulated the criteria on which basal readers have been constructed ever since (Goodman et al., 1988).

This scientific approach to instructional methodology quickly led to the introduction of scripted instruction books for teachers, many of whom were poorly educated and unprepared for the monumental "specialist" role assigned to them. For several reasons the manuals were designed to allow teachers to "do" rather than to "think." First of all, few administrators or supervisors were trained to support teachers in their instructional tasks, so teachers worked, for the most part, "on their own." Second, the manuals reflected the growing national interest in scientific methodology and were intended to increase productivity. Finally, many in the field believed that standardizing and routinizing the practice of teachers was important, and the manuals accomplished these goals.

The market for these instructional materials grew rapidly—and for understandable reasons. The publishers developed formats that were more attractive than any used before. The texts for children were colorful, and manuals for teachers provided step-by-step instruction. In many cases, "basal reading systems" expanded to include prepared work for children to do at their desks, skill testing, and entire classroom management systems.

As a result of new theories about learning and teaching, some variations in methodologies began to appear, but these variations tended to cycle in or out within the context of basal systems. For example, at one point, a methodology that was widely incorporated into reading series advocated a "look-say" method of reading; students were encouraged to capture words by sight rather than through a phonetic or letter-sound relationship. In 1955, in the widely read *Why Johnny Can't Read*, Rudolph Flesch denounced the reading texts currently in use but actually Flesch was criticizing the *poor design* of the reading materials that rejected the teaching of phonics rather than the theories on which the books were based.

At about the same time E. L. Dolch (1954), an earlier proponent of standardization, openly attacked the basal series movement by speaking out against the effort to "teacher-proof" materials and suggesting that such programs produced limited results. Another researcher, Jeanne Chall (1967), a staunch advocate of programs featuring strong phonological connections, questioned the scientific validity of basal materials after she conducted a four-year study of content in the materials.

Occasional criticisms of teachers' dependency on basal reading materials continued. Drawing on results of a series of studies, reading researcher Dolores Durkin (1974, 1975, 1978-79, 1981) attempted to modify teachers' reliance on the materials. Still, careful marketing, concern for standardization, and convenience all contributed to increasing, rather than decreasing, use. Although by all measures teachers were better educated, more prepared to exercise their own initiative in teaching reading, and less in need of the regimentation built into reading systems, 94 percent of the 10,000 elementary teachers surveyed by the Educational Products Information Exchange in 1977 relied on basal materials (Goodman et al., 1987).

The Commission on Reading

In 1983 the National Academy of Education's Commission on Education and Public Policy, with the sponsorship of the National Institute of Education, established the Commission on Reading. The Commission was mandated to "locate topics on which there has been appreciable research and scholarship. . .and gather panels of experts from within the Academy and elsewhere to survey, interpret, and synthesize research findings" (Anderson, Hiebert, Scott, & Wilkinson, 1985, p. viii). The Commission's work might have resulted in little more than a prosaic examination of research and a recital of common practice; but when it published *Becoming a Nation of Readers* in 1985, the Commission set the stage for a spirited reevaluation of the nature of reading and the process by which children learn to read. Only a short time before, the educational community had been advised that they were *A Nation at Risk* (Carnegie, 1983). Understandably, the Commission's report and research findings were read and debated extensively.

The Commission began by declaring that "Reading is the process of constructing meaning from written texts. It is a complex skill requiring the coordination of a number of interrelated sources of information" (Anderson et al., 1985, p. 7). The Commission supported this definition with a summary that advocated a proper balance between mastering the whole act of reading and practicing the component mechanical skills. The Commission's summary continues:

Children "read to learn" as they "learn to read."

■ **Skilled reading is constructive**. Becoming a skilled reader requires learning to reason about written material using knowledge from everyday life and from disciplined fields of study.

■ **Skilled reading is fluent.** Becoming a skilled reader depends upon mastering basic processes to the point where they are automatic, so that attention is freed for the analysis of meaning.

■ **Skilled reading is strategic**. Becoming a skilled reader requires learning to control one's reading in relation to one's purpose, the nature of the material, and whether one is comprehending.

■ **Skilled reading is motivated**. Becoming a skilled reader requires learning to sustain attention and learning that written material can be interesting and informative.

■ **Skilled reading is a lifelong pursuit**. Becoming a skilled reader is a matter of continuous practice, development, and refinement (Anderson et al., 1985, p. 18).

The Commission on Reading urged that instructors devote increased attention to the value of *early reading to young children*; that schools develop additional preschool and kindergarten programs focusing on reading, writing, and oral language; and that the educational community pursue increased efforts to strengthen comprehension instruction.

The Commission's report also addressed the issues of instructional materials used for reading and the pacing and methodology employed in the teaching of reading. The report expressed concern about lengthy phonics instruction; about the extensive use of workbooks and skill sheets used to develop isolated, discrete skills; and about contrived and frequently meaningless text used as the basis for instruction. The Commission expressed hope that the effective practices of the best reading teachers in the country could be identified and shared with others. Finally, in what seemed like the most fundamental concern raised, the report urged that children spend more time writing and reading independently.

An Emerging View

The attempt of the Commission on Reading to establish reading as part of a child's general language development represented something of a departure from standard practice. First of all, Commission members chose not to regard reading as one discrete skill to be isolated from other areas of literacy. While active investigation of the reading/writing process had been ongoing for quite some time, the results of this investigation signalled a clear shift in focus; they pointed to **literacy as arising from meaningful interchanges with adults and other members of the society.**

Second, this new focus reflected an interest in examining the world and perspective of the child. Where earlier research on children's thinking had tended to be laboratory-based, research on how children learn now expanded outward to home and community settings as well as natural school settings. Research also extended downward to include the study of younger children—infants and toddlers.

In pioneering work begun in 1966, New Zealand's Marie Clay stressed the gradual development of children's perceptual awareness of the customs involved in written English. She described, for example, occasions when creative writing activities appeared to be of special importance to the organization of reading behaviors.

Additional work by Kenneth Goodman (in Hall, 1987) in the U.S. and Frank Smith (1971, 1982) in Canada described reading as a natural process involving the reader in linguistic, cognitive, and social strategies. This work further suggested that children approach print in the same way that adults approach it—expecting print to have meaning. Rather than assuming that literacy was solely a perceptual process, both Goodman and Smith held that literacy involved a social perspective and that it was a cognitive activity. **Put simply, reading is more than letters to be un-puzzled (decoded). Reading has to make sense in the context in which it occurs.**

These researchers contended that when children work to understand print, they try different approaches; some efforts are successful, and some result in mistakes or errors. Kenneth Goodman and Yetta Goodman (in Hall, 1987) concluded that analyzing the errors, or "miscues," that children make in reading substantiated claims that children are "seekers after meaning, motivated by the need to comprehend," since most errors still preserve meaning.

This line of investigation, coupled with investigations into literacy before school and studies of "early readers" (Durkin, 1966; Bissex, 1980), had a major impact on the underlying assumptions that had served so long as the framework for much literacy instruction. Bissex (1980) documented her four-year-old son's progress in learning to read in *GYNS AT WRK: A Child Learns to Read and Write*. That this child came to reading primarily through writing reinforced the emerging holistic view on literacy. It also supported the findings of Durkin (1966) that indeed there were children who were not particularly gifted but who were reading before they arrived at school—before they had been formally instructed.

Such findings led educators and researchers to raise interesting questions: If learning to read *could* occur before or apart from carefully orchestrated "pre-reading skill" sequences, might reading be a naturally evolving process? And if such a natural process *could* occur, did teachers need to sequence reading instruction as strictly as they had in the past? Did they need to assume total responsibility for teaching a child to read? This reevaluation prompted an additional inquiry—troubling to some who had come to hold age six as *the* prescribed time for introducing reading instruction—into whether neural systems had to be sufficiently mature before teachers could safely attempt literacy-based activities.

Yetta Goodman's work offered some tentative answers to the questions posed by the continuing investigations. She suggested that, indeed, literacy-based activities did not need to be delayed until age six. Goodman contended that reading and writing were not primarily visual/perceptual skills involving mainly unit-sound relationships. She held, instead, that "reading consists of optical, perceptual, syntactic and semantic cycles each melting into the next as readers try to get to meaning as efficiently as possible using minimal time and energy" (in Hall, 1987, p. 7). Goodman maintained that children did not have to be taught to be literate. In fact, she said, "My research has shown that literacy develops naturally in all children in our literate society" (in Hall, 1987, p. 8).

The notion of "naturalness" continued to interest researchers. In several studies of early reading, researcher Elizabeth Sulzby (1981, 1982, 1985, 1986) asserted that while young children's engagement in literacy activities is not similar in all ways to the activities of adults, the engagement represents developing or emerging literacy skill. Sulzby found that as children encounter speaking, reading, and writing experiences in everyday situations, they try to figure out how relationships between the forms of expression work. This emerging understanding and the behaviors children demonstrate portray young children in the process of becoming literate—hence the term **emergent literacy.**

The new paradigm suggests a need for new assumptions. These new guiding principles have far-reaching implications for learning to read and write and for determining the most effective way to teach reading and writing. Conclusions from the work of William H. Teale and Elizabeth Sulzby (1986) offer the following six assumptions about literacy learning:

1. Literacy development begins long before children start formal instruction.

2. Literacy development is the appropriate way to describe what was called reading readiness; the child develops as a writer/reader.

3. Literacy develops in real-life settings for real-life activities in order to "get things done."

4. Children are doing critical cognitive work in literacy development during the years from birth to six.

Going to the Beach

This kindergartner's drawing, letters, depiction of some sounds, and interesting ideas combine to form a story:

"I will go to the beach and make a sand castle and go into the water and have a great little time." —Kindergartner

5. Children learn written language through active engagement with their world.

6. Although children's learning about literacy can be described in terms of generalized stages, children can pass through these stages in a variety of ways and at different ages (p. xviii).

Summary

We have touched on significant issues, events, research, and conclusions that have developed over the years and have contributed to our thinking about how children learn to read and write. Earlier assumptions about the literacy process—that reading and writing were primarily mechanical processes requiring carefully prefaced, sequenced, and timed instruction, and that early experience or cultural background was unrelated to school instruction—were prevalent and unchallenged until only recently. The impact of these beliefs on instruction was strengthened as a result of the basal reading systems that incorporated the assumptions and perpetuated them. That these reading materials became the standard delivery method for instruction was of more far-reaching significance than any theoretical differences that may have existed between published basal reading systems.

This examination of the historical background of literacy learning should help us evaluate the implications of the new theory of language development and the practices suggested by more recent views of literacy. A knowledge of where instruction has been is crucial to those who would give it a new direction.

3
▼

Approaching Learning in Language & Literacy

I n the first chapter we drew a parallel between approaching learning in language and literacy and taking a trip. Continuing this analogy, let us consider what might be involved in planning and taking a trip to, say, California. We would need to decide where in California we wanted to go—perhaps the ocean or California's mountains—and then we would need to decide when to go. After that we might take other logical steps in the planning process such as calling a travel agent, reading brochures, checking the bank balance, reviewing the calendar—in short, we would carefully consider major issues before just driving off or hopping on the first plane headed west!

As we approach language and literacy in the High/Scope K–3 Curriculum, we also need to make some fundamental preparations. We need to look first at where children are starting from and what they have done before coming to school, because research has shown that the foundations of language and emergent literacy are laid long before children walk through the school door.

We must also identify the early structures, forms, and products that children create along the route toward literacy as they begin to grasp the relationships between language and its symbolizations. This will heighten our interest in the trip. Also, we must be concerned with pacing

Go and hush the baby, Will.
It won't take long.
Go and hush the baby,
Sing him a little song.

— In *Go and Hush the Baby* by
Betsy Byars

and with coordinating skill development, so language will be interrelated with other learning.

And we must consider what we already know about how children learn—the "contour maps" that reveal the underlying features of the terrain. Finally, since most of the fun is in getting there, we should recognize that these advance preparations will help to ensure a pleasurable journey toward language learning.

In this chapter we consider the implications of what we know about emergent literacy and how those implications have helped to shape the High/Scope K–3 language and literacy curriculum.

Literacy Learning in the Home

The first reading of this subtitle may prompt one of two very different responses: denial or indifference. Some educators may still hold to the earlier assumption that, until children are six years old, they do not have the neural capacity to follow, or "track," print. These individuals may question any point of view that suggests that children have already acquired knowledge about both oral language and print forms of language before they come to school. Further, they may harbor such strong opinions about maturation and "readiness" that these opinions will dominate their perceptions of *what* should happen in school and *when* it should happen. Other educators accept the view that literacy emerges in infancy and in early childhood within the home setting—and take it for granted. They may ask, "So what difference does early learning make after the child is in school?"

In homes where adults communicate, work at jobs, and perform household tasks, language in oral and printed form abounds. Children in these settings acquire an early awareness of the forms of language that appear in their environment. Of course, children's language awareness is not likely to be complete; early attempts by children to use oral language and to write and read are almost certainly different than adults' conventional language activities.

Indeed, the earliest literacy experiences of children actually occur in the crib. These experiences provide basic building blocks for school literacy learning long before children sit at school desks. Think, for a moment, of infants "cooing" and "babbling" to parents during diaper changes—and parents "babbling" in response. Think of parents relating nursery and counting rhymes and singing jingles that name eyes, nose, and toes. These are entertaining activities, but they are also natural opportunities for language development, providing names, sounds, and verbal stimulation. Think of infants smacking their lips over favorite foods—and hearing the words "bananas," "pudding," and "cheese" applied to them. Think of toddlers stacking blocks with alphabet letters and emptying the cupboards of soup cans and boxes that spell out JELL-O™. While they play, children make countless associations with names, words, and symbols. Think of young children seeing "Colgate™" or "Crest™" logos every time they brush their teeth. And think of the associations young children make each time they pass the golden arches of "McDonald's™"! These are literacy learning events that occur at home and within the context of the family.

When parents add books to the environment of young children and begin to read aloud to them, the sounds recorded by symbols are also provided. These early, informal experiences do not guarantee that children will gain complete understanding about the nature of printed language. But convincing evidence demonstrates that well before school age, children understand that the story in a book derives from the *text* rather than from the *pictures*. Even when children generalize all logos on fast-food containers as "McDonald's™," it is clear that a relationship between ideas, thoughts, and print has been established.

Consider now three interesting lines of research from, respectively, Marie Clay, Elfrieda Hiebert, and Elizabeth Sulzby. In her early work Marie Clay (1975) observed that children write messages, often with an intent to communicate, long before they form letters. Clay noted that young children frequently scribble, draw pictures, or make marks that look a lot like letters, although the marks are not actual letters. These attempts by children to break apart and to combine elements of handwriting, spelling, and composing to generate written messages became the basis for Clay's further study.

"This is about people loving and then they get married and then they got a baby." — Kindergartner

Clay believed that children make an important breakthrough when they begin to see a relationship between language that is spoken and language that is written. As children continue observing and making additional discoveries about this relationship, they then start to experiment to determine which of the marks actually represent the ideas. Children's attempts eventually isolate some marks as more suitable than others, and the marks, drawings, or scribbles gradually grow to resemble the writing observed in the specific environment (e.g., English, Russian, Arabic). Clay (1975) found that certain principles guide the form that these marks take: Symbols recur, directionality appears, children invent ways to generate new statements from known elements, they inventory known forms, and they use contrasting forms—all as a result of informal literacy learning at home.

Another researcher, Elfrieda Hiebert (1988), discovered that as young children gain understanding of the *function* of written language in books and in their environment, they learn about the *forms* of written language as well. In summarizing the results of her research with entering kindergartners of varied backgrounds, Hiebert reported that children were able to name an average of 14 alphabet letters before they received instruction on letter names. This indicates that even without the school's guidance in connecting knowledge of letters and sounds to familiar print, children use the context of their environment extensively to provide meaning and thus to develop literacy.

The storybook reading of young children has also helped to specify exactly what children understand about story and print. Sulzby (1985) identified a developmental progression in the responses of children to the task of reading a familiar storybook. Children responded with speech that was closer to the formal language of books than to conversational speech, even though there were differences that paralleled age groups. Here again is evidence of literacy learning at home.

Acknowledging that literacy development begins at a young age invites us to compare the current view of literacy with the historical assumptions mentioned in Chapter 2. The view of emergent literacy clearly contrasts with the view of those who arbitrarily assign a unique occasion (e.g., entering kindergarten) or an age for "pre-reading" or "readiness" instruction. Pflaum (1986) concurs with the newer perspective when she observes that children display a range of incipient reading and writing behaviors well before the skills are fully formed and that this has resulted in a "blurring of the line between reading readiness and reading." This further supports the view that "readiness" is not separate and distinct from literate behavior.

For those formulating the approach to language and literacy in the High/Scope K–3 Curriculum, the implications of these theoretical foundations are compelling. Because school-age children have already been learning about oral and printed language since infancy, they come to the classroom prepared to extend their "learning in progress." Through the High/Scope K–3 approach, classroom staff ensure that children have ample opportunities for purposeful communication and plentiful print resources that are appropriate and functional. Educators must assume responsibility for recognizing where children are in their early literacy development and what needs to be done to support and enhance that development.

Writing and Reading Skills Develop in an Interrelated Fashion

Speaking, listening, writing, and reading are not, as we mentioned earlier, artificially separated in the lives of young children. Similarly, children's acquisition of skills in various areas cannot be artificially separated, although skills may temporarily move ahead in one area or lag behind in another. It is clear that children progress through stages or periods of emergent literacy in a way that may appear orderly at certain times but capricious at others. Yet the proficiency that children acquire in one skill area affects each of the other areas. This relationship, frequently described as **concurrent** rather than sequential, has interested researchers for some time.

Donald H. Graves (1983) contended that writing actually stimulates reading and is preliminary to reading. Durkin (1972) defined reading and writing as two forms of the same process—the act of writing being one of producing print, and reading representing a reaction to print. And again Sulzby (1986), in longitudinally studying the development of kindergartners' oral and written language, indicated that comprehension and production skills develop alongside lower-level skills—a concurrent rather than sequential relationship.

For a long time, though, the idea of a sequential ordering of skills was unquestioned: listening came first, then speaking, followed by reading, and after that writing. Accurate speech was thought possible only after children were able to hear and differentiate all the necessary sounds, and children's ability to compose stories was thought possible only after they had mastered the mechanics of handwriting. But research conducted by Emilia Ferreiro and Ana Teberosky attacked this view. Ferreiro and Teberosky set out to study children's knowledge and reasoning about written language. They criticized reading readiness tests that assumed a capacity for reading and writing was based on "certain linguistic aspects (such as correct articulation) and nonlinguistic aspects (such as visual perception and manual-motor coordination)" (Ferreiro & Teberosky, 1979/1982, p. 19, in DeVries & Kohlberg, 1987, p. 223).

Ferreiro and Teberosky challenged the widespread adherence to the idea of sequential skill development and the established testing programs that perpetuated this concept. Alphabet skills, for example, have traditionally been considered a critical component in the development of literacy. Historically, the alphabet was stitched into young girls' samplers, practiced in the frontier "loud school" mentioned in Chapter 2, and isolated as the basis for uncounted volumes of handwriting practice. Even in recent times, letter recognition activities have filled the majority of pages in kindergarten workbooks.

Conventional and unconventional forms express thoughts.

This emphasis on knowing and practicing alphabet skills has tended to "drive" instruction in a sequential manner; educators have viewed alphabet knowledge and the ability to write the alphabet as prerequisites to other writing skills. While knowledge of the alphabet is indisputably important for early reading, labeling it as a prerequisite means that, too often, teachers delay opportunities for writing and composing until after children have learned to recognize and name the letters of the alphabet and can form the letters with fine-motor skill. Concurrent development of alphabet learning, fine-motor skills and composing permits children to integrate learning in different areas.

Confusion arises from the fact that until recently, children's written forms were measured by adult standards and were considered *writing* only when they closely resembled the conventional forms of handwriting. In recent years, however, we have begun to realize that children's early forms of scribbling—the marks that children consider to be writing—*are* writing, in emergent form. In the context of emerging literacy, we now treat children's active explorations of the writing system as their speculation on how written marks can represent ideas, and this speculation does not necessarily wait for the conventional skill development.

In the seminal work *What Did I Write?* (1975), Clay articulated several principles that emerge from children's explorations with writing; these principles appear to help children distinguish writing from nonwriting. Clay found that children's experimentation with varied unconventional forms generates a number of ways of encoding thoughts into writing—scribbling, making wavy or letter-like forms, and stringing random letters together in patterned ways. Children combine the randomly chosen letters into more conventional forms, representing the initial sounds of whole words, syllables, and specified intermediate sounds. Gradually, the emergent learner "invents" a form of spelling or encoding. (We discuss this aspect of language learning in more detail in Chapter 5.)

Even the casual observer of young children in the act of writing recognizes that children move in and out of these forms as they write. Children often combine several unconventional and conventional forms, frequently mixing conventionally spelled words, scribbling, drawing, and invented spelling all in the same production. Through such in-and-out movement the more familiar, more comfortable, nonconventional forms are available to express more complicated thoughts, balancing the task demands between thought and production. Conversely, the less risky listing of familiar names or objects may be attempted using forms that are more experimental or at least have not been used to the point that they are natural or comfortable. For example, children may use conventional print to list names of family members, yet return to scribbling to write a story.

In its holistic approach the High/Scope K–3 Curriculum seeks to incorporate what we know about children's emerging writing and reading abilities. Since research indicates that reading and writing skills are interrelated and that the development of skills is not specifically a linear one, the curriculum emphasizes the "wholeness" of literacy understanding. Teachers encourage children to speak freely in their own language and dialect, to write naturally in their own way, and to read their compositions and the writing of others in their own emerging fashion. The curriculum does not separate the components of language into discrete fragments that are practiced in isolation. The whole language perspective argues convincingly that

"The name of this story is about Elizabeth."   — Kindergartner

language and literacy skill development is integrated in both thought and process.

Reading and Writing Have Functional Value

Most adults readily acknowledge a connection between their own reading and writing and "getting things done," but they may be less prepared to consider motivating factors for children. Indeed, children's early attempts at reading and writing often appear at first to be nothing more than imitation of adult work. However, on closer examination, it is clear that children often produce these early attempts to make something happen or to accomplish a task. Many adults recall instances when children have left notes for the tooth fairy or Santa Claus. These messages are designed to secure the same good will that a corporate executive seeks when writing a business letter to a client.

Parents do not usually teach children explicitly that writing a message or a list is a good way to get things to happen or that they will need to read in order to eat. Yet, even in homes where adults do little reading and writing and where parents do not actively encourage children to read and write, a great deal of functional reading and writing still occurs. For example, most adults read the labels on cans to decide which soup to prepare—and children watch them do it. Children observe carefully that one can yields chicken noodle soup and the other cream of broccoli. (And it is useful to know which is which if you do or do not like broccoli!) Adults scan checks for names and amounts and utter responses to bills and letters—and children observe the reactions the print produces. Adults also survey the TV listing for programs and channels—and children learn that there is a way to find out when and where to tune in "Scooby Doo." In the kitchen, recipes list ingredients that end up in chocolate chip cookies, and the take-out pizza menu clarifies whether "extra cheese" is available. Children who observe and participate in these activities begin to realize that reading and writing clearly make things happen!

Part of the functional value of literacy is that pleasure, too, is often a product or a by-product. Children return, time and time again, to a book they like—one that makes them laugh. They communicate by drawing or writing pictures that amuse others, and when they do so, they are *using* literacy skills to entertain themselves or others. When children follow printed directions for playing games, they use literacy skills to make sure that something they enjoy doing can happen. Similarly, when children listen to and read from religious writings, they use literacy skills to provide spiritual encouragement and knowledge.

In High/Scope classrooms the functional value of literacy is evident to children; it powerfully motivates their experiments and their investigations of literacy's conventional forms. Classroom activities involving speaking, listening, writing, and reading emphasize this connection: children listen to stories read aloud and then discuss the content, connecting it with other information. Writing provides an outlet for authentic expression and for accomplishing communication at a distance; reading offers entertainment, knowledge, and information, as well as insight into the thoughts of others; and speaking permits oral communication of emotions, information, and interpretations to peers in the classroom.

This functional connection is motivating to children, and it presents a clear opportunity for teachers to set up occasions that encourage exploration of the conventional forms of literacy. This does not suggest using regimented formulas or exercises but rather capitalizing on children's interests and matching instruction to individual learning styles. In this way teachers can expand the potential scope of children's literacy skill development while supporting the natural inquiry that drives children to want to learn new things.

...Poor little Chang was all out of breath from saying that great long name, and he didn't think he could say it one more time. But then he thought of his brother in the old well.

Chang bowed his little head clear to the sand, took a deep breath and slowly, very slowly said, "Most Honorable Mother, Tikki tikki—tembo-no-sa rembo—charibari—ruchi-pip—peri pembo is at the bottom of the well."

"Oh, not my first and honored son, heir of all I possess! Run quickly and tell the Old Man With The Ladder that your brother has fallen into the well."

— In *Tikki Tikki Tembo* by Arlene Mosel

Learning to Read and Write Is an Active, Constructive Process

As children encounter written language, they try to figure out how that language works, so they can use it themselves. They experiment with drawing or making marks that approximate the marks they have observed in their environment. Teale and Sulzby (in Strickland & Morrow, 1989) suggest that in so doing, children form and test hypotheses and attempt to discern the differences between drawing and writing. Experimenting with these early forms also helps children understand the meanings, structures, and cadences of written language. In addition, the experimentation assists children in learning the symbols of writing and in sorting out the relationships between the symbols and the sounds of oral language.

The image that is presented—one of children engaged in making sense of oral and written language—draws extensively from the work of several researchers. One interpretation of the theoretical position of philosopher Jean Piaget (in Pflaum, 1986) suggests that even the social knowledge that includes language skills is constructed within the individual. This view holds that developmental change is based both on biological processes of maturation and on the experiences of active children. It stresses the need to furnish children with appropriate objects and events that will provide strong experiences to use in building systems of understanding.

Ferreiro and Teberosky (in DeVries & Kohlberg, 1987) sought to understand the child's psychological experience and changes in conceptions of print and writing from the viewpoint of the learner. This study, which was carried out by asking children to comment on various forms of print, revealed how children transform materials through an active process of assimilation that involves progressive conceptualization and testing hypotheses. Ferreiro and Teberosky indicated that children do not begin their understanding of written language by mechanically associating sound responses with graphic stimuli.

The Soviet education and psychology scholar L. S. Vygotsky (in Pflaum, 1986) shares a Piagetian view of developmental trends in cognitive functioning. Vygotsky reasoned that children learn through maturation and the stimulation of social interactions. He described a "zone of proximal development" when describing the teacher's role. This zone "is the distance between the actual development level as determined by independent problem solving and the level of potential development as determined through problem solving under adult guidance or in collaboration with more capable peers" (Pflaum, 1986, p. 11). Briefly put, Vygotsky held that language is a major stimulus for conceptual growth and that this growth is assured through experiences—many guided and assisted by dialogues with adults.

A dominant theme in the work of these researchers is that children develop facility and understanding of oral and written language through *active* rather than passive involvement in experiences. Children do not automatically internalize or interpret experiences; rather, experiences are selectively blended with prior knowledge and with many other language and literacy events, contributing to a picture that gradually becomes more complete and more complex.

To a large extent children evaluate experiences or events according to what they see as proving useful for adults and other children. They also attempt or try different expressions in anticipation of certain reactions. For example, when a child announces that the sign placed on the bedroom door—complete with invented spelling and plenty of tape—means "KEEP OUT," it is likely that the child has seen someone else post a sign or a written message and has seen that the action accomplished a purpose. The child anticipates that a similar sign will produce a similar result.

"Keep out."

In this case if the result of the "KEEP OUT" sign is that others do, indeed, keep out, the child will probably post other signs—signs about other topics, perhaps, or signs produced in varied forms. On the other hand, if the sign is not read, if it is ripped off the door or ridiculed, or if the child is punished for taping the sign on the door in the first place, the child will see little reason for continuing to expand this form of communication.

Recognizing that children are active participants in the process of constructing meaning about reading and writing is important for at least two reasons. First, this view places children in positions of authority; they have a measure of control over the hypotheses they will use to test the situations they experience. Meaning and understanding are constructed within children's own cognitive structures. The second reason derives from the fact of children's empowerment: children need not be instructed directly to become literate but can rely on their own resources for learning.

Children themselves ultimately make sense of the experiences in which they are engaged—but teachers and parents play important roles in creating an environment full of opportunities for children to pursue literacy skills. The environment in which language and literacy learning flourishes is an environment where children find useful literacy tools within reach, where adults and children demonstrate written and oral language frequently, where literate acts contribute to accomplishing day-to-day work, and where reasons and motivation for actively participating are present. In such an environment parents and teachers acknowledge and accept the power children hold for controlling their own learning. Nevertheless, adults must take the initiative to stimulate children to rethink, adjust, and expand their developing aptitudes. In the classroom setting it is especially important that interaction among all children and adult participants is encouraged and supported.

Teachers in High/Scope K–3 classrooms recognize and support the active nature of children's language and literacy development in several ways:

■ Teachers encourage children to explore oral and written language.

■ Teachers help children to work cooperatively as well as independently.

■ Teachers use a whole language perspective to promote complete and integrated understanding of language.

■ Teachers differentiate instructional opportunities in daily workshops.

■ Teachers provide and organize materials that support the naturally occurring interests of children.

■ Teachers support children's growth in understanding and assist children in extending their skills through dialogue and participation.

■ Teachers aid children in reviewing their experiences in order to test and expand their understanding.

The process is a vital and a dynamic one. Children act on and in an environment supported and arranged with them in mind. And, while children do not directly internalize information about oral or written language, they constantly incorporate what they learn about it into the knowledge they already have. Creating and maintaining an environment rich in opportunities for growth in literacy skills makes the role of the High/Scope teacher challenging and appealing.

The Family's Involvement in Children's Language Development

In the High/Scope environment we view the family as the child's partner in developing literacy learning and as the school's partner in providing settings in which literacy can flourish. In this way the forms of language—listening, speaking, writing, and reading—and their functional aspects are bound together with the people in the children's world. The whole language perspective argues against artificial separation of forms and artificial separation of those who participate in the process of learning.

Families demonstrate their involvement in language and literacy development in several ways. **Reading regularly to children is one excellent way for parents to help with language skills.**

■ Parents should plan to read with their children at a regular time each day. When a specific time is set aside for reading, e.g., after dinner or before bedtime, children understand that reading is valued. Children learn that they can depend on this event; they do not need to renegotiate each day. Reading at the same time for about the same length of time also means that longer selections can be read "in installments" and children will be able to look forward to hearing the story's conclusion.

■ Parents and children should select a special place where the daily reading occurs. A comfortable chair, the end of the couch, pillows on the floor, at the kitchen table, or on the bed are all places with pleasant associations. The television or telephone should not interfere.

■ Parents should endeavor to find good reading material. Libraries and bookstores often distribute reading lists of noteworthy children's literature, and children can often borrow books from school. Parents should be encouraged to make use of material in the home—articles from the newspaper, comic strips, family magazines, and jokes from *Reader's Digest* are examples.

■ Parents should tie the reading in with activities the family has experienced. Reading stories about camping, visits to the zoo, or family events such as the birth of a brother or sister or the death of a pet becomes considerably more valuable when the stories are connected to memories of family camping trips and family occasions.

■ Parents should talk *with* their children—not just *to* their children—when they are reading. Parents should discuss what they have read and encourage children to relate the feelings and experiences the stories evoke. While parents should not sound as though they are "testing," they should encourage children to predict what they think might happen in the story. Parents should also encourage children to re-tell and to summarize what they have read.

Another way to enhance the family's involvement in all aspects of language and literacy development is for **parents to model their own reading and writing for their children.** Again, this is an indication that the parents value literacy and that they use reading and writing to do the jobs necessary for organizing the house and earning a living. Such modeling also demonstrates adult levels of fluency and suggests to children what they can aspire to.

Not every exchange will be fluent; sometimes parents may confront unknown or unfamiliar terms in reading. But when parents look up pronunciations and definitions in the dictionary, they demonstrate to children in the most helpful way that achieving literacy is a lifelong process. When children realize that their own risk-taking efforts to learn to read and write are quite similar to the process their parents are engaged in, children are encouraged and validated in their attempts.

The family assists the home-school partnership when they **support the emergent literacy process at home.**

■ Parents should demonstrate an openness for children's exploration of writing forms. Early writing should be viewed as a developing and unfolding process. Children should be encouraged to try forms and spellings without pressure to be correct each time. Since children are less likely to risk writing if they sense that their attempts are only acceptable when perfect, parents should suggest "give-it-a-try." Young children are open to seeking out ways that more nearly approach conventional forms when they have many opportunities to "write their own way."

■ Parents should support children's early attempts to read. The earliest efforts of children to read from familiar or favorite story books are unlikely to be "word perfect." Parents should work to build an atmosphere of acceptance and encouragement for trying out reading strategies, such as looking at the pictures as well as at the print, retelling the story, and thinking aloud about what might happen. Children should be encouraged to consider what might make sense and to feel free to use their memory and recollection about favorite phrases when they are reading.

■ Parents should provide appropriate paper, pencils, and other writing tools. They should provide a safe, well-lighted place where reading and writing materials can be stored and where children can plan to work.

Anne's Explanation

After a strong beginning, four-year-old Anne dictated a story that was too demanding to write in her own way:

> ~~TO ANNE~~ I HOPE YOU
> LIKTHIS PIKCHR. LOVE —
>
> This is me. I am with Daddy. We are skating outside in the ice storm. The power is off. That's why we are skating outside on the ice that the ice storm brought. It looked like each branch was a seperate snow flake all covered with ice.
>
> Daddy falls down on one of the logs that has fallen down on the ice. So then I picked him up. I had to hold his hand the rest of the time we skated.
>
> Mommy is in one window and Cole is in the other. They dont like it because they have to be somewhere where there is no power.
>
> Then we left. It was raining. In my hands are some clips that ~~stood or~~ hold on umbrella (It isn't invisible, but I just didnt want to show it) Then we went home. We sat down with mommy & Cole. Lightning came. After that, mommy and Cole and I went upstairs and crawled in bed.
>
> Then Daddy came up and picked up the flashlight. As soon as he turned it on... on came the power. Mommy got realy excited and did her "WE HAVE POWER" dance.
>
> The end.

■ Parents should plan to support children's initiatives in writing and reading. They should understand that young children sometimes want to write and sometimes want someone to take their dictation. This is especially true when what children have to write about is more complex and advanced than their skills for recording it.

Finally, **family members are encouraged to visit High/Scope classrooms regularly.** When family members are physically present in the classrooms, there is indisputable evidence that they value literacy: they have scheduled their work to make the visit possible. Parents acquire substantial information when they see the relationship between the forms of oral and written language, i.e., when they see how speaking, listening, writing, and reading relate to one another. The family members have an opportunity to see the materials and activities that have been selected for children. In addition, the participation of family members in the classroom provides information to teachers about the background of the family and offers insight that helps teachers plan instruction.

Summary

We have looked at how the theoretical foundations of acquiring language and literacy are demonstrated in practical situations, and we have initiated the process that will permit us to translate what we know in theory into actual classroom practice. The High/Scope approach to language emphasizes not only that children's early experiences at home are important for commonly accepted cultural, social, and emotional reasons but also that they are valid early experiences in reading and writing. We stress the importance of both home and school learning that is functional for the children who are involved. And we believe that to implement a total whole language perspective, children should have well-selected resources at their disposal, to aid them in developing all forms of oral and written language.

4
▼

Creating a Classroom Environment for Literacy Development

Because language and literacy are social activities best experienced through interaction with others, the classroom environment should be designed to facilitate such interaction. In this chapter we consider three aspects of designing High/Scope K–3 classrooms that are of special importance for literacy development:

- Choosing furniture and arranging the room
- Selecting and grouping materials and equipment
- Organizing time and scheduling the day

He was shortish, and oldish. And brownish. And mossy. And he spoke with a voice that was sharpish and bossy.

"Mister!" he said with a sawdusty sneeze, "I am the Lorax. I speak for the trees."

— In *The Lorax* by Dr. Seuss

Choosing Furniture and Arranging the Room

Few schoolrooms today contain desks and seats that are bolted to the floor as they were years ago. The rationale for more flexible seating arrangements has come from many directions—but in particular from those concerned with the development of language and literacy. Of course, the classroom must meet basic physical standards by providing space for children to move safely in and out and

Sample Room Arrangements in K–3 Classrooms

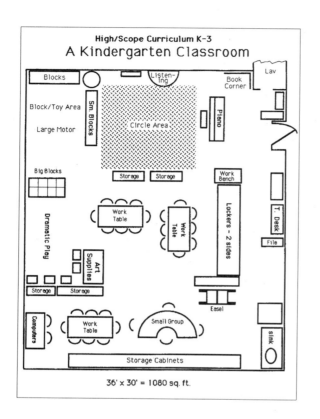

High/Scope Curriculum K-3
A Kindergarten Classroom

36' x 30' = 1080 sq. ft.

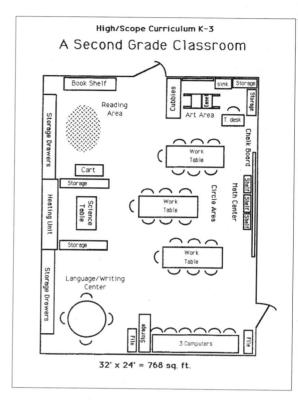

High/Scope Curriculum K-3
A Second Grade Classroom

32' x 24' = 768 sq. ft.

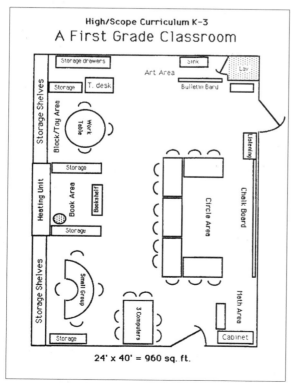

High/Scope Curriculum K-3
A First Grade Classroom

24' x 40' = 960 sq. ft.

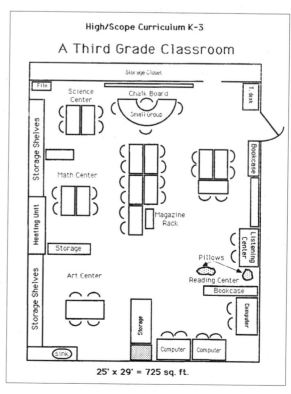

High/Scope Curriculum K-3
A Third Grade Classroom

25' x 29' = 725 sq. ft.

around the room; adequate ventilation and lighting; and comfortable, adjustable furniture that can accommodate the typical size range of children at a given grade level. In addition, we arrange classrooms so children and teachers can see each other, share information, solve problems cooperatively, and gauge emotional reactions to conversation. These activities are all crucial to enhancing language development. Eye contact between children and teachers is necessary for effective interactions, and teachers arrange seating with that goal in mind. Whenever possible, desks or tables should face each other to maximize collaboration and cooperative learning.

We organize High/Scope classrooms to facilitate three kinds of activities: **whole-class activities, workshop activities involving teacher-led and independent small groups,** and **individual activities.** Flexible furniture arrangements make it possible to create space for specific functions:

- Space in a carpeted area where the whole class gathers informally on the floor to listen to stories, enjoy music, and have discussions

- Space where quiet activities involving games, reading, and conferences take place

- Space for specialized activities, such as using hollow blocks, creating art projects, doing carpentry work, and engaging in dramatic play

- Space for computers and audiovisual equipment used in language and music

The arrangement of classroom furniture will vary, of course, according to the grade level. States or districts generally set minimum requirements for floor space; fixed features such as radiators, air conditioners, floor-to-ceiling windows, and access to outdoor classroom spaces also contribute variations. The classroom floorplans shown here illustrate arrangements of furniture and space that take the forgoing considerations into account in kindergarten and grades 1, 2, and 3.

Storage units, cabinets, and bulletin boards contribute to a language-rich classroom environment by making materials accessible to children; further, they can help to create an orderly and attractive atmosphere in the classroom. Teachers capitalize on these classroom tools by making sure that they offer opportunities for exercising literacy skills. For example, in a classroom focused on language and literacy,

- Books and reading materials are organized on open shelves or cupboards, so they are appealing and children can easily see what is available.

- Materials are stored and labeled so children can easily see where to return them after use.

- Tubs or containers hold printed materials for small groups to use.

- Tape recorders, record players, listening stations, computers, etc., are placed near accompanying tapes, records, books, and software.

- Writing materials and instructional aids are displayed and stored where children use them.

- Bulletin boards are placed at the eye level of children so that titles, labels, and displays become additional print resources for the classroom.

- Display areas such as tables and countertops are cleared so children can use them to display their own work and to see the results of others' work.

Language and Literacy Activity Centers

These centers, which group materials into areas focused on language and literacy development, feature materials that appeal to the senses and that provide children with hands-on experiences. The materials are developmentally appropriate and cover the range of skills expected in any heterogeneously grouped early childhood classroom.

By focusing children's attention on writing and by organizing writing materials in one location, the classroom **writing center** allows children to participate in many forms of writing. Children identify this center by an easy-to-read sign, and the center demonstrates to children that writing is valued to such an extent in the classroom that space is defined to support it. Although the materials themselves may change with the grade level and with the time of year, several different kinds of writing tools are available at all levels. For example, kindergarten students beginning the school year use unlined paper and a variety of pencils, crayons, and markers; by the end of third

Some Signs of the Times!

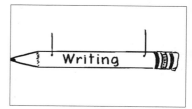

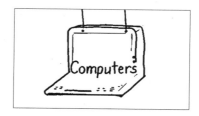

Children share ideas, solve problems, and have fun when desks are grouped.

grade appropriate writing materials for students include lined paper, notebooks, typewriters, pens, and a wide range of additional items.

Suggested materials for a writing center include *paper*—unlined, lined, construction, scrap pieces, craft, chart, oak tag; *writing tools*—pencils, pens, markers, crayons, chalk; *equipment*—typewriter, chalk boards, wipe-off boards, magnetic letters, print and stamp sets, glue, scissors, tape, stapler, paper clips; and *other resources*—envelopes, telephone directories, order pads, calendars, folders, stickers, stamps, carbon paper, junk mail, books. Many of these materials, grouped together as a Publishing Center, serve as a convenient place to bind children's books.

The **reading center** highlights an assortment of print materials that children can read independently, share with other children, or use in small teacher-led groups. The sign over this center indicates that materials are available; it advertises that in this area of the room children can find books of many types, magazines, newspapers, child-authored work, and reading materials brought from home—to name only a few.

The **computer center** is an important component of a High/Scope classroom because of the natural connection that exists between computers and the production of written language. For several reasons computer resources are best centered in the classroom, rather than housed in a separate laboratory setting. Locating computers in the

Materials are available at the Writing Center.

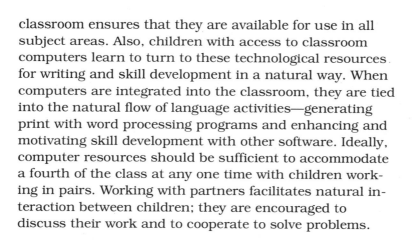

A lawnchair makes a comfortable place to read.

classroom ensures that they are available for use in all subject areas. Also, children with access to classroom computers learn to turn to these technological resources for writing and skill development in a natural way. When computers are integrated into the classroom, they are tied into the natural flow of language activities—generating print with word processing programs and enhancing and motivating skill development with other software. Ideally, computer resources should be sufficient to accommodate a fourth of the class at any one time with children working in pairs. Working with partners facilitates natural interaction between children; they are encouraged to discuss their work and to cooperate to solve problems.

Integrated activity centers for social studies, science, math, and art also are integral components of the same High/Scope classroom environment that supports growth in language and literacy. Oral and written language are intentionally integrated with content areas to stress natural relationships and to decrease the artificial separation of subject matter and skills that was described

First graders use computers independently.

in an earlier chapter. In this way, language and literacy permeate all curriculum areas, leading children into explorations in science, social studies, art, and mathematics. As a result, children have ample opportunities to use their developing skills in language and literacy. In particular appropriate resources, such as trade books, games, and equipment for carrying out projects and conducting research, serve to extend children's writing and reading skills.

Other Print Resources in the Environment

Many resources and materials appear naturally in the home and in school—and many of them deserve emphasis in the classroom. For example, the signs and labels that display children's names and identify places, materials, and buildings are continuing reminders of the usefulness of written language. When kindergartners enter a classroom, they see their names on a list of students and they see their names on cubbies or lockers where they hang their sweaters. These young children see signs identifying activity centers and naming the animals that live in cages; they see print messages that describe the weather and the calendar. And kindergartners soon learn that signs for the "Bathroom," "Office," and "This Week's Menu" are especially useful!

Throughout the early elementary years these print resources serve an important purpose in the classroom. First- and second-graders learn many words from signs and announcements in their rooms. Early elementary students experience print on classmates' T-shirts and on lunch boxes, and these examples of print expand the models available for writing and reading. The varied character of ornamental and colorful typefaces also reinforces the understanding that, even in its more unusual forms, print carries meaning. Children learn that in capital and lowercase form, in manuscript and cursive, and in varied sizes, "D" is the first letter of the word "dog."

No doubt about where the back packs should go!

The teacher should not take sole responsibility for providing names and signs for the classroom environment. Children should be encouraged to write whatever interests them and to label materials they share with others or projects they have completed. Morning kindergartners enjoy leaving messages for the afternoon class; ongoing communication about what is developing in the block center can often engage children for several days. Third- graders find it useful to label the parts of a science experiment that is in progress so others entering the room know what is happening. First- and second-graders take pleasure in taping notes to the wall with messages about where to store the "*bag*" packs.

Selecting Materials

As we mentioned earlier, reading and writing centers in High/Scope classrooms should include materials that allow active participation of children, stimulate children's sensory involvement, and encourage a hands-on approach to learning. The emphasis on participation is particularly important because it motivates children to become active agents in their own natural literacy development. The following five categories of language and literacy materials will help to focus the selection process:

- Children's literature
- Basal reading series
- Computer software
- Other print resources
- Nonprint resources

Children's Literature

We turn first to children's literature since it serves as the primary reading and language development resource in the High/Scope whole language curriculum. As most teachers are aware, the variety of well-written and well-illustrated storybooks is so extensive as to be almost overwhelming. Deciding which books to include in the room is a demanding task—but an enjoyable one. Useful criteria for choosing books likely to have a positive impact on young children include literary content, the nature and quality of the illustrations, the subject matter, the manner in which the subject is treated, and the way the book is designed and put together.

Few teachers have enough time to satisfactorily research each of these dimensions, so reading lists developed and published by professional organizations can prove helpful. The International Reading Association, the National Council of Teachers of English, and the National Association of Education of Young Children are examples of groups that publish comprehensive, cumulative lists of high-quality children's literature. Several journals also review books upon publication; the reviews in *The Horn Book*, *Language Arts*, *The School Library Journal*, and *The Reading Teacher* provide thorough evaluations of books and illustrations, together with suggested age or interest levels.

Bookstores and libraries frequently compile reading lists on specific topics and lists of books that have received special awards. These lists might include categories such as the following:

- Caldecott award books
- Newbery award books
- Picture books
- Folk tales
- Biographies
- Anthologies
- Classics
- Family topics (birth, death, divorce, etc.)
- Dinosaurs
- Easy-reading books
- Mythology
- Poetry
- Reading aloud

Children enjoy reading from a wide selection of trade books.

- Multicultural awareness
- Natural world
- Sports

The wealth of good children's books makes it convenient to develop a whole language program around books children choose to read. Thinking about ways in which particular books can help children acquire and extend skills in speaking, listening, writing, and reading is also important. In the High/Scope K–3 Curriculum the learning opportunities or objectives that help children develop skills in language and literacy are described as **key experiences.** (See Chapter 5 for complete treatment of using the key experiences.) Because teachers plan instruction around the key experiences in speaking, listening, writing, and reading, books that have specific textual features addressing these experiences can be effective additions to the classroom library. Well-selected books not only present pleasant, entertaining stories but also offer excellent opportunities for language learning in areas such as **developing vocabulary** (e.g., *Eating the Alphabet* by Lois Ehlert); **experiencing patterned language** (e.g., *Brown Bear, Brown Bear, What Do You See?* by Bill Martin, Jr.); **discovering elements and strategies useful for understanding narrative text** (e.g., *The Three Pigs* by Paul Galdone); **studying expository form and style and learning strategies for understanding what is read** (e.g., *Tadpole and Frog* by Christine Back and Barrie Watts); and **developing fluency** (e.g., repeated or innovative re-readings of Arnold Lobel's well-loved *Frog and Toad Are Friends*).

Other examples of children's literature lend themselves well to working on specific phonological elements. For example, Verna Aardema's *Bringing the Rain to Kapiti Plain* provides numerous opportunities to hear the "long" sound recorded by "a" within the natural confines of a rhythmic, read-aloud tale.

When children's literature is used as a teaching resource, primary emphasis is placed on the literary quality of the text. Teachers read the books aloud first—often several times—to assure that children have an opportunity to enjoy and appreciate the story itself. After this, teachers may point out features specific to the text; they encourage children to search out repeated sounds, letters, words, phrases, and elements of punctuation, capitalization, and structure. Later, teachers plan to bring in other examples from literature and other print resources to aid children in generalizing their discoveries about directionality of print, sounds, repetition, and rhyme. An important consideration is that the children's interest and ability to choose literature that "holds" them is combined with the teacher's knowledge of literature and decisions to have it available for classroom use.

Big books are appealing resources primarily for children in kindergarten and first grade. These enlarged texts make it possible for groups of children to see both printed text and illustrations as the books are read aloud—in much the same way that one or two children might typically share a book of regular size. Teachers should select big books that have special appeal because of high-quality illustrations, simplified plots, and specific text features that encourage children to identify letters or recognize words and phrases.

See Appendix A for an introductory listing of books divided into several categories and designed to fill varied purposes.

Child-authored books are important materials to include in reading centers. Teachers should encourage children to produce their own original stories and their own versions of best-loved books after they have heard and read the books repeatedly. Children's familiarity with the structure of these stories often provides a starting place for "spin-offs" or derivations. Favorites such as P. D. Eastman's *Are You My Mother?* lend themselves to fanciful retellings and permit personalization of the storylines. The child-authored books are especially useful materials since the natural interest of children has produced them and

Big books produce big smiles!

*Child-authored books make reading interesting and exciting for children;
they enjoy writing and illustrating their own stories.*

generates continued involvement with them. Varied binding techniques available in the classroom make it possible
for children to produce professional appearing productions. Binding with a dry mount process, using a punch
binder, or using other sturdy materials adds dignity to the
work of child-authors.

Taken together, these varied forms of children's literature provide for holistic language and literacy instruction
that offers highly individualized materials and covers a
full range of language skill development. Educators
should consider children's literature an essential resource
for building a whole language program.

Basal Reading Series

Basal reading texts represent another potential source of
instructional materials for the High/Scope K–3 language
and literacy curriculum. Many factors may come into play
when basal series are chosen. Some states mandate the
purchase of materials that reflect a particular point of
view. Some districts adopt series that fulfill the expectations of the communities. And some elementary schools
choose basal series that are in keeping with the perspectives of administration or staff. Whatever the reasons influ-
encing the selection of basal reading texts, those
responsible for making the decision must carefully consider the content of these materials. They must also make
certain that recommended uses of the series support the
whole language approach of the High/Scope Curriculum.

Basals can be **substantively useful** when textbook material provides an underlying theoretical framework that is consistent with a whole language perspective. Teachers can then combine the main substantive topics for instruction with children's literature and other print resources. Rather than relying solely on basal materials for reading instruction, teachers add many other materials for general reading and for extending literacy skills.

Using basals as the sole resource in all areas of language instruction is not recommended and is not compatible with the High/Scope whole language approach. But when teachers use basal materials in a variety of substantive ways, they can choose features from the series that are congruent with the whole language philosophy. The following questions are useful to consider when analyzing basal materials for possible selection and/or use.

What is the philosophical framework of the series? The whole language perspective views speaking, listening, writing, and reading as interrelated forms of language and literacy. The perspective stresses the integration of experiences so that children may use a combination of semantic, syntactic, and phonic cues to help them interpret oral and written language. Basal materials should reflect this perspective both in format and in presentation of the mechanical aspects of writing and reading. Respect for the natural language of children and encouragement for viewing language holistically in all forms should be evident.

What is the overall nature and range of the reading selections? When examining the selections included in a basal series, teachers should look for well-developed, high-quality children's literature—appropriate to the grade level—and stories that have proven appeal for children. Some basal series feature reading selections that fail to develop elements of character, setting, and plot sufficiently, thus preventing readers from identifying fully with the stories (Anderson et al., 1985). The text should include stories that are long enough to offer interesting reading built on strong narrative, and stories should offer opportunities for children to become involved in the story lines.

Expository text should be presented in a way that is "considerate"—i.e., printed in a way that helps children identify main ideas, explanatory information, and summaries.

Controlled vocabulary, which is useful in early reading, should not be limited to the extent that it detracts from sense or meaning. Some basal series suffer from a sparsity of well-written text and from a tendency to shorten and abridge text to such a degree that the flavor of a story cannot be adequately developed (Anderson et al., 1985). Teachers should be certain that the text engages children in "reading" and not "reading about reading," which happens when text is used solely to advance the development of skills.

What is the instructional design of the series? The design of a reading series should reflect concurrent rather than sequential skill development. For example, writing skills in the whole language perspective develop alongside speaking, listening, and reading skills, so opportunities for writing should be an integral part of the program. The series should also allow for the individualizing of the skills sequence to accommodate differences in children's abilities and interests. By focusing on children as unique individuals, teachers assess in a continuous manner and emphasize skills that are appropriate. The basal series should acknowledge the reality that the acquisition of skills, while generally predictable in a developmental format, may vary considerably from child to child.

Similarly, since children's basic background knowledge is frequently limited and inadequate for interpreting a given text, children should be permitted choices about what they read. Arbitrary timing that withholds the opportunity to read a story from the back of the book limits the child's involvement. Teachers should be prepared to allow the children's purposes for reading and the functional reasons for which children select reading to determine much of the instructional design of the series. Flexibility is especially important so that the material can be tailored to the needs of individual populations of children. Teachers should be aware of these concerns and plan to add or delete material according to the children's needs.

What is the methodology employed? Too often, reading methodology "wars" have been waged over the issue of "all" or "none" in the matter of teaching phonics. A whole language perspective is inclusive; it views semantic, syntactic, and phonic cues as useful and important for learning to encode language into symbolic form, for decoding the written form, and for returning language to its oral form. Teachers should evaluate basal series to be sure that they acknowledge and incorporate all semantic, syntactic, and phonic strategies.

Series should present phonics instruction, when needed, as an enabling resource, rather than as an end in itself. Phonics instruction should be used only as long as needed and within the context of text that emphasizes meaning. Care should be taken to assure that the material related to phonics is accurate, that the generalizations children learn about phonics are useful, and that the introduction of new material is paced appropriately. In general, basal materials should stress the view that all speaking, listening, writing, and reading skills emerge from less developed, unconventional forms toward forms that more nearly approximate the skill level of adults. Skills development materials such as workbooks and skill sheets should reflect this philosophy. Teachers should look for basal formats that differentiate instruction. These systems should make flexible clustering of children for instruction convenient. Basal systems that advocate static groups or systems that make no provision for wide ranging skill and ability levels in early elementary classrooms are equally suspect.

Additionally, teachers should look for a focus that encourages children to assume some control of their own learning efforts. In all stages of the basal program—but especially in early writing and reading—children should be encouraged to try different forms, attempt new processes, and take risks while experimenting with ideas and information that may become generalizable.

A willingness to permit children some choice in selecting reading material of interest and a commitment to helping children extend their skills when they are ready should be apparent. It argues against using single-source reading textbooks. In fact, Sulzby (April 1990) summarizes this position succinctly, "It seems to be far more important for children to have the freedom to read widely across different types of books rather than to be tied to reading from one textbook" (p. 19).

When educators do include basal reading series among the instructional materials in High/Scope K–3 classrooms, it is with the understanding that the issues raised here have been comfortably resolved. In this way, the selective and substantive use of basal series may assist teachers in developing whole language programs; for these teachers, the series provides a framework that can be coordinated with a wealth of books and other instructional resources.

Computer Software for Language and Literacy

Software chosen from the **computer center** should be evaluated as carefully as any other materials brought into the classroom. In fact, many of the same questions considered when evaluating basal reading series apply as well when selecting software. Software supports natural language and literacy development and skill acquisition in several ways.

■ **Word processing programs** enable children to view the computer as a convenient writing tool. Some word processing programs permit children to explore unconventional writing forms by providing a special computer device called a "mouse" that enables children to form scribbles, to draw, or to make other marks that approximate conventional forms of print. Other programs offer children opportunities to produce enlarged print and to use other simple techniques for engaging in early writing and reading. Word processing programs enable children to write and spell and thus make it possible for children to produce compositions that are longer and more complex than compositions written by hand.

■ **Skills instruction** software is used by children who are ready to profit from such instruction because they are conventionally literate, i.e., they can interpret and compose text that others can read. The types of skills practiced are appropriate for the children's stages of development.

■ **Guided practice and tutorial assistance** software programs are useful for supporting children's increasing ability to move freely from one reading strategy to another. Such practice solidifies the progress children are making at being able to decode unfamiliar words, recognize words, and comprehend what is presented. The guided practice also provides opportunities for children to strengthen their writing skills.

■ **Problem-solving** software programs provide children with opportunities to strengthen and extend their skills in sequencing, comparing and contrasting; studying causes and effect; and engaging in critical thinking.

■ **Entertainment** software incorporates many of the features described here, but is used primarily for pleasure.

Some High-Quality K–3 Programs

The following programs meet several of the criteria for high-quality **kindergarten–grade 1** programs:

■ *Muppet Slate* (Sunburst) (Word Processing)
■ *Magic Slate* (Sunburst) (Word Processing)
■ *Color Me* (Mindscape) (Drawing)

These programs allow the youngest children to explore forms of print by drawing, scribbling, and using letter-like forms; they also invite children to extend their experi ences to conventional print activity.

Older children also enjoy the programs listed above which are basically word processing and drawing programs. Because of older children's movement toward conventional literacy, they seek programs that help them write stories, develop familiarity with the alphabet, strengthen letter/sound relationships, expand word recognitions skills and understanding.

In addition to *Muppet Slate* and *Magic Slate*, other software can be used to help children in **grades 2–3** write stories, develop familiarity with the alphabet, and strengthen understanding of letter/sound relationships. These programs include the following:

■ *Sound Ideas* (Houghton Mifflin)
■ *Fun From A to Z* (MECC)
■ *Children's Writing & Publishing Center* (The Learning Company)
■ *Explore-a-Story Series* (D. C. Heath)

Additional recommendations for K–3 computer software programs are provided in Appendix B.

Children enjoy independent play activities that involve working with the alphabet.

Supplementary Print Resources

The list of supplementary print resources that can enrich the literacy environment of classrooms is so long and so varied that we include only a sample here. These materials reflect the interests of children and vary with the time of the year, the geographic location, and the perspective and creativity of the teacher. In most cases, rotating the materials helps solve the storage problem and keeps the interest level high. Magazines such as *National Geographic* have continuing appeal, but yesterday's newspaper has the same appeal for children that it has for adults—limited! A January newspaper announcing a snowstorm is useful only for papier maché in May. These materials might be included not only in a reading or writing center but also in a dramatic play center or a science, social studies, or math center.

Supplementary print resources are easily grouped to enrich many literacy experiences:

■ Current newspapers (to read), old newspapers (to cut up), magazines, children's magazines, comic books, telephone directories, maps, tourist brochures, how-to-do-it manuals, cookbooks

■ Advertising supplements, coupons, play money, signs and posters, business cards, stationery and order forms, appointment books, address labels, calendars, menus, fast food containers, placemats, napkins, soft drink cups, food packaging containers, card-catalogs

■ Catalogs, shopping bags, T-shirts with messages, gift wrap, sales slips

■ Baby books, scrap books, mail, photograph albums

Nonprint Resources

Finally, teachers should make an effort to bring many nonprint resources to the early childhood classroom to supplement other printed materials. In choosing non-print materials to round out a language-rich classroom environment, teachers should consider the following general guidelines:

Prop boxes and dress-up clothes offer great resources for dramatic enactments. And what fun results!

■ Materials should tie in with the whole language key experiences of speaking, listening, writing, and reading: *puppets, tapes and recordings, musical instruments, typewriters, materials that encourage dramatic play (costumes, dress-up clothes, masks; real kitchen equipment, telephone).*

■ Materials should have proven appeal to children: *puzzles, stamp sets, art materials, construction and manipulative sets, stickers.*

■ Materials should demonstrate potential for being used in open-ended ways that encourage problem solving, thinking creatively, and employing a playful and game-like approach: *sequence cards, photographs, playing cards, umbrellas, coffee cans, tote bags, trays, boxes.*

■ Materials should enable children to use various senses in experiencing them: *wooden or magnetic letters, writing and drawing tools, food for cooking and eating, clay, fabrics of different textures, music tapes.*

Organizing and Scheduling Instruction

The third aspect of the classroom environment that holds special importance for language learning involves the ways that teachers organize instruction and schedule the school day. Classroom organization and scheduling instruction play major roles in facilitating literacy learning since, as we discussed earlier, children acquire and extend language skills through actual daily usage that accomplishes specific tasks and provides pleasure in the process.

Language occurs naturally in High/Scope classrooms as children and teachers interact informally. Opportunities for communication involving subjects like friends, families, and exchanges about pets and lost teeth are potentially among the most useful in the classroom. But in High/Scope classrooms language is also used in more formal settings; these settings are organized and designed to ensure adequate attention to all oral and written forms. Of course, teachers organize school time according to the constraints of district guidelines and the age level of the children. And even within these wide parameters, the vagaries of bus schedules, "pull-out" programs, and the timetables of special assignment teachers make the notion of following a schedule easier said than done.

Teachers must be sure to set aside time each day for the **whole class** to meet as a group to share conversation and feelings, hear stories read aloud, and discuss events. In these whole-class settings children have wide ranging opportunities to sing, dramatize stories, and solve problems.

At all grade levels, teachers also should schedule time when **small groups** of children meet to work on topics that have special interest for them. In these small groups teachers plan instruction that is individualized according to the developmental needs of the children. We use the term **"workshop"** to describe these group times because the attitude workshops foster is one of active participation and involvement on the part of the children.

Language Workshops

In High/Scope classrooms language workshops replace the more limited notions of "reading groups" or "seat-work time" that accompanied earlier interpretations of reading and writing instruction. Rather than relying on static recitation, round-the-circle reading, or skill sheets, teachers use workshops to provide children with opportunities to experience and acquire skill in all forms of language. Teachers and children share the responsibility for learn-

Half-Day Kindergarten Sample Schedule

8:30–8:50
Opening/circle

8:50–9:30
Plan-do-review

9:30–10:30
Language/math workshop

10:30–11:00
Outside play/snack/physical education

11:00–11:30
Music/story

11:30
Dismissal

Full-Day Kindergarten Sample Schedule

8:30–9:00
Opening

9:00–9:45
Plan-do-review

9:45–10:45
Language/math workshop

10:45–11:15
Music, movement

11:15–11:45
Lunch

11:45–12:00
Prepare for outside

12:00–12:30
Outside play

12:30–1:00
Circle or theme activity

1:00–1:40
All read/all write

1:40–2:00
Physical education

2:00–2:20
Story

2:20
Dismissal

ing. Teachers assume a responsibility for planning instruction around broadly defined learning objectives that are primary or **key experiences**. These key experiences, defined more completely in the following chapter, provide the framework that helps teachers gain an in-depth understanding of the High/Scope approach. Yet children share the responsibility for learning as active, working participants.

For example, in the language workshop the teacher may choose to emphasize extending auditory skill with six or eight children. They may be clustered around a big book that the teacher uses to emphasize repetitive phrases. In another part of the room, other children play a game designed to reinforce skills that have been introduced earlier. Other children may be reading or writing, using materials available in centers that they chose and following plans that they made. Still other children may be using language-related software at the computer center or listening to taped stories at a listening center.

These informal and flexible groupings of children rotate during the language workshop time period, permitting the children's interest to remain high and making it possible for the teacher to supervise activities and children throughout the room.

Because teachers organize the room with cooperative experiences in mind and because they arrange materials so children can use them independently, this type of multiple activity setting is possible and practical. Teachers find that children adapt quickly to the workshop setting. Children look forward to the variety of experiences offered by the workshop—working with the teacher, working independently, working with a partner, and working with several children to solve problems. Being part of flexible working configurations is stimulating for children; they have many different kinds of opportunities to gain insight and to collaborate with peers.

Teachers appreciate the chance to work intensively with small clusters of children so they can gauge skill levels and offer adequate opportunities for children to practice skills. Teachers anticipate that participation in these instructional groups changes freely. Teachers also note that independence is fostered when children work in small groups on language and literacy development skills and solve problems that naturally develop as they interact with peers.

First Grade Sample Schedule

8:30–8:50
Opening

8:50–9:10
Music

9:10–10:30
Math workshop

10:30–10:40
Story time

10:40–11:10
Whole-group reading

11:10–12:10
Language workshop

12:10–12:35
Lunch

12:35–1:05
Science/social studies

1:05–1:30
Physical education

1:30–2:50
Plan-do-review

2:50
Dismissal

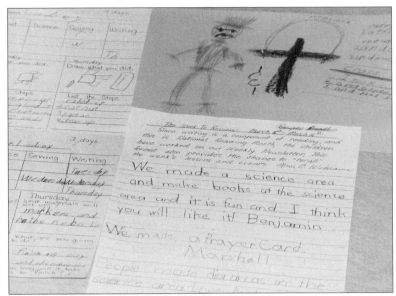

Children may plan where they will work by writing sentences or filling in a planning form.

Plan-Do-Review

At all grade levels it is important for children to have opportunities to work independently during some part of each day. They times are included in the schedule as **plan-do-review**.

The plan-do-review sequence has become a hallmark of High/Scope programs at all age levels. In this setting teachers help children plan independent activity, support children as they engage in the activity, and encourage children to review their work and relate it to earlier knowledge. As such, it holds a prominent place in the K–3 curriculum.

As the sample schedules indicate, the time of day and the length of time allotted to plan-do-review vary according to grade levels and local scheduling needs. What is consistent, however, is the perspective that the plan-do-review process promotes. Children use language in all forms as they plan and organize their interests and activities so they become purposeful. Similarly, children use all forms of language when they pursue individual interests, e.g., building with blocks, painting pictures, playing games, reading and writing in journals, and researching innumerable science topics. Finally, children continue using language when they review and represent the work they have done. They may talk or sing about the work, read what they have written during work time, or write reflections on

Second Grade Sample Schedule

8:10–8:40
Opening/Center sign-in

8:40–9:10
Science/social studies/music

9:10–10:05
Math workshop

10:05–11:05
All read

11:05–11:35
Physical education

11:35–11:55
Calendar and wash-up

11:55–12:25
Lunch

12:25–12:45
Story time

12:45–1:45
Language workshop

1:45–2:50
Plan-do-review

2:50
Dismissal

the problems they have encountered while they worked independently.

Teachers in High/Scope K–3 classrooms find as many ways to help children with this purposeful planning as there are teachers! Some teachers meet with the whole class and involve children briefly in the experience of deciding where they plan to spend time and what they plan to do. Some teachers prefer to meet with small groups, so they can explore in more depth the reasons why children plan to work in a certain center or area of the room. Some teachers of older children encourage children to explain their choices to peers or write sentences and paragraphs that focus on their interests and the reasons for particular choices.

The time children spend "doing" work is time that is filled with opportunities for oral and written language. Children have conversations with other children and with the teacher during their work time. Children explore the wealth of materials in all the centers and use these materials in ways that express their developmental stages. To expand their understanding, they have opportunities to independently explore the useful connections between what they have known and done before and what they currently are doing.

As teachers help children to reflect on or review the activities they have completed, they have additional resources for testing the language hypotheses discussed earlier. Teachers solve the logistics of this review period as creatively as they organize the planning segment. Some teachers encourage children to use oral language—for instance, to explain a painting, demonstrate how an experiment was conducted, or read a letter written to a favorite author. Teachers at other grade levels encourage children to write about what they have done—in drawings, or emerging or conventional print, in many forms of journals, and on signs left with their work.

Summary

We have explored the environment of High/Scope K–3 classrooms, and this perspective has served to underscore the pervasiveness of language and literacy in this setting. The climate engendered when oral and written language are valued is a stimulating one. When the room is ar-

Third Grade Sample Schedule

8:30–8:55
Opening exercises

8:55–10:05
Math workshop

10:05–10:40
Physical education

10:40–12:20
Language workshop

12:20–1:05
Lunch

1:05–1:40
Music/science/social studies

1:40–2:50
Plan-do-review

2:50
Dismissal

ranged to facilitate all forms of language use, when the materials are selected to interest children and make their learning both effective and pleasurable, and when the day is scheduled to allow varied forms of interaction, the wholeness of language is validated.

In Part Two of this guide we present an overview of the High/Scope key experiences in language and literacy (Chapter 5), and then offer suggested activities, which are grouped under the three major language and literacy key experience categories (Chapters 6–8). Developmentally appropriate assessment techniques and procedures are discussed in Chapter 9.

▼

Part 2

Key Experiences, Activities, & Assessment

5
▼

Key Experiences in Language & Literacy Development

The **High/Scope K–3 key experiences** in the whole language curriculum are fundamental learning objectives that contribute to children's mastery of oral and written language. These experiences are not, however, narrowly focused objectives that are numbered and checked off once they have been taught. Rather, the key experiences are useful guides that repeatedly generate literacy activity. Because these experiences consistently promote growth in language skills, they can and should be repeated frequently. Each time a child participates in a key experience, there is potential for broadened learning and interpretation of what has been learned; these experiences are not repeated solely to provide additional skill practice.

Some educators may immediately associate the key experiences with scope and sequence charts, but that is inaccurate. High/Scope defines the key experiences in language and literacy as **learning goals** that help teachers identify and build on children's individual strengths—e.g., "Children putting facts and understandings into their own words," "children writing in the content areas," or "children reading their own compositions." High/Scope's key experiences are quite different from skill lessons that concentrate on teaching specific skills, such as identifying homophones or forming contractions.

…Wilbur never forgot Charlotte.

Although he loved her children and grandchildren dearly, none of the new spiders ever quite took her place in his heart.

She was in a class by herself.

It is not often that someone comes along who is a true friend and a good writer.

Charlotte was both.

— In *Charlotte's Web* by E. B. White

The concept of key experiences acknowledges the progressive nature of language and literacy development, but research on this topic adds an important qualifier: *while a general continuum of literacy behaviors can be discerned, there is no predictable, consistent linear progression of skill acquisition.* This means that children are certain to observe and make connections between spoken and written language in their minds before they write continuous text and poetry. Yet, on the other hand, children may approach learning to read by writing before they read—a way that strikes many as convoluted. We can distinguish a general sequence of growth events and can set typical language and literacy expectations for kindergartners through third-graders, but we cannot lay out a predetermined path down which each child will walk. The High/Scope key experiences are **milestones in children's language and literacy development**, not incremental markers. A chart at the end of this chapter contains a complete list of the High/Scope whole language key experiences in the areas of speaking and listening, reading, and writing.

Although in a whole language perspective "the language is kept whole so that all the necessary data for language learning will be present" (Goodman, 1989, p. xi), we have to endure temporarily some artificial separations in skill acquisition to articulate useful milestones in language and literacy learning. Therefore, in the next three chapters we direct attention first to **key experiences in speaking and listening**, then to those in **writing**, and then to those in **reading**—*with the understanding that all of these domains are nevertheless interrelated.* Also, each chapter contains descriptions of **learning activities** that are *vehicles for instruction*, generating opportunities for teachers to individualize instruction according to children's specific interests or developmental patterns and providing appropriate opportunities for skill practice. The activities are arranged in broad developmental categories. The chart on the next page presents a complete listing of the language and literacy key experiences.

High/Scope K–3 Curriculum:
Key Experiences in Language & Literacy

In a language-rich environment where purposeful and supportive communication and use of print resources and children's literature predominate, children shall be

Speaking & Listening

Speaking their own language or dialect

Asking and answering questions

Stating facts and observations in their own words

Using language to solve problems

Participating in singing, storytelling, poetic and dramatic activities

Making and using recordings

Recalling thoughts and observations in a purposeful context

Acquiring, strengthening, and extending speaking and listening skills:

- Discussing to clarify observations or to better follow directions
- Discussing to expand speaking and listening vocabulary
- Discussing to strengthen critical thinking and problem-solving abilities

Writing

Observing the connections between spoken and written language

Writing in unconventional forms:

- Scribbles
- Drawings
- Letters—random or patterned, possibly including elements of names copied from the environment
- Invented spellings—of initial sounds, syllabic sounds, concluding sounds, and intermediate sounds

Writing in conventional forms

Expressing thoughts in writing

Sharing writing in a purposeful context

Using writing equipment (e.g., computers, typewriters)

Writing in specific content areas

Acquiring, strengthening, and extending writing skills:

- Letter formation
- Sentence and paragraph formation
- Capitalization, punctuation, and grammatical sage
- Spelling
- Editing and proofreading for mechanics, content, and style

Expanding the forms of composition:

- Expressive mode
- Transactional mode—expository, argumentative, descriptive
- Poetic mode—narrative poetry

Publishing selected compositions

Reading

Experiencing varied genres of children's literature

Reading own compositions

Reading and listening to others read in a purposeful context

Using audio and/or video recordings in reading experiences

Reading in specific content areas

Acquiring, strengthening, and extending specific reading skills:

- Auditory discrimination
- Letter recognition
- Decoding—
  phonetic analysis (letter/sound associations, factors affecting sounds, syllabication);
  structural analysis (forms, prefixes, suffixes)
- Vocabulary development

Expanding comprehension and fluency skills:

- Activating prior knowledge
- Determining purpose, considering context, making predictions
- Developing strategies for interpreting narrative and expository text
- Reading varied genres of children's literature

6
▼

Speaking & Listening: Key Experiences & Activities

Speaking, and listening to others speak, are fundamental experiences in High/Scope K–3 classrooms.
These experiences form the underpinnings of the
language-rich environment that in many important ways
parallels the home environment where children's language
was initiated and acquired. In Chapter 1, as we looked at
the way children acquire language, we focused on the natural quality of the interactions that surround purposeful
communication in the home. *It is this naturalness that
High/Scope classrooms seek to emulate.*

The supportive verbal interaction that develops between children and teachers and among children themselves occurs because there is a common understanding
that language helps people function. Verbal interaction
helps children and teachers accomplish work and learning. These exchanges help speakers restructure their
knowledge in order to communicate and help listeners
broaden their interpretation of what they are hearing.
This social interaction is a strong means for becoming
literate. Researcher Elfrieda Hiebert declares, for example,
"Substantive talk is . . . not, a frill; it is a primary means
for becoming literate." (Hiebert, 1990, p. 503).

Because the furniture in the High/Scope classroom is
arranged so children and teachers can see each other, the
classroom environment (Chapter 4) facilitates speaking

*…You have gone downtown
to do some shopping.*

*You are walking back-
wards, because sometimes*

*You like to, and you bump
into*

a crocodile.

What do you say, dear?

Excuse me.

— In *What Do You Say, Dear?*
by Sesyle Joslin

and listening. Children talk with other children when they explore the realistic materials grouped into activity centers. To understand others' points of view and follow directions, children are encouraged to listen to the conversation of other children and adults. And children are guided to learn more about discussing and "talking about talking about reading and writing" (Hiebert, 1990, p. 502).

Teachers in High/Scope classrooms are alert to problems that develop when classroom conversation escalates to the point of distraction and becomes nonproductive, and they employ appropriate management strategies. But teachers are also aware that artificially quiet classrooms and unrealistic demands for children to walk through school halls with with little or no conversation are counterproductive, preventing children from gaining self-control and expanding appropriate language use.

Many activities in the classroom extend receptive and expressive language. Some are **whole-class experiences** that occur spontaneously when children gather for circle time or opening activities. Children speak about what happens at home, tell stories about cats having kittens, and share their culture with others. Children learn about pronunciation, about word order, and about word meaning, all within the context of purposeful communication. Teachers also initiate conversations about local or national current events, calendar and weather, and plans for school activities. And, of course, teachers select for reading aloud good examples of children's literature that offer, among other advantages, the stimulation of expanded vocabulary.

Workshops are useful occasions for establishing conversational tone and for facilitating the collaboration that arises between interested conversational partners. When children have opportunities to ask and answer questions, they gain knowledge about negotiating meaning and understanding. The workshop conversations expand children's knowledge of the names of places, objects, and functions. The conversations help children categorize information, restate facts, summarize arguments, and internalize knowledge. The workshops also provide opportunities for children to engage in "strategy" instruction. For example, teachers work with small groups of children using both listening and dialogue to develop text meaning in "reciprocal teaching" (Palincsar & Brown, 1989).

The High/Scope approach underscores the idea that children need frequent opportunities to use oral language to solve problems; one effective format for initiating this process is the **plan-do-review** sequence. Teachers encourage children to use speech in order to translate their interests and their generalized desire for action into purposeful plans. Children are then encouraged to follow up on their plans by participating fully in the work time, using *speaking and listening* as tools for participation. For example, we expect children in a High/Scope classroom to talk and listen while they play math games, to discuss as they measure the growth of plants at the science center, to speak out loud as they read jokes to friends, and to listen with care when other children share their writing or reading with them. These are naturally occurring examples of conversation that extend children's understanding of their planned work. Not surprisingly, one way children review what they did during work time is by orally describing their work to other listening children. Sometimes this oral description occurs naturally in small-group conversation, and at other times it includes a complete representation of the event. In these instances, children may add voice recordings or tapes, singing, dancing, or dramatizing what was done.

Examples of activities specifically designed to engender **speaking and listening** experiences are presented in this chapter. In each case, **selected High/Scope key experiences** are noted, but only as rough guidelines, because the activities are designed to lead to these outcomes as well as to a variety of other outcomes. The activities can be repeated in varied situations with groups of different sizes. Suggestions for grade levels are included but need not be interpreted strictly, because teachers will find ways to simplify some ideas or expand others to meet the developmental levels of children in the classroom. The order of these activities is not predetermined, in keeping with the fluid nature of literacy skill development. Nevertheless, some activities automatically suggest a preferred time of the year, and others build cumulatively to develop a theme. Also, each activity includes suggestions on various ways to extend the learning experiences.

Grades K–1

Speak Up!

Children speak in a playful setting.

Materials

Large ball, space for children to sit on the floor in a circle

Activity

Teachers:

- Invite children to form a circle on the floor.
- Introduce the idea of rolling a ball to children, asking them to speak their names aloud as they have a turn.
- Reassure children who are hesitant or fearful.

Teachers and children:

- Play the game, taking turns rolling the ball to different participants, waiting for each person to "speak up." (Teacher models speaking for hesitant children and continues the game.)
- Expand the concept so children respond with complete sentences, e.g., "My name is Sam."
- Expand the concept so children respond with first and last names, e.g., "My name is Sam Smith."
- Expand the concept so the child who rolls the ball asks the question that is answered by the child who receives the ball: "Who are you?. . .""I am Sam Smith!"

Questions to Ask

Are there other ways we could play this game? What could we ask people when we roll the ball to them? Is there a way we could change this game so we could play it outside? If we played this game outside, would we speak in the same way?

Key Experiences

- Speaking their own language or dialect
- Asking and answering questions
- Stating facts and observations in their own words

Extension

1. Teachers and children add other kinds of information—eye color, age.

2. Teachers and children make the concept more complex by using the turn-taking, game format to practice skills—simple math facts, alphabetical order, etc.

3. Children develop new turn-taking games to meet their interests.

Grades K–1

Give It a Name!

Children make signs and nametags for places, features, and toys in the classroom.

Materials

Oaktag strips, index cards, "Post-It™" notes, construction paper strips; masking tape or hole punch, string or yarn

Activity

Teachers:

- Engage children in conversation about how useful their names are—and how difficult it would be if they could not be identified with names.

Teachers and children:

- Pretend that a common item in the classroom, e.g., the chair you are sitting on, does not have a name.
- Explore possibilities for giving important things in the classroom print names, e.g., the rug, the sink.
- Plan to use appropriate material to make and fasten print signs for items in the classroom.
- Plan to label materials in math, science, social studies centers

Children:

- Select materials and items to be labeled.
- Write names in their own way and attach them to the items.
- Share names by reading to classmates and adults.

Questions to Ask

What would happen if I wanted to talk to _____ and he was with a lot of other children, and he did not have a name? Do you think names are necessary? Why? How do you think you got your name? Your nickname? Do cars, trucks, airplanes, shops, or stores have names? Discuss.

Key Experiences

- Stating facts and observations in their own words

- Using language to solve problems

- Observing the connections between spoken and written language

- Writing in unconventional forms:
  - Scribbles
  - Drawings
  - Letters—random or patterned, possibly including elements of names copied from the environment
  - Invented spellings—of initial sounds, syllabic sounds, concluding sounds, and intermediate sounds

- Writing in conventional forms

- Using writing equipment (e.g., computers, typewriters)

- Writing in specific content areas

- Reading and listening to others read in a purposeful context

- Acquiring, strengthening, and extending specific reading skills:
  - Auditory discrimination
  - Letter recognition
  - Vocabulary development

What about toys, food in the grocery store, programs on TV, places in your neighborhood—are these named?

Extension

1. Teachers and children discuss variations on names with interested children, e.g., a classroom toy may be named "the horse" or "Woody," etc.

2. Teachers encourage children to negotiate spelling as they name items in the classroom.

3. Teachers encourage children to collaborate as they decide what to name the items.

4. Teachers and children plan a "Mixed-up Name Day." Participants wear name tags with silly names and use them to identify one another.

Grades K–1

It's Green Day—or Week!

Language, math, science, music, movement, social studies, and art combine to develop color awareness, concepts, and vocabulary.

Materials

Classroom materials and supplies—paper, fabric, toys, art supplies, books, e.g., *Little Blue and Little Yellow* by L. Lionni; materials brought by children from home

Activity

Teachers:

- Plan and announce a Color Day, e.g., "Green Day."
- Invite children to wear green clothing and to bring something green from home.
- Plan a healthful snack featuring colorful foods, e.g., celery, honeydew melon, grapes, zucchini, olives, or lime-flavored drink.
- Plan a display of labeled green items, adding items brought by the children.
- Collect and read aloud books that incorporate the color.
- Search for sensory and concrete activities and experiences that children can do independently, e.g., using green clay, mixing colors to produce green, painting with green paint, looking through green cellophane. Arrange necessary materials in a center.

Teachers and children:

- Make lists of green items, call attention to labels, identify the print symbols that record the concept of "green."
- Explore additional words for describing color and properties of color, e.g., "chartreuse," "forest green," "shade", "hue", "tint."
- Consider making a book called "The Big Green Book," including illustrations and text of green classroom items, green items from home, green items from outside, things that could never have

Key Experiences

- Speaking their own language or dialect
- Asking and answering questions
- Stating facts and observations in their own words
- Participating in singing, story-telling, poetic and dramatic activities
- Observing the connections between spoken and written language
- Writing in unconventional forms
- Writing in conventional forms
- Using writing equipment (e.g., computers, typewriters)
- Writing in specific content areas
- Experiencing varied genres of children's literature
- Acquiring, strengthening, and extending specific reading skills:
  - Auditory discrimination
  - Letter recognition
  - Vocabulary development

been green, things that might surprise us if they were green, etc.

- Introduce sensory materials that are in the center; predict what might happen, e.g., when children mix food coloring; consider special handling needs, e.g., a clay board should be used with the green clay; consider special cleaning at conclusion, e.g., washing out the green paint brushes and hanging up the wet tempera painting.

- Share books, extending and deriving additional writing activities from them, e.g., make green eggs for a snack after reading *Green Eggs and Ham* by Dr. Seuss.

Children:

- Engage in a wide range of activities at all content centers.

Questions to Ask

What green things are in the grocery store? Can you think of five green things in your bedroom?

Extension

1. Teachers expand ideas for books that can be derived from the topic, e.g., "A_____ may be green but a dog is brown."

2. Teachers choose movies about color, e.g., *The Gruesome Gray Monster*.

3. Teachers and children plan color walks to shopping center, in neighborhood, etc.

4. Teachers and children plan similar productions for other colors.

Note: The range of activities is so extensive that plenty of time should be available for exploring as long as children remain interested. Some of the activities are introduced in whole-group settings, extended for several days in workshops, and incorporated into long-lasting independent interests. The opportunity for challenging students should be uppermost in mind when planning the workshops.

Grade K–3
Let's Cooperate!*

Children collaborate in telling a story and finding ways to represent the story.

Material

Tape recorder, hoola hoop or large pot, clay

Activity

Teachers:

- Explain that everyone will be involved in making up and recording a story.
- Turn on tape recorder and position children on floor or at low table around hoop or large pot; provide children with egg-sized piece of clay to warm in their hands.

Teachers and children:

- Model the idea of adding an ingredient to the "story pot," e.g., "One day I was out in the country right on the edge of a stream." "Stir" this ingredient into the pot and invite another person to add either another ingredient about the setting or an ingredient about characters, or about the problems and events the characters have experienced.
- All together, stir more suggested ingredients in and then tell the story that emerges from this collaboration.
- Listen to a taped recording of the story and decide what else might be "stirred in" to clarify the story, complete the story, make it more spooky, etc.
- Encourage children to form the hand-warmed clay into some representation of the story.
- Explore the idea of incorporating information from other content areas, e.g., problems presented in a story may be solved using math concepts or scientific analysis. The focus of the activity is to develop a story, and the activity should not deteriorate into contrived variations. Nevertheless, it is helpful for children to recognize the connections between literature and other areas of study.

Key Experiences

- Participating in singing, storytelling, dramatic activities

- Making and using recordings

- Acquiring, strengthening, and extending speaking and listening skills:
  - Discussing to expand speaking and listening vocabulary

Children:

- Share their representations as they retell the story.
- Use the cooking pot format to tell stories of their own choosing.

Questions to Ask

I'm going to "stir up" a story—what shall I begin with? Shall I stir in the setting, or one of the characters, or something that happens in the story? When you use the warmed clay to make something about the story, will you choose something that happened to someone in the story, will you make something to show where the story took place, or will you make one of the characters in the story?

Extension

1. Teachers begin a story appropriate to a season of the year or to a major study theme.

2. Teachers and children use the taped version of the story to stage a dramatic enactment.

3. Teachers and children expand the concept to include videotaped versions of their cooperative storytelling efforts.

Note: This activity works well in language workshops where teachers select key experiences, e.g, narrative text comprehension strategies, vocabulary development. After children understand the format, know how to use the tape recorder, and are comfortable, they may wish to extend it to the plan-do-review process.

---

*This activity was suggested by Betsy Evans, Head Teacher and Director of The Giving Tree in Gill, MA.

Grades K–3
Puppet Pets

Children use puppets to express feelings, communicate, and tell stories.

Materials

Assorted animal puppets; stage is optional

Activity

Teachers and children:

- Experiment with manipulating various puppets.
- Consider characteristics of puppets.
- Manipulate two puppets, individually or with partners.
- Initiate conversation and story-telling between puppets; introduce setting, plot, character.

Children:

- Continue using puppets.
- Individually or cooperatively, tell a story with puppets; include setting, plot, character.
- Share puppet presentations with classmates and with the teacher.

Questions to Ask

What kind of puppets have you seen? How do they work? How could you show that the puppet is angry? Sad? Happy? What kind of things are easy to do with puppets and what are difficult? What makes a good story for puppet shows?

Extension

1. Children add scenery as a background for the puppet stage.

2. Children write stories for retelling.

- Speaking their own language or dialect
- Asking and answering questions
- Stating facts and observations in their own words
- Participating in singing, story-telling, poetic and dramatic activities
- Recalling thoughts and observations in a purposeful context

3. Children share spontaneous or revised presentations with other groups.

4. Teachers invite professional puppeteers to demonstrate their craft and art.

5. Teachers show movies and read books to the children about professional puppet groups.

Grade K–3
Channel "YOU"

Children use the simple prop of a television monitor to speak in a variety of ways, settings.

Materials

Large cardboard box, e.g., appliance, paper products, or a simple puppet stage. Any other appropriate additions—scenery, microphone, costumes, props, classroom television set; the poem "Channels" from *A Light in the Attic* by Shel Silverstein

Activity

Teachers:

- Obtain a large box or puppet stage to serve as a classroom television prop.
- Read the poem "Channels" by Shel Silverstein to the children.

Teachers and children:

- Discuss television programs that are regularly enjoyed by members of the class.
- Identify the different types of program formats, e.g., news, comedy shows, documentaries, dramatizations of stories, interviews with famous people, weather reports and forecasts, sports.
- Explore the feasibility of constructing a classroom television set from the large box or puppet stage. Discuss the features that would be needed, e.g., large monitor area which would feature cut-out, performance space, on/off switch, channel knobs, remote control device, volume and color adjustments.
- Consider the kinds of programming that could be shown on the "classroom channel"—interviews with children, news report from the school, puppet plays, children reading their own compositions.
- Explore the idea of children developing news reports on science, social studies, or math topics to strengthen the connections between all areas of learning.

Key Experiences

- Speaking their own language or dialect
- Asking and answering questions
- Stating facts and understandings in their own words
- Acquiring, strengthening, and extending speaking and listening skills:
  - Discussing to clarify observations or to better follow directions
  - Discussing to expand speaking and listening vocabulary
  - Discussing to strengthen critical thinking and problem-solving abilities
- Writing in specific content areas
- Reading in specific content areas.

- Collect the materials needed to make the television set.

Children:

- Construct the set and plan the television programs.
- Present classroom television programs on varied topics.

Questions to Ask

How do you feel about television programs? What kind of programs do you watch at home? Are there programs that your family chooses not to watch? Why? If you did not have a television set at home, what might you do with the time you usually spend watching your favorite programs? What do you think makes a good television program? What topics would you consider in making television programs that would appeal to the children in this room and how would you provide accurate information to others "tuning in" the classroom channel?

Extension

1. Teachers encourage children to use the idea of presenting a television documentary, a news report, or an interview as a way of summarizing work they have completed in a theme area.

2. Children present programs on their classroom television channel for other classes and for parent nights.

Note: This activity might be initiated with the entire class, extended in the small-group language workshops, and expanded to be available throughout the day in all subject areas and in the plan-do-review sequence.

Grade 1–3

Have a Good Weekend!

Develop a "Weekend Backpack" or kit to send home with children for the weekend, to accompany a child who will be absent for a trip, or to encourage a child who is recuperating from illness.

Materials

Backpack, sturdy battery-powered tape recorder and tape, small spiral-bound notebook, unlined newsprint tablet, assorted pencils, crayons, markers. Optional materials—map, television guide, newspaper, museum guide, inexpensive and easily operated camera, black and white film, etc.

Activity

Teachers:

- Assemble appropriate equipment and materials obtained with the help of the Parent-Teacher Association, from budgeted funds, or financed by contributions. Fit whatever is selected into the backpack and provide the necessary school identification.

- Clarify the procedure for replacement of the backpack and its contents in the event it is lost or accidentally damaged.

Teachers and children:

- Brainstorm ideas for materials people take with them when they plan a trip, when they have to enter the hospital, or when they attend any type of special event.

- Discuss the Weekend Backpack, emphasizing that it will be available on a rotating basis—to support someone who is ill or absent from school for some other reason, or to record a child's weekend experiences.

- Discuss the care and responsibility that is involved with checking out the Weekend Backpack.

- Brainstorm events that might be interesting ones to "review."

- Brainstorm ways that such events could be recorded and reviewed, e.g., recording a description of a trip, including some music heard, some sounds experienced; writing a summary or story of

Key Experiences

- Stating facts and observations in their own words

- Making and using recordings

- Recalling thoughts and observations in a purposeful context

- Acquiring, strengthening, and extending speaking and listening skills:
  - Discussing to clarify observations or to better follow directions
  - Discussing to expand speaking and listening vocabulary
  - Discussing to strengthen critical thinking and problem-solving abilities

- Writing in unconventional forms
  - Scribbles
  - Drawings
  - Letters—random or patterned, possibly including elements of names copied from the environment
  - Invented spellings—of initial sounds, syllabic sounds, concluding sounds, and intermediate sounds

- Writing in conventional forms

- Writing in specific content areas

- Expanding the forms of composition:
  - Expressive mode
  - Transactional mode—expository, argumentative, descriptive
  - Poetic mode—narrative poetry

- Reading in specific content areas

an event a child experienced; or making a drawing of the hospital room where a child is recuperating.

■ Discuss the sign-out procedure and develop a priority system, e.g., illness, a family trip, taking an airplane trip for the first time, a weekend at home.

Children:

■ Check-out the Weekend Backpack and try to find as many ways as possible to use their **speaking**, **writing**, and **listening** skills to record and review life experiences.

■ Share their weekend, vacation, or hospitalization experiences by using recordings, writing, and reading.

■ Continue exploring topics of personal interest.

Questions to Ask

Why do you think people like to share with others their memories and recollections of trips? Why do you think people like to take photographs of weddings, trips to the beach, vacations, etc.? Have you ever had to spend time in the hospital or at home recovering from an illness? What did you miss most about not being at school?

Extension

1. Teachers develop different packs—a bag just for hospital use, a "mini" version in a smaller pack with no tape recorder, or a standard "take-turns-every-weekend" pack.

2. Teachers and children discuss ways to include all subject areas e.g., by bringing mementos back for math or science centers, books about places visited to add to social studies or theme centers, etc.

3. Teachers and children look for ways to share experiences with other classes. For example, children share recordings made of the sound of waves as they crash on the beach, a poem written while sitting on the beach, a bag of shells collected along the beach, photographs of the sunset, brochures describing the beach area, maps detailing the locale, drawings made while watching sea gulls, and ideas for continued study.

4. Teachers and children explore ways to follow up on the events and experiences recorded, e.g., finding library books that provide additional information, encyclopedias to clarify specific interest, etc.

■ Acquiring, strengthening, and extending specific reading skills:
  • Auditory discrimination
  • Letter recognition
  • Decoding—*phonetic analysis* (letter/sound associations, factors affecting sounds, syllabication); *structural analysis* (forms, prefixes, suffixes)
  • Vocabulary development

7
▼

Writing: Key Experiences & Activities

Writing is another fundamental literacy experience in High/Scope K–3 classrooms for the simple and compelling reason that children become writers by writing. As children make connections between spoken language and written language, they extend their understanding to include the symbolic forms used to capture speech. Children typically make these connections during naturally occurring events at home, well before they enter school. Children hypothesize about the connections, and the evidence they accumulate expands their speculations about written language. Children initially wonder where the message resides—and it is sometime later that they separate out print from picture and concentrate on understanding the text.

When children enter High/Scope kindergarten classes, they see clear evidence of the connections between spoken and written language. For example, teachers write down the children's spoken language, transforming utterances into symbolic, printed form. Teachers model writing—print production—and call attention to features of the print as well as to the corresponding oral form. Teachers read aloud from print and direct attention to the process of moving from one form to another. Thus, the connections between oral and written language are not taken for granted; they are solidified and reinforced through repeated experiences in and out of the classroom.

"... I'm writing a letter to Amy.

"I'm inviting her to my party," Peter announced.

"Why don't you just ask her? You didn't write to any-one else," said his mother.

Peter stared at the sheet of paper for awhile and said, "We-e-el-l, this way it's sort of special."

— In *A Letter to Amy* by Ezra Jack Keats

"Once upon a time a mama was doing work and Freddy Cougar came into her house and ate her all up. Pretty soon she came to life and her little girl was happy." — Preschooler

Children are encouraged to explore for themselves the symbols that hold functional value, and teachers are prepared for the same range of children's explorations that accompany the development of oral language, i.e., the earliest results of these explorations are approximations of adult forms. When learning to speak, infants experiment with many sounds. They may settle on a phrase like "Da-da bye-bye" as a way of conveying the message "Daddy went out of the room." We do not expect children to arrive at fully developed and conventional speech in their early attempts. Similarly, the developing symbolic forms children use to encode oral language into written form appear unconventional by adult standards.

Early writing development takes many unconventional forms; the forms may approximate the appearance or direction of print and be "scribble," wavy or letter-like in appearance—not recognizable as letters at all. Drawing is often included and considered as part of the text. The "pretend writing" may even be viewed differently by the same child at different times.

Symbols used in early writing incorporate principles found in conventional writing, such as recurring or repetitive forms and horizontal placement, and they often possess some of the features of letters.

Early writing development often incorporates both letter-like units and letters in random order or patterned in intricate schema. Elements of print found in the environment, especially on commonly seen signs such as "K-mart™," McDonald's™," "STOP," and "Ford," easily become integrated into early writing exploration.

Children who are encouraged to investigate writing and other elements of the print world often move on to attach phonemic meaning (differentiated sounds) to the graphemic meaning (written units). Given the quirkiness of the English alphabetic system, it is a difficult task, at best, to make these associations, and unless children are actively encouraged to explore letter-sound relationships, they may not make the attempts. In fact, children who are instructed to produce only conventional, adult forms of writing are limited unnecessarily and miss an important set of experiences.

High/Scope teachers find it useful to keep broad behavioral milestones in mind as they observe children using early unconventional writing forms. They understand that just as children progress through general literacy development in individual ways, they progress through the phases of early writing in individual ways.

The work of Temple, Nathan, Burris, and Temple (1988) points to five commonly observed stages during which children explore and invent spelling systems for themselves. These stages may appear in three-year-olds who have had many reading and writing experiences; they may appear over a four-year period beginning in preschool and ending in second grade; or they may simply appear as vestigial elements, barely recognizable at all. The stages include the following:

- Prephonemic spelling
- Early phonemic spelling
- Letter-name spelling
- Transitional spelling
- Conventional spelling

Big, Bad Freddy Cougar; Playing Ball in the Park; A Dog Show

In the illustration at left (page 88), a preschooler's repetitive, horizontal forms resemble adult cursive writing. Drawing, print-like marks, and scribble appear together in a kindergartner's story (directly below). A carefully drawn picture is read as a story in the third illustration, also produced by a kindergartner:

"The name of the story is the boy and girl who played ball in the park." — Kindergartner

"This dog is in the dog show." — Kindergartner

In the *prephonemic spelling stage*, children string together letters that are formed accurately but that bear no relation to represented speech sounds. In overall appearance these letter strings approximate the words children see in their environment.

Early phonemic spellers attempt to represent speech sounds with letters while they continue to operate with limited facility. Children isolate a sound or two in a word, yet finish the word with unrelated letters.

The transition to the next stage, *letter-name spelling*, reflects a higher degree of sophistication. Children conceive of words as entities that may be broken down into components. They represent these component parts—phonemes or sounds—with letters, acknowledging the relationship between the sounds and the print symbols that record the sounds.

Transitional spellers gradually extend facility with letter-sound representation by moving from initial sounds to syllables and on to final sounds; eventually, they include intermediate sounds as well. During this period, children become aware of the features of conventional spelling.

With practice, children synthesize these features and the features emerge as *conventional spelling* forms.

The "how" of writing is important to teachers in High/Scope K–3 classrooms because of the connection with the "what" of writing—composition. High/Scope teachers consider this relationship an integral part of the whole language curriculum and emphasize its importance by providing opportunities for children to write regularly—in their own way and on topics of their own choosing. Teachers initiate these opportunities in kindergarten by encouraging children to sign in each day, write in journals, and write stories their own way. This emphasis on writing remains unchanged throughout the elementary grades, with the only difference being the conventional forms children employ and the more complex topics children select. Even when children are developing the print and spelling generalizations, they are also developing as writers. For example, as they invent spelling, they work through the phonic skills, becoming stronger in their ability to generalize and make exceptions, as they continue to emphasize meaning (Hansen, 1987).

A Game and a Visit

Well-formed letters appear conventionally but have no connection to speech sounds in the first illustration; in the second, some sounds are represented but limited facility with the concepts means that other words are completed with unrelated letters.

"Me and my friend was going to play hide and go seek. Then my mom gave me and my friend some money and after that we went in the house and played with my toys. Then her and me went back outside."
— Kindergartner

"I would like to go to my friend's house." — Kindergartner

> THE SNAK ATE ₱ MISE
> WE WATCT HEM ETE ₱ MISE
> THE FIRST MOWS WAS ATEON
> BY THE HEPE
> THE LAST MOWS WAS-ATEON
> BY THE BUT
>
> Rebecca L

"The snake ate four mice. We watched him eat four mice. The first mouse was eaten by the head. The last mouse was eaten by the butt."
— Kindergartner

Workshops offer a natural forum for extending children's writing experiences. Teachers often integrate writing activities into the day as assignments for children—writing letters, writing stories, writing about feelings, making lists, writing responses to books read. Teachers also encourage children to make entries of their own choosing in any of several kinds of journals. With these activities High/Scope teachers establish a supportive writing environment that enables children to express their own thoughts in a variety of written formats—formats that permit children to accomplish purposeful work.

Teachers understand that writing, as defined by researcher Donald Graves (1983), is a process rather than a one-dimensional event. Teachers assist children through steps in the process: *prewriting* experiences where children brainstorm on topics and information, *drafting* tentative first versions, *revising* through review, *editing* with the help of interested classmates and conferences, and possibly *publishing* the work. High/Scope teachers are aware, as Graves and other researchers emphasize, that spelling, punctuation, capitalization, and grammar are considered secondarily, after prewriting and drafting. These later skills are standardized through a process of active revising, editing, and proofreading.

The Snake Eats Mice; and Beetle Juice Goes Shopping!

The illustration at left treats an unconventional topic in an almost-conventional manner!

In the illustration below, several initial and concluding sounds are represented conventionally: "B(bee) DL(tle) J(jui) S(ce) UT (went to) D(the) S(store)." But some sounds are not yet perceived accurately—e.g., "D" for "the."

"Beetle Juice went to the store."
— Grade 1

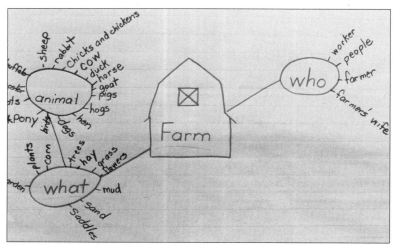

"Prewriting" experiences enable children to brainstorm on various topics of interest, thus allowing them to draw upon their prior knowledge.

Children learn to work through this editing process in small workshop groups, but they are able to extend the process to individual work. In the workshops children interact with other children about literacy issues: they experience the reactions of others who have read their writing; they learn whether others understood what they wrote or even if they could read it; they find out whether others share the same opinion; and they determine whether others have the same background experiences.

Children may also discover that classmates challenge their spelling and have trouble understanding where the sentences begin and end. This becomes a powerful and authentic reason to work at generalizing spelling rules. The process of readjusting hypotheses about spelling, grammar, and punctuation engages the writer and those who react to the writing. In all these examples the children who write and the children who react to writing learn through collaborative effort.

High/Scope teachers also schedule writing conferences to help children evaluate the samples of ongoing work in writing folders and portfolios (Chapter 9). Together, teachers and children may work through problems of finding writing topics, difficulties with grammar and spelling, techniques for revising and editing, and ways that expand the substance and forms of composition.

"Conventions"

Conventional forms of writing and spelling emerge as children generalize their writing experiences.

"I saw a bear and this is what he said, 'Hi, Sweetheart.' The bear is brown. The next morning I went walking. The bear was still asleep. Then the bear woke up. I said 'Oh-oh.' Then he said 'Good morning.' "   Grade 2

"I saw a duck walk and said 'Hello' and I look around and said 'Who said that?' And then I look down. It was a duck and the duck said, 'Have you seen a duck around here?' I said, 'You are a duck.'"   Grade 2

All About Pandas — *"I know special things about pandas. Many pandas are big and healthy. When baby pandas are born they look like pink mouse. And sometimes baby pandas are born they have no fur. Many people in China have made laws not to kill pandas. They need food to live for there little cubs. Pandas can do many somersaults and they play a lot. Many people have killed pandas, and many have disapear. Some people do not want these pandas to die."* — Grade 3

In the examples at left, children participating in workshops derive writing topics from literature discussions. "All About Pandas" (directly left) is the topic for expository writing meant to be shared with other children. "The Pain" (below left) is the topic for expressive writing inspired by a child's feelings about the trials and tribulations of having an older brother.

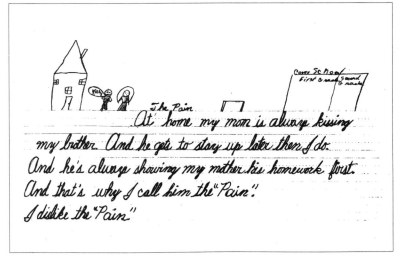

The Pain — *"At home my mom is always kissing my brother. And he gets to stay up later than I do. And he's always showing my mother his homework first. And that's why I call him the 'Pain.' I dislike the 'Pain.'"* — Grade 3

Children collaborate to edit text written at the computer.

Some teachers find that workshop times work well for these individual conferences; other teachers set aside time during plan-do-review. Conferencing is an important part of the writing process, and teachers work out the details related to timing and scheduling in creative ways.

We suggest activities that demonstrate how teachers can encourage the writing process in High/Scope classrooms. One activity, "The Author's Chair," suggests a generic format for use when children share their writing as author or as listener. Writing researcher Jane Hansen recommends this activity for helping children grapple with articulating and understanding meaning (Hansen, 1987).

The key experiences around which the activities are developed are broad and lead easily to variations and extensions. More important than any specific activity itself, however, is the fundamental approach that views the writing process as an aspect of whole language, a larger process that develops just as the children who engage in it develop as writers.

This teacher uses a writing conference to develop a child's unique skills.

…There in the center of the web, neatly woven in block letters was a message. It said:

"SOME PIG!""

— In *Charlotte's Web* by E. B. White

Teachers are encouraged to simplify activities for children when necessary and to expand activities to provide challenge and stimulation for other children. In each case the grade level indicated is only a suggestion.

Grades K–1
Walk Around the Print

Children walk around the schoolroom, building, playground, neighborhood, or shopping area—observing, naming, and discussing items that feature print.

Materials

Examples of print that carry meaning for children, e.g., room signs, classroom name lists, children's T-shirts, bulletin board captions, calendars; signs for "gym," "kitchen," "Principal," name of school building; names on school equipment, fences; neighborhood street signs, STOP sign, traffic lights; familiar store or restaurant names

Activity

Teachers:

- Announce the "Print Walk" and speculate about what kinds of items that have print on them might be found.
- Engage children in conversations about different examples of print.

Teachers and children:

- Walk, using opportunities to identify signs, features of print, names.
- Talk about what is seen, touch print, compare forms of print and names.
- Discuss familiar features, e.g., "That letter is the first letter in your name, isn't it, John?"
- Read children's T-shirts, lunch boxes, labels on shoes.
- Emphasize that reading in this way is like reading in books.

Children:

- Read—whenever and wherever!

Key Experiences

- Speaking their own language or dialect

- Stating facts and observations in their own words

- Acquiring, strengthening, and extending speaking and listening skills:
  - Discussing to clarify observations or to better follow directions
  - Discussing to expand speaking and listening vocabulary
  - Discussing to strengthen critical thinking and problem-solving abilities

- Observing the connections between spoken and written language

- Acquiring, strengthening, and extending specific reading skills:
  - Auditory discrimination
  - Letter recognition
  - Decoding—*phonetic analysis* (letter/sound associations, factors affecting sounds, syllabication); *structural analysis* (forms, prefixes, suffixes)
  - Vocabulary development

Questions to Ask

Do you have anything to read at home besides books? How do you know that this is reading? Do you have anything "on" you—right now—that we can read? Does anyone have an "A" on himself or herself? Does anyone have a letter in his or her name that appears on the STOP sign, for example?

Extension

1. Teachers encourage children to take their own "print walk" at home. Teachers encourage children to bring disposable print materials from home to add to the centers.

2. Teachers and children develop a bulletin board with clothing items featuring print—appropriate for children to read.

3. Teachers and children plan a "Read My T-Shirt Day." Everyone in the school is asked to wear shirts with appropriate print.

Grades K–2

From A to Z

Children use varied materials to experience the alphabet in multiple ways.

Materials

Pasta (cooked or uncooked), alphabet cereal, "Gummi Bears™" letters; paper plate or waxed paper; books, including *Eating the Alphabet* by Lois Ehlert

Activity

Teachers:

- Read *Eating the Alphabet* aloud to children several times.
- Direct attention to print and to the alphabet.

Teachers and children:

- Discuss fruits and vegetables mentioned in the book.
- Consider other ways to "eat the alphabet," e.g., SpaghettiOs™, cereals, pasta, Gummi Bears™ products.
- Explore possibilities for recognizing and forming alphabet letters with available materials. (Discuss which materials would be edible—e.g., cooked spaghetti, cereal, candy letters—and which would not, e.g., uncooked pasta)

Children:

- Explore materials independently.
- Form letters from cooked spaghetti; collect and arrange other letters in alphabetical order or combine into words; match lower-case with capital letters; form sentences.
- Share experiences with other children and with the teacher.
- Save what might be needed for another occasion.
- Eat the rest.

Key Experiences

- Observing the connections between spoken and written language
- Writing in conventional forms
- Using writing equipment (e.g., computers, typewriters)
- Acquiring, strengthening, and extending writing skills:
  - Letter formation
- Acquiring, strengthening, and extending specific reading skills:
  - Auditory discrimination
  - Letter recognition
  - Vocabulary development

Questions to Ask

How many ways can you think of to "eat the alphabet"?
Do you think you could write with spaghetti? Have you
ever read your cereal or soup?

Extension

1. Children glue uncooked pasta or cereal letters,
names, words, or stories to paper.

2. Children produce edible collages with edible print.

3. Teacher reads *Strega Nona* by Tomie de Paola to
generate discussion about pasta; following that, children
help cook pasta.

4. Teacher and children plan an "alphabet lunch";
they include alphabet soup or pasta, cheese cut in
alphabet shapes, etc.

5. Teacher and children use alphabet cutters to make
cookies.

Grades K–3

The Author's Chair

Children sitting in an "Author's Chair" share their writing with an interested audience.

Materials

A comfortable place in the classroom—a chair, grouping of pillows, etc.—where children share their writing with other children; a sign that identifies the "Author's Chair"

Activity

Teachers:

- Arrange a place where writers can regularly go to share their written work with interested listeners.

- Explain that the "Author's Chair" is a place reserved for authors—those who have written something they would like to share with interested listeners.

- Explain that listening to an author share his or her writing is an important job and that careful listeners help the author make writing that is clear, interesting, useful, and enjoyable.

Teachers and children:

- Consider the "ground-rules" for sharing writing, e.g., when, how many children are involved, how long.

- Discuss the format, e.g., making constructive comments.

- Experiment; several authors share their writing and others in the group offer constructive comments.

Children:

- Participate as authors who want to share their writing.

- Participate as listeners/commentators.

Key Experiences

- Recalling thoughts and observations in a purposeful context

- Expressing thoughts in writing

- Sharing writing in a purposeful context

- Acquiring, strengthening, and extending writing skills:
  - Letter formation
  - Sentence and paragraph formation
  - Capitalization, punctuation, and grammatical usage
  - Spelling
  - Editing and proofreading for mechanics, content, and style

Questions to Ask

How do you know whether others understand what you've written? What are some things you need help with when you write? Does it help you to hear things read aloud that have been written? Why?

Extension

1. Teachers occasionally take the "author" role, encouraging children to question and make suggestions.

2. Teachers discuss techniques for improving clarity, strengthening meaning, structuring the story, etc., in language workshops.

Note: Many opportunities to develop these writing, speaking, and listening skills occur in the class workshops. As children learn how to consider various topics and to listen carefully as topics are presented, they learn and generalize the conventions involved. Teachers should encourage children to focus their attention so the sharing of writing does not become "the blind leading the blind."

Grades K–3
A B C's

Children create alphabet books on varied topics after exploring a wide range of available alphabet books.

Materials

Writing materials, computer, facilities for binding books; alphabet books such as the following:

> *ABC Museum of Fine Arts, Boston* by Florence Cassen Mayers: Harry N. Abrams, Inc.
>
> *Alligator Arrived With Apples* by Crescent Dragonwagon: Macmillan
>
> *Animalia* by Graeme Base: Harry N. Abrams, Inc.
>
> *Aster Aardvark's Alphabet Adventures* by Steven Kellogg: Morrow
>
> *Eating the Alphabet* by Lois Ehlert: Harcourt, Brace Jovanovich
>
> *Guinea Pig ABC* by Kate Duke: Dutton
>
> *Have You Ever Seen . . . ?* by Beau Gardner: Dodd, Mead and Co.
>
> *Q is for Duck* by Mary Elting & Michael Folsom: Clarion Books
>
> *Where Is Everybody?* by Eve Merriam: Simon & Schuster

Activity

Teachers:

- Read a wide variety of alphabet books aloud to children.

- Engage children in predicting what picture or event will be used to illustrate the letters.

- Provide a quantity of alphabet books of varied subject matter and reading levels for children to use independently.

Teachers and children:

- Discuss the alphabet book format, comparing topic variations.

- Select a familiar topic; brainstorm words that are important to that topic, e.g., "Our classroom."

Key Experiences

- Writing in specific content areas

- Acquiring, strengthening, and extending writing skills:
  - Letter recognition

- Experiencing varied genres of children's literature

- Reading own compositions

- Reading and listening to others read in a purposeful context

- Reading in specific content areas

- Acquiring, strengthening, and extending specific reading skills:
  - Auditory discrimination
  - Letter recognition
  - Decoding—*phonetic analysis* (letter/sound associations, factors affecting sounds, syllabication; *structural analysis* (forms, prefixes, suffixes)
  - Vocabulary development

- Together, seek to complete an alphabet format by selecting an entry for each letter, e.g., A—apple in lunch box, B—books, C—coats in cubbies, D—desks, etc.

Children:

- Working in groups or independently, choose a topic, then brainstorm for appropriate words.
- Produce individual or group alphabet books for the chosen topic.
- Share writing; edit; publish.

Questions to Ask

What topics might be good ones to use for making our own alphabet books? Why? What do you like in your favorite alphabet books? Are there topics in science, social studies, or math that could become unusual—and interesting—alphabet books?

Extension

1. Teachers and children share more complicated alphabet books such as *The Ultimate Alphabet* by Mike Wilks: Henry Holt and Co.

2. Children share their books with younger or older students.

3. Children and parents develop a "My Family ABC."

Note: This activity works well in the class workshop settings. The children develop and expand these skills with continued practice and in independent work.

Grades 1–3

Make and Take a Book

Children make four-page, folded books, and use them to write thoughts, stories, etc.

Materials

Paper, scissors, "Fold-a-Book" directions, glue, markers, crayons, pencils, computer

Activity

Teachers and children:

- Prepare for writing by planning and "brainstorming" subjects or topics that are of interest.

Children:

- Choose paper.
- Follow directions for folding a book.
- Choose writing materials.
- Write (draft) thoughts on their chosen topics.
- Share writing with others in the "Author's Chair" or workshops.
- Revise (edit).

Questions to Ask

What kinds of books do you like to have others read aloud? What kinds of books do you like to read yourself? Why? What do you think are important features in a book? Who is going to be the author of this book? Who is going to be the illustrator? Do you have favorite authors and illustrators? Could you share some of their books?

Extension

1. Combine several books for longer stories.

2. Cut apart computer-generated stories for text on large format books.

3. Try other forms of making books, e.g., lunch bags, folded sheets, paper plates, punch/binder, etc.

Key Experiences

- Writing in unconventional forms:
  - Scribbles
  - Drawings
  - Letters—random or patterned, possibly including elements of names copied from the environment
  - Invented spellings—of initial sounds, syllabic sounds, concluding sounds, and intermediate sounds

- Writing in conventional forms

- Expressing thoughts in writing

- Sharing writing in a purposeful context

- Acquiring, strengthening, and extending writing skills:
  - Editing and proofreading for mechanics, content, and style

- Reading own compositions

- Reading and listening to others read in a purposeful context

Fold-a-Book

Use any size paper. Large sheets of newsprint work well

1. Fold paper in half lengthwise.

Fold in half again.

Fold in half again.

2. Open to step 1 lengthwise fold. Cut narrow strip A to C on fold of two middle sections.

3 Open the slit.

4. Refold side D with pinches to make a fold. Crease the outside.

5. Pull points D and B out while pushing A and C to the middle to make a plus sign.

6. Bring points D and B toward you.

7. Bring remaining page toward you to make a book.

8. Crease the book edge.

9. To make a book with more pages, paste two books together.

Acknowledgment: This sharing of fold-a-books is a way of thanking the many teachers who have used them to help children enjoy reading and writing. We do not know the original origami reference; the folding format has been, and continues to be, passed on from teacher to teacher.

Reprinted with permission of the International Reading Association from the following: The Reading Teacher, *March 1990, p. 526.*

Make and Take Lots of Books!

Children make many different kinds of books to expand the possibilities for publishing their own compositions.

Materials

Construction paper, wallpaper, maps, giftwrap paper, remnant paper from printers, oak tag, grocery or lunch bags, paper plates, product containers, fabric; notebook rings, key chains, shower curtain rings, plastic fasteners, large paper fasteners, punch binder/plastic spiral binders, dry mount press; laminator or clear plastic film; scissors, glue

Activity

Teachers:

■ Assemble materials for making books in a convenient location in the classroom.

■ Look for opportunities to use the writing/editing/publishing process in all curriculum areas.

■ Consider ways to expand publishing children's writing to reflect the topic, literary style, and interest of children.

■ Look for ways to make the books published by children functional, i.e., sturdy enough so that many children can use them in the reading center, attractive enough so that other children are interested in reading them, convenient enough so that children can check them out and share them at home.

Teachers and children:

■ Explore books that lend themselves to derived versions, e.g., *Brown Bear, Brown Bear, What Do You See?* by Bill Martin, Jr. Rereadings of this book suggest children's spin-offs such as *Gray Ghost, Gray Ghost, What Do You Hear?*; the pattern inherent in the book leads children to create new

Key Experiences

■ Writing in unconventional forms:
  • Scribbles
  • Drawings
  • Letters—random or patterned, possibly including elements of names copied from the environment
  • Invented spellings—of initial sounds, syllabic sounds, concluding sounds, and intermediate sounds

■ Writing in conventional forms

■ Expressing thoughts in writing

■ Sharing writing in a purposeful context

■ Using writing equipment (e.g., computers, typewriters)

■ Acquiring, strengthening, and extending writing skills:
  • Letter formation
  • Sentence and paragraph formation
  • Capitalization, punctuation, and grammatical usage
  • Spelling
  • Editing and proofreading for mechanics, content, and style

■ Reading own compositions

■ Reading and listening to others read in a purposeful context

versions. (See Children's Literature Resource Lists, Appendix A).

- Explore concepts that are familiar to the children, e.g., happiness, sadness. Encourage children to discuss, write, and illustrate these concepts as ways of expressing their prior knowledge.

- Explore additional concepts that are part of children's activities and are useful in instructional settings, e.g., over, under, below, through, sizes, and shapes. Encourage children to discuss, write, and illustrate these concepts as ways of expressing their prior knowledge and incorporating additional understandings.

- Explore sequenced action in experience stories and classroom events, e.g., writing about and illustrating all the steps involved in making apple-sauce, making a papier mâché classroom animal, or planting a class garden.

- Explore topics from all content areas and decide what kinds of books can be made to develop and relate information obtained from those explorations, e. g., number books, books outlining patterns of change in science, comparing the properties of materials, or books about historical events or people.

- Explore and expand the children's vocabulary by focusing on nouns, adjectives, adverbs, and verbs, e.g., "Snakes slither, birds fly, sharks swim, kangaroos hop, and I walk!"

- Explore collections of environmental print found in packaging and examples of family-generated literacy, e.g., letters, notes, and photographs.

Children:

- Work through the pre-writing, drafting, editing processes and then publish the work in a functional format.

Questions to Ask

How would you go about publishing your writing? Do you have ideas about making the book sturdy enough for lots of children to read? What attracts you to a book? Do you look for certain things when you are choosing books to read?

Extension

1. Teachers involve parents as volunteers to assist children in publishing and preparing materials in advance that children can use independently.

2. Teachers add library-style pockets to books, have children prepare library cards, and develop a checkout system for individually made or class-produced books.

3. Teachers and children read books to other classes or arrange an exchange system between classes.

Product covers serve as sturdy publishing covers.

Simple shapes, derived from the text content, add interest to the project.

Shower curtain rings, notebook rings, punch binding, large paper fasteners, and report fasteners serve well; dry mounting, if available, offers variety.

Folded construction paper, paper plates, folded grocery bags, and lunch bags are sturdy materials for mounting edited text. Colored paper glued to the original paper makes books more durable and interesting

Grades K-3
Write a Letter to ...

Each child writes a letter to someone. The possibilities are endless, e.g., a parent or relative, the author of a favorite book, someone who participated in a field trip, an "alien," or someone who lived many years ago.

Materials

Paper, pencils, markers; typewriter or computer

Activity

Teachers:

- Briefly discuss the circumstances that occasion this letter, e.g., a field trip, a book discussion, a school event.

Teachers and children:

- List questions, concerns, and issues prompted by the topic.
- Brainstorm on topics that might be included in a letter to the chosen person or group.

Children:

- Choose paper, tools.
- Write (draft) the letter.
- Share letters with others.
- Revise (edit) the letter.

Questions to Ask

What might we ask (say to, request, comment, etc.) this person in a letter? Why? Have you ever gotten a letter like this? Shall we mail the letters? What would we need to do to send the letter in the mail? Do you think we will get an answer?

Key Experiences

- Writing in unconventional forms:
  - Scribbles
  - Drawings
  - Letters—random or patterned, possibly including elements of names copied from the environment
  - Invented spellings—of initial sounds, syllabic sounds, concluding sounds, and intermediate sounds

- Writing in conventional forms

- Expressing thoughts in writing

- Sharing writing in a purposeful context

- Using writing equipment (e.g., computers, typewriters)

- Acquiring, strengthening, and extending writing skills:
  - Letter formation
  - Sentence and paragraph formation
  - Capitalization, punctuation, and grammatical usage
  - Spelling
  - Editing and proofreading for mechanics, content, and style

Extension

1. Read storybooks that include writing letters or receiving answers to mail.

2. Read books that detail the parts of letters and the elements of properly prepared envelopes.

Grades 1–3
Dear Author ...

Children write letters to authors of favorite books.

Materials

Paper, pencils, pens, typewriter, computer, crayons, envelopes, stamps; favorite books; resource book from library with addresses for publishers, authors

Activity

Teachers:

- Pose questions about a favorite book written by a contemporary author, e.g., "I wonder how the author happened to write about the main character?"

Teachers and children:

- Pose additional questions about books that are favorites of the whole class or of individual children.
- Speculate about the answers to the questions.
- Consider asking the author questions about the books.
- Plan writing a letter to an author, inquiring about features of the book or commenting on favorite aspects.
- Discuss the format of the letter—paper/pencil, computer, etc.
- Discuss the editing process and publishing or mailing the letter.

Children:

- Choose a favorite book.
- Plan and write a letter to the author.
- Share writing with classmates; edit.
- Prepare letter for mailing.
- Wait—with hope!—for an answer.

Key Experiences

- Writing in unconventional forms:
  - Scribbles
  - Drawings
  - Letters—random or patterned, possibly including elements of names copied from the environment
  - Invented spellings—of initial sounds, syllabic sounds, concluding sounds, and intermediate sounds

- Writing in conventional forms

- Expressing thoughts in writing

- Sharing writing in a purposeful context

- Using writing equipment (e.g., computers, typewriters)

- Acquiring, strengthening, and extending writing skills:
  - Letter formation
  - Sentence and paragraph formation
  - Capitalization, punctuation, and grammatical usage
  - Spelling
  - Editing and proofreading for mechanics, content, and style

- Expanding the forms of composition:
  - Expressive mode
  - Transactional mode—expository, argumentative, descriptive
  - Poetic mode—narrative poetry

- Publishing selected compositions

Questions to Ask

In addition to the type of question suggested earlier, try questions about the setting or plot of the story, e.g., Do you think the author of this book ever lived in Australia? Why do you think the author chose to tell the story this way? Why do you think the author chose to arrange the events in this order?

Extension

1. Teachers and children create a bulletin board with pictures of favorite books or book jackets, letters written to authors, and responses.

2. Teachers and children pretend to be the authors of fables and folktales, answering questions speculatively. For example, "Thank you for your letter about *Little Red Riding Hood*. Yes, when I was a little girl I had a beautiful red cape and that is why I decided to have the main character in my story have one, too!"

- Experiencing varied genres of children's literature

- Acquiring, strengthening, and extending specific reading skills:
  - Auditory discrimination
  - Letter recognition
  - Decoding—*phonetic analysis* (letter/sound associations, factors affecting sounds, syllabication; *structural analysis* (forms, prefixes, suffixes)
  - Vocabulary development

Grades 1–3
Buddy Journal

Two students keep a diary journal by writing back and forth to each other.

Materials

Stapled unlined or lined paper or notebooks; pencils, pens, markers

Activity

Teachers:

- Introduce the idea of keeping diaries or journals.
- Talk about the reasons for keeping diaries and the different formats of diaries.
- Introduce the idea of exchanging journals with "buddies" or of friends keeping a diary or journal together.

Teachers and children:

- Agree on the frequency of writing in the diaries or journals, e.g., daily, three times a week.
- Set a time limit for completion of the cycle, e.g., two weeks.

Children:

- Choose a "buddy"—a friend with whom they can converse comfortably.
- Introduce themselves in writing in their own journals.
- Exchange the journal with the "buddy."
- Begin each writing session by rereading the last entry and responding to it.
- Change "buddies" at the conclusion of the cycle.

Key Experiences

- Writing in unconventional forms:
  - Scribbles
  - Drawings
  - Letters—random or patterned, possibly including elements of names copied from the environment
  - Invented spellings—of initial sounds, syllabic sounds, concluding sounds, and intermediate sounds

- Writing in conventional forms

- Expressing thoughts in writing

- Sharing writing in a purposeful context

- Expanding the forms of composition:
  - Expressive mode
  - Transactional mode—expository, argumentative, descriptive
  - Poetic mode—narrative poetry

- Reading own compositions

- Reading and listening to others read in a purposeful context

- Acquiring, strengthening, and extending specific reading skills:
  - Auditory discrimination
  - Letter recognition
  - Decoding—*phonetic analysis* (letter/sound associations, factors affecting sounds, syllabication; *structural analysis* (forms, prefixes, suffixes)
  - Vocabulary development

Questions to Ask

What do you think will be difficult about keeping this kind of journal? How is this kind of journal different from a diary you may have kept at home? How will you choose your buddy for this journal?

Extension

1. Teachers include themselves in the rotation.

2. Teachers intersperse other forms of journals into the classroom, e.g., individual diaries, dialogues with the teachers, learning logs, reflections, etc.

Note: Keeping journals is a valuable experience for children in early elementary classrooms. Nevertheless, teachers should be aware of considerations about the sharing of information in journals, the issues of privacy, and even the legal ramifications. Teachers should, therefore, have clearly defined purposes in mind when assigning journals and have guidelines for reading, sharing, or reporting the entries.

Grade 1—3

Read All About It!

Children identify the print and text features of newspapers and experience reading and writing different sections of newspapers.

Materials

Newspapers—neighborhood, local, and national; newsprint; writing tools—typewriters; computers; butcher paper; tape; glue or rubber cement

Activity

Teachers:

- Collect daily and Sunday editions of newspapers. Arrange the papers and other materials in an attractive center.

- Introduce the newspapers to the children, allowing ample opportunities for them to explore what is known and familiar, e.g., the comics, pictures of news events they have also seen on television, letters and words.

Teachers and children:

- Examine the print features of newspapers, e.g., capital and lower-case letters, size and styles of print, words, sentences, and paragraphs.

- Examine the physical features of newspapers, e.g., columns, lay-out, comics, photos, artwork, and organization of topics.

- Discuss the terminology that is useful for working with newspapers, e.g., headlines, columns, advertisements, features, comics, mast head, sports, editorials, entertainment schedules.

- Discuss the different styles of writing and the different forms of text, e.g., comics, features, headlines, sports, book reviews, local or international news, advertisements.

- Brainstorm ideas for a class newspaper, e.g., masthead.

- Brainstorm ideas for news and feature topics.

Key Experiences

- Expressing thoughts in writing

- Using writing equipment (e.g., computers, typewriters)

- Writing in specific content areas

- Acquiring, strengthening, and extending writing skills:
  - Letter formation
  - Sentence and paragraph formation
  - Capitalization, punctuation, and grammatical usage
  - Spelling
  - Editing and proofreading for mechanics, content, and style

- Expanding the forms of composition:
  - Expressive mode
  - Transactional mode—expository, argumentative, descriptive
  - Poetic mode—narrative poetry

- Publishing selected compositions

- Reading and listening to others read in a purposeful context

- Reading in specific content areas

- Acquiring, strengthening, and extending specific reading skills:
  - Auditory discrimination
  - Letter recognition
  - Decoding—*phonetic analysis* (letter/sound associations, factors affecting sounds, syllabication; *structural analysis* (forms, prefixes, suffixes)
  - Vocabulary development

- Brainstorm ideas for items to announce and advertise, or for editorial topics.
- Brainstorm "staff roles," e.g., editor, manager, lay-out, copy.

Children:

- Draft articles, features, sports stories, comic sections, etc.
- Edit writings with peers, a group of students, or a teacher.
- Proofread edited writing, compile in newspaper format, and copy.
- Possibly market.

- Expanding comprehension and fluency skills:
  - Activating prior knowledge
  - Determining purpose, considering context, making predictions
  - Developing strategies for interpreting narrative and expository text
  - Reading varied genres of children's literature

Questions to Ask

Do you have newspapers at your house? How do people at your house use the newspapers? (Be prepared for all types of answers: e.g., reading the want ads, lining bird cages, training dogs, and cleaning windows!) What do you know about newspapers? Do you think newspapers are a recent invention? Who pays for newspapers and how does this system work? How do newspapers get to all the places we find them, i.e., grocery stores, newsstands, homes and apartment buildings, farms, cities across the country? What kinds of information can be found in a newspaper?

Extension

1. Consider timing this activity to correspond with "National Newspaper Week." At this time some newspaper publishers make special materials available; some permit limited field trips to observe publication.

2. Encourage children to expand the class newspaper to include information on all the content areas, e.g., reporting on science and math activities, writing about new students in the classroom, describing a class trip.

3. Encourage children to learn more about interesting, important events that have been reported in newspapers, e.g., an earthquake, a local sports event, an event in another country.

4. Encourage children to discover what happened on the day of their birth by looking in a local library for a copy of a national newspaper of that date.

5. Encourage children to research local historical events by re-reading old newspapers, e.g., a hurricane, a bank robbery.

6. Children may take a trip to a library and learn to read from a microfiche reader or take a trip to the newspaper office and learn about the "morgue."

7. Help children explore whether the class newspaper could be copied and made available to parents, teachers, and other children at the school.

8. Encourage children to explore career options in newspaper publishing; possibly invite a newspaper reporter, an editor, a circulation manager, or a publisher to visit the class and discuss their roles.

9. With the children, look for additional activities that use newspapers—the classified advertisement pages for tempera art projects, folded paper for hats, papier mâché, etc.

10. Help children explore the need to recycle newsprint and learn how newsprint paper is made.

Note: The learning opportunities surrounding newspapers are so extensive that this topic should be introduced to the whole class, expanded in workshops, and extended for children in individual and group occasions over several weeks.

Grade 1-3

Poetry, Please!*

Description: Children explore image and metaphor as they investigate form and content in poetry.

Materials

Poetry in many forms including collections on varied topics; paper; writing tools; hand lens; computers.

Activity

Teachers:

- Collect poetry for class use, looking for poems that relate to the interest, lives, experiences, and culture of the children.

- On frequent occasions share poetry with children. These occasions may be in conjunction with other reading-aloud experiences.

- Involve children in exploring the meaning of poetry by asking them open-ended questions, e.g., "How do you feel about what the author of that poem wrote? Can you think of a way to describe that feeling?"

Teachers and children:

- Explore the language options or literary conventions that are present in many examples of poetry, e.g., imagery, metaphor, similes.

- Explore the idea of picturing feelings and thoughts within oneself. Introduce children to this idea by having them examine their hands, arms, legs with a small hand lens; call attention to the external physical features that all can see. Then ask children to "look inside themselves" to picture not only physical features of bone, blood and muscle but also to investigate what is in their imaginations, their feelings, their dreams, their thoughts.

Key Experiences

- Expressing thoughts in writing

- Sharing writing in a purposeful context

- Acquiring, strengthening, and extending writing skills:
  - Letter formation
  - Sentence and paragraph formation
  - Capitalization, punctuation, and grammatical usage
  - Spelling
  - Editing and proofreading for mechanics, content, and style

- Expanding the forms of composition:
  - Expressive mode
  - Transactional mode—expository, argumentative, descriptive
  - Poetic mode—narrative poetry

- Publishing selected compositions

- Experiencing varied genres of children's literature

- Reading and listening to others read in a purposeful context

- Using audio/or video recordings in reading experiences

- Acquiring, strengthening, and extending specific reading skills:
  - Auditory discrimination
  - Letter recognition
  - Decoding—*phonetic analysis* (letter/sound associations, factors affecting sounds, syllabication; *structural analysis* (forms, prefixes, suffixes)
  - Vocabulary development

- Suggest a basic poetic structure:

> Inside me is (color)
> like (something of that color)
> Inside me is (sound)
> like (what does it sound like?)
> Inside me is (feeling)
> like when (. . .)
> Inside me is (a fear)
> like when (. . .)

- Brainstorm some other poetic forms, valuing the creative process as much as the aptness of the final product.
- Encourage children to make similes based on their feelings as expressed in language.

Children:

- Write similes.
- Combine writing in a poetic structure.
- Share writing with others.
- Revise and edit selected writing.
- Proofread and publish selected writing.

- Expanding comprehension and fluency skills:
  - Activating prior knowledge
  - Determining purpose, considering context, making predictions
  - Developing strategies for interpreting narrative and expository text
  - Reading varied genres of children's literature

Questions to Ask

What are some of the things that the author of this poem is trying to say? What images does the author of this poem use to help explain feelings and to describe sounds, colors, etc. What do you see in this poem? How do you feel about it? What do you love? What do you fear? What do you dislike?

Extension

1. Children might compile anthologies of some of their similes.

2. Children might illustrate their similes.

3. Help children become aware of other poetic conventions—meter, rhyme, etc. These conventions should only be viewed as additional tools for children to use in relating their thoughts through language.

Note: Valuable resources for teachers:

Glazer, J. I., & Lamme, L. L. (1990). Poem picture books and their uses in the classroom. *The Reading Teacher, 44,* 102–109.

Koch, K. (1970). *Wishes, lies and dreams.* New York: Harper and Row.

Koch, K. (1973). *Rose, where did you get that red?* New York: Random House.

Temple, C., Nathan, R., Burris, N., & Temple, F. (1988). *The beginnings of writing.* Boston: Allyn & Bacon, Inc.

Tiedt, I. M. (1983). *Teaching writing in K–8 classrooms: The time has come.* Englewood Cliffs, NJ: Prentice-Hall, Inc.

Poetry suggestions:

De Regniers, B. (1988). *Every child's book of poems.* New York: Scholastic Books.

Ginsburg, M. (1982). *The sun's asleep behind the hill.* New York: Greenwillow Books.

Koch, K., & Farrell, K. (1985). *Talking to the sun.* New York: Henry Holt.

Prelutsky, J. (1990). *Something big has been here.* New York: Greenwillow Books.

---

*The general concepts of this activity are excerpted and derived from Cariello, M., (1990). "The Path to a Good Poem That Lasts Forever": Children Writing Poetry. *Language Arts, 67,* 832–838.

8
▼

Reading: Key Experiences & Activities

The process of reading is complex, and the skills that combine to produce motivated, fluent readers are involved. But just as we said that children learn oral language by using language and children learn to write by writing, now we add "children learn to read by reading."

One advantage of High/Scope's developmental approach to whole language instruction is that it takes into account the determination of learners to construct meaning for themselves. We view children as powerful agents in the complex process of becoming literate. What children want to know—what interests them, what helps them derive meaning from printed text, what spurs them on to master the reading material—provides a significant motivator for acquiring literacy skill. It also demonstrates that teachers do not have total control over the involved skills that combine to produce fluent readers.

For many years and in many programs teachers adhered closely to the recommendations set by basal systems for the organization of literacy instruction. Frequently letter recognition and letter-sound relationships were viewed only as preparation or "readiness" for the main act of reading, which would follow at a later time. The decisions about when to teach the alphabet, when to introduce skills, and when to teach vocabulary were predetermined and nonnegotiable. And finally, read-

...Frog hurried home.
He found a pencil
and a piece of paper.
He wrote on the paper.
He put the paper in an
envelope. On the envelope
he wrote "A LETTER FOR
TOAD."

...Frog said, "I wrote
'Dear Toad, I am glad
that you are my best friend.
Your best friend, Frog.'"

"Oh," said Toad, "that
makes a very good letter."

Then Frog and Toad went
out onto the front porch
to wait for the mail.
They sat there,
feeling happy together.

— In *Frog and Toad Are Friends*
by Arnold Lobel

ing text, often selected according to "readability" formulas rather than for literary value, was inserted into the curriculum as the vehicle for delivery of preplanned instruction in specific skills.

The High/Scope K–3 whole language curriculum reorders this sequence so the skills and strategies that children need in order to understand what they choose to read are presented when the children need them. Instruction is offered when a child needs to learn, not when the school decides to teach. The evidence of research on how children learn and the principles underlying the concept of emergent literacy argue strongly for this approach.

To feel comfortable with this position, teachers must understand how children learn language and acquire language skill. Teachers must be well-versed in the details of phoneme-grapheme correspondence, in knowledge about strategies that assist children in becoming thoughtful readers, and in appropriate pedagogical and methodological techniques. Scope and sequence skill lists and many widely available supplementary materials answer specific questions about distinct phonic elements and how they should be introduced and taught, but teachers must be prepared to coordinate this knowledge into a framework of children's development and apply the knowledge holistically.

The goal of this curriculum guide, and especially of this section on the key experiences, is less providing details of skill acquisition and more of providing a larger framework for applying the teacher's knowledge on behalf of children who are active in learning to read. We look at establishing a **literacy set**—the set of factors that provides a foundation for reading—through conceptual preparation. We look at assisting guided reading and we look at ways of encouraging independent reading. To address these issues, we develop guidelines that suggest key events and opportunities all children should experience.

...The letters had never thought of this. Now they could really write—say things.

They said things about the wind, the leaves, the bug.

"Good," said the caterpillar approvingly. "But not good enough."

"Why?" asked the letters, surprised.

"Because you must say something important," said the caterpillar...

— In *The Alphabet Tree* by Leo Lionni

Establishing a Literacy Set

New Zealand educator Don Holdaway, writing in his important book *The Foundations of Literacy* (1979), describes a series of factors that contribute to a literacy set, which is the substructure all reading instruction is based on. There are these factors:

■ *Motivational factors*—Expectations of print developed through children's repeated experiences with books and other print resources and through encouragement to produce written language

■ *Linguistic factors*—Familiarity with written dialect in oral form, i.e., syntactical structures, vocabulary, intonation patterns, and semantic rules

■ *Operational factors*—Strategies for handling written language, e.g., using context and the purpose of text, integrating cues, and gaining insight into how reading works

■ *Orthographic factors*—Knowledge of the conventions of print, e.g., directionality, letter forms, phonetic principles, structural analysis

These factors establish a set or stage for all that follows in reading. They are part and parcel of an enriched environment, but teachers do not necessarily teach them directly. Rather, teachers begin to weave these factors together as they lay the foundation for literacy by preparing children conceptually for reading.

In High/Scope classrooms teachers initially prepare the stage when they arrange their rooms to facilitate language use, when they set up schedules to facilitate whole-group discussions, when they build on the learning and understanding children exhibit, when they integrate learning opportunities through the entire curriculum, and when they develop workshops and independent work opportunities.

Reading Aloud

When teachers compile careful selections of children's literature and other appropriate reading and writing materials, the literacy set is expanded. Teachers then make a commitment to *reading aloud* to children; they consider reading aloud time an integral part of each school day in the early elementary years. High/Scope teachers find that reading aloud to third grade children is just as valuable as reading to kindergartners; the only variations are the nature and length of the reading selections. Teachers point to the fact that when they read aloud, they not only bring children into the world of story and literature, but they also usher children into a world of information, feelings, and experiences.

Harold decided one evening to take a trip through the alphabet, from A to Z ... and he left his yard, taking his purple crayon and the moon along.

To get very far he was going to need a lot of words.

B is for Books. He could find plenty of words in a pile of big books. He was ready for anything.

—In *Harold's ABC* by Crockett Johnson

Guidelines for Classroom Reading*

Reading of Storybooks to Children	Reading of Informational Texts to Children	Reading of Picture Phrase Books

Reading of Storybooks to Children

Before Reading

- Show the cover of the book to the children. Encourage predictions of the book's content.
- Discuss the book's author and illustrator.
- Allow children to discuss their own experiences that are related to those in the book.
- Discuss the type of text the children will be hearing (folktale, fable, fantasy, realistic fiction).
- Introduce children to the main characters and setting.
- Set the purpose for the children to listen to the story.

During Reading

- Encourage children to react to and comment on the story as they listen.
- Elaborate on the text, when appropriate, in order to help children understand the written language used in the story and the critical story components.
- Ask questions occasionally to monitor children's comprehension of the story.
- Rephrase the text when it is apparent that children do not understand the ideas.
- At appropriate points in the story, ask children to predict what might happen next.
- Allow children to voice their own interpretation of the story.

After Reading

- Review the story components (setting, problem, goal, resolution).
- Help children make connections between events involving the main character and similar events in their own lives.
- Engage children in a follow-up activity that involves thinking about the text.

Reading of Informational Texts to Children

Before Reading

- Determine children's level of understanding of the topic presented in the text through methods such as leading a discussion about the picture on the cover or children's experiences with the topic.
- Provide demonstrations of difficult concepts.
- Set a purpose for listening.
- Establish a link between children's experiences with the topic and what they will be learning from the text.

During Reading

- Ask questions periodically to check children's understanding of the text. Questions that actually appear in the text might provide excellent opportunities for discussion and demonstration of the topic.
- Extend new concepts to children through demonstrations, concrete examples, or pictures while reading the text information.
- Encourage comments about the demonstrations and pictures so that children talk about unfamiliar concepts.
- Provide suggestions about activities children might engage in later that will encourage them to explore the topic further.

After Reading

- Allow children to ask questions about the text.
- Help children see how informational text can be used to learn more about their own worlds.
- Offer follow-up activities that will tie text concepts to children's experiences.

Reading of Picture Phrase Books

Before Reading

- Let children know that these books are ones they will be able to read if they listen and look carefully at pictures and print.
- Have children attempt to read the print on the cover. Talk about words they already know.
- Let children predict what the book might be about based on the title and the cover picture.
- Have children talk about their own experiences that are related to the book topic or theme.
- If children cannot see the print, provide multiple copies or enlarge the book.

During Reading

- Allow children who are able to read along.
- Challenge children to identify words in the text.
- Ask children how they are able to recognize the words they have identified.

After Reading

- Briefly review the content of the text, drawing upon the experiences of the children to highlight specific events or sequences.
- Repeat the text, having the children join in as they recognize the words.
- Let children explore the print by having them attempt to write words from the book.
- Extend the presentation by having children act out the text, draw pictures to go along with the text, or compose a similar text.
- Provide opportunities for children to read the book on their own.

*These guidelines are reproduced with permission of Jana M. Mason and the International Reading Association from: Mason, J. M., Peterman, C. L., & Kerr, B. M. *(1989)*. Reading to kindergarten children (tables 1–3). In *Emergent literacy: Young children learn to read and write*. Newark, DE: International Reading Association.

In family settings reading aloud is one of the earliest literacy experiences. The act of reading provides satisfaction and pleasure to both parents and children, and informal and natural learning about literacy occurs. Many of the factors Holdaway (1979) discusses are experienced in reading stories informally—e.g., learning about book format, pages, illustrations and text, left/right progression, intonation patterns, following plot, and components of print.

When children listen to another person reading, they hear the forms of language, become aware of the predictable structures of dialogue, and learn about the emotional capacity of language. Children learn the vocabulary that expresses culture and builds a sense of story. Reading aloud strengthens the auditory and visual memory of children, arouses their interest in unfamiliar topics, and develops a bond between reader and listener.

Children generally attempt to emulate those literacy experiences that have been the most positive. This means that the first books children will probably try to read are those they have heard read repeatedly—encouragement for those who have read *Go Dog Go*, *Good Night Moon*, and *Koala Lou* more times than they can count!

Language Experience

We also believe that an important part of setting the literacy stage—especially in kindergarten—involves **recording in written language the oral language of children**. A teacher's recording of the dictated messages of children serves an important purpose: to call attention to the possibility of transforming oral language into written form and to have a textual record. This text becomes valid, appealing material for children to read.

Dictated experience stories, recorded by the teacher, provide opportunities for children to see language in written form before they are able to produce print conventionally themselves. The vocabulary is the vocabulary of children, and the written record of this discourse is effective print text. When teachers write a child's experience story or group experience stories, they incorporate important examples of the wide range of emergent literacy activities that are effective in developing the conceptual preparation for other reading.

...Earl's got a hat with a real horse feather.

He wears socks made of chicken leather...

Earl knows all the letters in the Zulu alphabet.

He caught wild boars in a butterfly net.

Earl's too cool for me.

— In *Earl's Too Cool for Me* by Leah Komaiko

Reading Children's Own Compositions

Teachers also **encourage children to write their own stories and compositions in their own way**. The lessons of research on early reading and writing are clear: many children are interested in reading because they have been encouraged to explore their interest in writing. Gibson (1989) discusses children's experiments with writing approximations, print practice, and alphabetic writing as activities that are particularly strong during the years between age two and age eight—roughly through the completion of third grade. As before, this early writing experience produces valuable reading text.

Children's natural interest in writing should be integrated into the reading process. To write in isolation is a waste of time if the associations between producing print and reading print are not strengthened. The High/Scope whole language curriculum stresses these connections by clearly articulating the need for children to read and write for authentic reasons and for the genuine desire to communicate purposefully. The teacher provides incentives that supply many such reasons: writing about one's feelings to share them with others; writing a letter to someone to offer information, express appreciation, or request help; writing in a journal to document one's activities or to dialogue with another person; writing a story to share story elements with others; writing directions for completing a task.

These authentic reasons for writing (and therefore authentic reasons for reading what is written) are not reserved for higher grade levels. Kindergartners have purposes and reasons for expressing genuine feelings just as first-, second-, and third-graders do. Whether the form of writing is unconventional or conventional is of little consequence. Similarly, early reading may take unconventional forms. Children often rely to some extent on memory, use the illustrations, and employ patterned language and repeated phrases to approximate conventional reading. **What is essential in setting the literacy stage in High/Scope classrooms is that we encourage children to write in order to express themselves; simultaneously, we encourage children to read what they have written and what others have written to them and for them.**

Assisting Guided Reading

Gibson (1989) and Holdaway (1979) both underscore an important point that is valuable for teachers to remember: *Beginning readers need support and assistance as they enter the world of print.*

Consistent with High/Scope's constructivist philosophy, children in High/Scope classrooms are encouraged and supported by adults to actively engage in making sense of print. Teachers encourage children to make many attempts to understand the rules that govern print (e.g., sounds have a relationship to letters); to learn the conventions of reading and writing (e.g., spacing between words); and to recognize which attempts are generalizable (e.g., lowercase and capital letters have consistent value, regardless of print size). For children to be truly free to take risks, they must feel secure that their efforts and approximations are acceptable and one of the ways this is accomplished is by allowing children to share some early reading experiences with other readers.

Reading with printed text and taped version provides some assistance as well as modeling fluency.

We suggest several ways that **shared reading** can work in a whole-group situation, in workshops, or with partners:

■ **Repeated rereadings of favorite stories**. Children read along as the story is read aloud; this is especially convenient with enlarged text and "big books."

■ **Choral readings**. Children emphasize the rhyme or rhythm by joining in familiar refrains.

■ **Listening tapes with books**. Children follow the print version while listening to the taped version.

■ **Reading pairs**. Children read in unison or take turns.

■ **Echo reading**. Children read what has been previously read by another.

■ **Reader's theater**. Children read aloud, with feeling, the dialogue portions of stories.

In each of these examples, totally accurate, word-for-word reading is less important than the fact that children are practicing reading in comfortable and enjoyable situations. Some of the risk of a perfect performance is re-

Children listen attentively when a classmate reads aloud from a favorite book.

duced while the collaborative exchange assures increased interest and appeal.

Assisting Independent Reading

We recognize that for children to move beyond emergent and beginning stages of reading, a solid literacy set must be established and the classroom environment must unequivocally support independent reading. We return to the report *Becoming a Nation of Readers* and emphasize two crucial recommendations that appear at the report's conclusion: "Teachers should devote more time to comprehension instruction," and "Children should spend more time in independent reading" (Anderson et al, 1985).

High/Scope teachers must be prepared to grant children opportunities to search out what they want to read, to provide reasons and functional purpose for reading, to assist children in developing reading strategies, and to provide occasion for practicing what has been learned about reading. To accomplish these objectives, teachers must help children organize their thinking *before* they read, help children think *while* they read, and help children review what they have read *after* they finish. In many ways, this process is similar to the spirit of High/Scope's plan-do-review sequence.

Teachers must help children activate whatever *prior knowledge* they possess so this information becomes a useful resource for interpreting the reading text. Teachers activate children's prior knowledge through conversations, brainstorming sessions, and the use of open-ended, thought-generating questions. In situations where teachers realize children have undeveloped or inadequate background knowledge for understanding what they read, teachers should look for ways to provide additional experiences. They may read other books to the children, show movies, videos, and film strips, plan field trips, or bring visitors to class. Building up a store of background knowledge is a critical requirement for children who are constructing meaning from printed text.

Teachers should also help children look forward to what they read and make *predictions* about what they expect to encounter in any reading text. Illustrations and the format of the print text offer assistance for children as they preview the kind of reading before them. Children need to develop varied strategies for reading different genres of writing—stories, poetry, maps, articles, and graphs. Many of these strategies are skills developed during reading workshops.

Teachers also support independent reading by helping children expand *vocabulary* and learn strategies for attacking words they do not know. Some words have consistent phonic or structural elements that can be decoded, and children can be helped to practice generalizable rules for decoding phonetically. Some words are interpreted through context; strategies such as semantic mapping where children explore the relationships between familiar and unfamiliar words can be of assistance. Other words are specialized, so children should be helped to understand a specific event and connect it to unfamiliar words. In the independent reading process teachers must encourage children to use strategies, apply generalizations, or consider rule exceptions that are appropriate for the nature of the tasks at hand.

In all of these examples teachers should provide instruction about features of text children are confronting and provide practice for the newly acquired skills. This practice, often a part of workshops, should involve additional material but in the context of reading, not in isolation from meaningful text. We encourage teachers to use the activities that follow this section and to adapt games, puzzles, movement, music, and art activities to provide additional playful and pleasurable practice occasions.

The same thoughtful approach is important as children engage in the reading process—teachers should make it possible for children to *discuss what they read.* These opportunities occur comfortably during workshops. Teachers sometimes pair students and the partners discuss their reading; sometimes teachers find that several children have read the same book and can discuss the book as a group; sometimes teachers discuss informally with a child in the reading center while others in the workshop group are working through different issues. High/Scope classrooms make any of these possible options.

Strategic reading. Comprehending what is read is not an automatic response to decoding words. Rather, as the state of Michigan's definition of reading suggests, "Reading is the process of constructing meaning through the dynamic interaction among the reader's existing knowledge, the information suggested by the written language, and the context of the reading situation" (Michigan State Board of Education, 1988). For the development of independent reading children need to *use strategies* to weave together their prior knowledge, the nature of the text they are reading, and their purpose for reading.

High/Scope teachers return to the workshop times as occasions for assisting children in becoming strategic readers. Within the context of meaningful text—not in skill and drill format— children look for narrative elements in story (setting, character, and plot) and use that framework as a guide for thinking through stories. Similarly, teachers employ any of a number of strategies for guiding understanding of expository text—e.g., directed reading/thinking activities, expository text mapping. Reciprocal teaching activities that encourage children to generate questions, summarize, clarify, and predict are examples of other self-monitoring focuses (Palinscar & Brown, 1989).

Sometimes these strategies are woven into playful activities, and other times they are approached as a detective looks for clues—with dogged persistence. However, the payoff for learning the strategies is a powerful one because children learn how to learn—and this opens a multitude of doors.

During the independent reading process, teachers also help children develop additional strategies for learning what to do when they become "stuck" or when they need to "fix up" misunderstandings. When children are encouraged to take chances and try new techniques, they need an arsenal of additional techniques or strategies available to them. For example, if a child has tried to decode a word unsuccessfully—because it was not phonetically consistent—a "fall-back" position or another strategy is necessary. The child needs to try something else, e.g., what is known about unstressed syllables. The child might also try thinking about the context and what might add meaning to the text.

Newman (1985) tells the story that the following question was asked of teachers attending a workshop: "When you are reading and you come to something you do not know, what do you do about it?" The teachers responded with a long list, including suggestions to use the context, skip the word and return later, substitute a word that seems to maintain the meaning, or even to try to read something else on the same topic. In contrast, when the teachers were asked, "What would you do to help a student having difficulty reading?," they responded with suggestions that offered a different perspective. They encouraged that children look again at the prefixes and suffixes or look again for familiar small words within the word. Finally, teachers said they would say the unknown word for them.

Adults use the flow of language to assist them—the whole rather than the parts—and employ what they already know to see if reading makes sense; they expect to self-correct when it does not make sense. We conclude from this example that teachers should approach the task with children as they approach the task themselves. That is, they should spend time helping children develop a variety of cues, rather than relying solely on the time-honored, but not totally effective, recommendation "Sound it out."

High/Scope teachers naturally assist children in reviewing and in making connections between what they have read and the strategies they have used as they encounter new material. During reading review children distill their thinking to focus on main ideas and on cause and effect. The review strengthens the bonds developed between strategies used to understand, and the final outcome both reaffirms the purposes for reading and reassures children about their reading abilities.

...The next Saturday afternoon, when Laura and Jack were starting to meet Mr. Nelson, she saw him coming across the footbridge. Something white was in his hand. Laura flew down the knoll. The white thing was a letter.

"Oh, thank you! Thank you!" Laura said. She ran to the house so fast that she could not breathe. Ma was washing Carrie's face. She took the letter in her shaking wet hands, and sat down.

"Pa's all right," Ma said. She snatched her apron up to her face and cried.

— In *On the Banks of Plum Creek* by Laura Ingalls Wilder

Children read enthusiastically what interests them.

A fluent process. Teachers urge children to read independently so that all the parts coalesce and the *reading process becomes a fluent one*. Children gain this facility through repeated opportunities to practice and to build on what has been learned throughout the emerging literacy experiences. After mastering conventions, acquiring skills, and defining purposes and strategies, children find that the reading process becomes almost automatic and thus, fluent.

Teachers supporting independent reading make a variety of reading material available, ensure that children have plenty of time to read, and encourage reading for pleasure rather than making it a skill-oriented, competitive experience. Clearly this approach means that teachers seek ways to extend reading skills in all other content areas. Whenever possible, teachers and children integrate reading and writing into major project and theme learning (Katz & Chard, 1989).

The key experiences in reading are specifically designed to develop a literacy set through conceptual preparation, shared reading, and independent reading. The key experiences reflect three important principles:

■ **Literacy learning is approached from whole to part,** i.e., the whole message is important and inclusive; as

the message clear. Letters, sounds, words, phrases, sentences, and paragraphs receive focus to make meaning clear.

■ **Literacy learning is integrated into the whole of other learning**. Reading is a dynamic process that enables and empowers children to explore their world. This means that reading is not reading for itself; it is integrated with science, social studies, music, art, mathematics, and all other content areas. In fact, children are often drawn *to read* in order to fulfill their interest in science, social studies or the arts and they are similarly drawn *to explore* science, social studies and the arts more fully because of their introduction through reading. Children read for authentic reasons in all areas—not to fulfill arbitrary requirements but to gain the understanding they seek.

■ **Literacy learning is motivating and pleasurable for its own reasons**. Children learn to read so they can read what interests them. The activities in the classroom that provide learning experiences are initiated by the learner, reinforced in positive ways, supported by adults, and guided by the pleasure that is inherent in literature.

As in the speaking, listening, and writing key experiences, minimal attention is devoted to specific grade levels. In High/Scope's open framework curriculum there is ample opportunity for informal groupings and systematic small group literacy instruction that need not be grade level restricted. On the other hand, within a grade level, there is still ample opportunity to view children as individuals whose literacy development demands support and nurture but rejects rigid, lock-step progress.

The following activities are representative of many other activities that are guided by these principles. In many instances, using one or two of the activities will open the doors to whole collections of ideas, books, and materials that are appropriate and interesting. Teachers engage in their own dynamic, growth-seeking processes to build up pedagogical and methodological resources. Teachers are urged to look at these activities as models that can be simplified or made more complicated by shifts in questions, more or less teacher participation, and subtle changes of materials. These activities are included to stimulate teachers' searches for other activities—activities that encourage children to explore more fully the myriad paths to literacy.

Grades K–1
Morning Message

Children share reading of functional messages; the messages are teacher-produced and adapted to children's skill levels.

Materials

Chalkboard, chart pad, chalk, or markers

Activity

Teachers:

- Write a brief introductory message to children on the chalkboard or chart pad, e.g., "Hi, boys and girls."

- Guide children to read the message, noting the strategies they employ.

- Acknowledge to children that the print on the board is a way of symbolizing or recording what is also spoken.

- Repeat messages as children's interest warrants.

- On another occasion, expand the simple message, e.g., "Good morning, boys and girls."

- In a casual way, after rereadings, sweep your hand beneath the message, to indicate its left-to-right progression.

Teachers and children:

- Jointly explore the morning message each day, looking for known features, noting new or unfamiliar elements, and employing familiar strategies for identifying words and phrases.

- Share the reading of gradually more complex messages, including messages that add features of punctuation, sentence structure, capitalization, etc. For example, "Today we have a surprise. Can you guess who is coming to visit?"

Key Experiences

- Observing the connections between spoken and written language

- Writing in unconventional forms:
  - Scribbles
  - Drawings
  - Letters—random or patterned, possibly including elements of names copied from the environment
  - Invented spellings—of initial sounds, syllabic sounds, concluding sounds, and intermediate sounds

- Writing in conventional forms

- Expressing thoughts in writing

- Reading and listening to others read in a purposeful context

- Reading in specific content areas

- Acquiring, strengthening, and extending specific reading skills:
  - Letter recognition
  - Decoding—*phonetic analysis* (letter/sound associations, factors affecting sounds, syllabication; *structural analysis* (forms, prefixes, suffixes)

Children:

■ Read the message independently.
■ Write an answer to the message.
■ Take turns writing the message.

Questions to Ask

Who can help us read the message this morning? Are there parts of the message that you have seen before? How were you able to figure out what the morning message had to say? What ideas do you have for figuring out what the message could say tomorrow?

Extension

1. Teachers match features of the message with skills encountered and genres of literature, e.g., predictable or patterned format, narrative or expository style.

2. Teachers encourage children to leave messages for individual children in classroom mailboxes.

3. Teachers expand vocabulary to include pertinent content and provide opportunities to practice newly acquired phonic skills.

Grades K–1

It Happened Like This...

Children participate in an experience story.
Children's group experience is recorded by the
teacher for review, reading, and rereading.

Materials

Chart pad, markers; chalkboard, chalk

Activity:

Teachers:

- Encourage children to orally recall an experience or event.

- Encourage children to reflect on the experience, noting any similarities to other experiences or events; encourage children to reflect on any new or unusual aspects about the experience.

- Encourage children to sequence the events.

- Suggest writing what the children have expressed, so a record of the experience can be shared.

Teachers and children:

- Agree on organization, e.g., chronological, sequential.

- Children dictate phrases and sentences; the teacher records them as continuous print text. For example:

    We picked apples at the farm.
    We counted the apples.
    We sorted the apples.
    We graphed the apples.
    We washed the apples.
    We cut the apples into pieces.
    We cooked the apples in a pan.
    We stirred the apples.
    We mashed the apples in a colander.
    We made applesauce!
    We ate the applesauce.
    M-m-m-m-!

- Share the reading of the story, repeating the reading as interest warrants.

- Indicate left-to-right progression of phrases and sentences.

Key Experiences

- Speaking their own language or dialect

- Stating facts and observations in their own words

- Participating in singing, storytelling, poetic and dramatic activities

- Observing the connections between spoken and written language

- Writing in unconventional forms:
  - Scribbles
  - Drawings
  - Letters—random or patterned, possibly including elements of names copied from the environment
  - Invented spellings—of initial sounds, syllabic sounds, concluding sounds, and intermediate sounds

- Writing in conventional forms

- Expressing thoughts in writing

- Sharing writing in a purposeful context

- Reading own compositions

- Acquiring, strengthening, and extending specific reading skills:
  - Auditory discrimination
  - Letter recognition
  - Decoding—*phonetic analysis* (letter/sound associations, factors affecting sounds, syllabication; *structural analysis* (forms, prefixes, suffixes)
  - Vocabulary development

- Discuss prominent patterned phrases, sentence structure, repetition of print elements (punctuation, capitalization), and phonemic segments that are obvious.
- Look for other print text that incorporates these identified features and share reading of them.
- Discuss independent reading of this text and the possibility of illustrating the story.
- Discuss the possibility of writing a similar story independently.

Children:

- Reread, illustrate, write their own stories.
- Share the drafts with classmates, edit the writing, and possibly publish new stories.
- Share stories with classmates.

- Expanding comprehension and fluency skills:
  - Activating prior knowledge
  - Determining purpose, considering context, making predictions
  - Developing strategies for interpreting narrative and expository text
  - Reading varied genres of children's literature

Questions to Ask

What happened . . . what did we do today?

Extension

1. Children identify frequently noted capital and lower-case letters and words they can read.

2. Teachers explore the idea of action words being used to describe what took place, i.e., verbs such as "count," "cut," "mash." Dramatize action words to assure understanding and include other words that might have been used or other actions that could have occurred, e.g., "throw" or "threw."

3. Teachers choose additional books about the topic, e.g., *Apple Pigs* by Ruth Orvach and *Rain Makes Apple-sauce* by Julian Scheer; compare content between the books.

4. Teachers and children collect other experience stories written by the children. Bind the stories as books and add them to the classroom library.

Note: While writing an experience story is a general format (the idea can be used repeatedly), it is not meant to occur at one sitting; it might begin in a whole-group time, be extended in class workshops over several days, and then be extended to independent work at another time.

Grade K–1
Read It Your Way!*

Teachers model and introduce the emergent reading of storybooks.

Materials

Storybooks that have proven attraction for children

Activity

Teachers:

- Select a collection of familiar storybooks and other books that are likely to appeal to young children.
- Read books; reread them as interest suggests, stopping at predictable points to encourage children's participation.

Teachers and children:

- Gather in a comfortable place; after reading a book chosen by the children, offer to read another book. Model an *enthusiastic* reading style. Announce that during the week the children—and teacher(s)—will have many opportunities to read favorite books.
- Explain that the books are available for independent reading and identify the place where books are displayed and stored.
- Emphasize that children can read in their own way, i.e., reading aloud, describing pictures, reading with another child. Explain that not all children will be able to read every word or to follow the conventions used by adults.
- Encourage children to record the name of each book they read on a sheet, card, or other form, along with their own name. Accept each child's unconventional or conventional writing style for these records, since the goal for this exercise is as much to encourage children to develop a pattern of accountability as it is to develop the list of books read. Enclose the lists in the children's assessment portfolios.
- Later, suggest that children share books with a "buddy." The experience of sharing is more important than any word-for-word reading.

Key Experiences

- Experiencing varied genres of children's literature

- Reading and listening to others read in a purposeful context

- Acquiring, strengthening, and extending specific reading skills:
  - Auditory discrimination
  - Letter recognition
  - Decoding—*phonetic analysis* (letter/sound associations, factors affecting sounds, syllabication; *structural analysis* (forms, prefixes, suffixes)

- Expanding comprehension and fluency skills:
  - Activating prior knowledge
  - Determining purpose, considering context, making predictions
  - Reading varied genres of children's literature

- On another occasion, invite children to read to a buddy, taking turns. Monitor and encourage turntaking, providing the children with strategies for sharing longer books to avoid long periods of listener inactivity.

- Explore ways children can connect what they are reading with what they are considering in other the areas of math, science, and social studies. Similarly, encourage children to search out books that reflect their current interests in other content areas.

Children:

- Continue to read independently and to make a list of the books read and shared with others.

Questions to Ask

What would you like to read today?

Extension

Teachers use "Silent Sustained Reading," "Drop Everything and Read" or other projects to organize independent reading at regular time each school day.

Note: The importance of this activity lies in establishing an ongoing framework for children's independent reading and in developing an atmosphere that encourages children's emergent reading abilities, whatever their developmental level. At least once a week the teacher models the reading process, possibly in a language workshop, calling children's attention to specific features of the stories, problems encountered, and emotions. The reading climate developed within this loose, flexible structure establishes that reading is to be a regular experience, that the choice for what is read is the child's, that there will be opportunities to share the reading experience from the *child's* perspective—at his or her specific emergent or conventional development stage. Children also assume responsibility for recording, in their own ways, what they read.

---

*This activity is derived from Sulzby, E., & Barnhart, J. (1990). The developing kindergartners: All our children emerge as writers and readers. In J. S. McKee, (Ed.), *The developing kindergarten: Programs, children, and teachers*. Ann Arbor: MiAEYC.

Grades K–1
What Did You Hear?

Children hear literature read aloud that features prominent use of phonic elements.

Materials

Trade books featuring prominent phonic elements. The following examples are taken from a list* developed by educator Phyllis Trachtenburg (1990):

Short A: *Angus and the Cat* by Marjorie Flack and *The Cat in the Hat* by Dr. Seuss.

Long A: *Bringing the Rain to Kapiti Plain* by Verna Aardema and *The Paper Crane* by Molly Bang.

Short and long A: *Caps for Sale* by Esphyr Slobodkina.

Short E: *The Little Red Hen* by Paul Galdone and *Yeck Eck* by Evaline Ness.

Long E: *Ten Sleepy Sheep* by Holly Keller and *Never Tease a Weasel* by Jean Soule.

Short I: *Willy the Wimp* by Anthony Browne and *Whistle for Willie* by Ezra Jack Keats.

Long I: *The Bike Lesson* by Stan and Jan Berenstain and *Why Can't I Fly* by Rita Gelman.

Short O: *Drummer Hoff* by Barbara Emberley and *Fox in Socks* by Dr. Seuss.

Long O: *Roll Over!* by Mordicai Gerstein and *White Snow, Bright Snow* by Alvin Tresselt.

Short U: *Seven Little Ducks* by Margaret Friskey and *Umbrella* by Taro Yashima.

Long U: *The Troll Music* by Anita Lobel.

Many books that are examples of the way consonants record sounds, e.g., /m/ as in *Madeline* by Ludwig Bemelmans.

Activity

Teachers:

- Collect and read aloud books so children can enjoy stories.

- Reread books that contain prominent phonic elements.

Key Experiences

- Experiencing varied genres of children's literature

- Acquiring, strengthening, and extending specific reading skills:
  - Auditory discrimination
  - Letter recognition
  - Decoding—*phonetic analysis* (letter/sound associations, factors affecting sounds, syllabication; *structural analysis* (forms, prefixes, suffixes)
  - Reading varied genres of children's literature

- Encourage children to attend to phonemic segments through repeated readings of continuous text.

Teachers and children:

- Playfully identify phonemic segments that are similar, e.g., short *a* in "cat" and "hat."
- Gradually identify symbols that record sounds.
- Provide additional opportunities for children to identify consonant and vowel sounds in natural usage and text.
- Provide additional material that permits children to use the information in new settings.

Children:

- Continue reading independently or collaboratively.
- Look for additional examples of books to demonstrate consonant or vowel elements.

Questions to Ask

What is a sound that you hear? Have you heard a sound like that before? Where? Do you have a sound like that in your name? Do you know what letter records that sound? What is the sound that ____ records? Do you know of other words that have a sound like the sound you heard in _____?

Extension

1. Teachers provide big books and other print materials so children continue their search.

2. Teachers provide a range of material, at varying levels of difficulty, to encourage children's generalizations of their newly acquired sound discrimination.

3. Teachers expand the concept to include rhyme books.

*Reprinted with permission of Phyllis Trachtenburg and the International Reading Association. Appears in Trachtenburg, P. (1990, May). Using children's literature to enhance phonics instruction. *The Reading Teacher,* 648–654.

Grades 1–3

Compare the Pigs!

Children compare versions of The Three Pigs *by mapping the structures of the stories.*

Materials

Copies of *The Three Pigs* in various versions, e.g.,

The Three Little Pigs by Paul Galdone:

The Three Little Pigs by James Marshall

The True Story of the 3 Little Pigs by A. Wolf as told to Jon Scieszka

The Three Little Pigs by Walt Disney

Story-mapping formats

Activity

Teachers:

- Read the standard version aloud to the children, perhaps several times.
- Read alternate version(s).

Teachers and children:

- Compare versions, discuss similarities and differences.
- Explore the idea of mapping the elements of stories as a way of focusing on the story structure.
- As a group, map the structure of one version using one of the Story Maps on the following page.

Children:

- Map the structure of other versions.
- Consider the implications of character, setting, and plot.
- Look for other versions to add to the comparison.

Key Experiences

- Experiencing varied genres of children's literature

- Expanding comprehension and fluency skills:
  - Activating prior knowledge
  - Determining purpose, considering context, making predictions
  - Developing strategies for interpreting narrative and expository text
  - Reading varied genres of children's literature

Questions to Ask

Why do you think there are so many versions of this story? Which parts of the story seem to vary? Why might this be? How do you feel about the ending in this story? Does it make a difference if the endings vary? Do you have ideas for unusual endings for this story?

Extension

1. Children write new versions of *Three Pigs* and illustrate them.

2. Children dramatize any versions or use puppets to enact favorite versions.

3. Children vote on favorite versions and graph results.

4. Teachers and children expand the idea of comparing versions of other favorite stories, *The Three Billy Goats*, *The Gingerbread Boy*, or *Cinderella*, for example.

5. Teachers and children compare versions of stories from other countries and speculate on reasons for variations.

Story Map 1

Who?

Where?

What?

First

Next

Next

Then ...

The End!

Story Map 2

Who is in the story?

Where does the story take place? When?

What is the problem?

What happened first ... next?

How was the problem solved?

Story Map 3

(Title)

Main Characters:

Other Characters:

Setting—time and place:

Problem(s):

Resolving the problem,

Beginning:

Middle:

End:

Grades 1–2

Draw a Map*

Children represent elements in narrative form by drawing a story map.

Materials

Children's books; paper, crayons

Activity

Teachers:

- Select and read a storybook.
- Engage children in a discussion about the book, predicting what might happen and commenting about events.
- Engage children in reviewing the whole story.
- Reread as interest warrants.

Teachers and children:

- Discuss story elements, including characters, setting, problem or events, solution, ending.
- Compare elements of the story with another familiar story to verify the commonality of elements.
- Jointly, identify elements that could be drawn or mapped.
- Explain the format illustrated on the following page, and gather materials.

Children:

- Independently or cooperatively map the story by drawing pictures of the story elements.
- Share story maps with classmates.
- Choose other books to map.

Questions to Ask

What are the elements in this story—who is in the story? Where does the story take place and when? What happens? Is there a problem? How is the problem solved? Did the story end the way you thought it might? How else

Key Experiences

- Stating facts and observations in their own words
- Using language to solve problems
- Writing in unconventional forms:
  - Scribbles
  - Drawings
  - Letters—random or patterned, possibly including elements of names copied from the environment
  - Invented spellings—of initial sounds, syllabic sounds, concluding sounds, and intermediate sounds
- Writing in conventional forms
- Expressing thoughts in writing
- Experiencing varied genres of children's literature
- Reading and listening to others read in a purposeful context
- Expanding comprehension and fluency skills:
  - Activating prior knowledge
  - Determining purpose, considering context, making predictions
  - Developing strategies for interpreting narrative and expository text
  - Reading varied genres of children's literature

might the story have ended? Do all stories have the same elements? Is it easy to illustrate all of the elements in a story? Which ones?

Extension

1. Teachers plan workshops to clarify the concepts and techniques of illustrating story elements.

2. Teachers discuss in workshops the assistance that knowing this much about a story offers for understanding both this story and other similar stories.

3. Teachers suggest additional ways to map stories.

4. Teachers extend story-mapping to include "TV productions."

5. Teachers extend story-mapping to include dramatic representation.

---

*This activity was suggested by Pat Kingfield, Grade 1 teacher, Urbandale, Iowa.

Grades K–3

How Do You Feel?

Children read and discuss books of varied genres that deal sensitively with human emotions.

Materials

Children's literature, including such titles as:

A Baby Sister for Frances by Russell Hoban: Harper and Row

Everett Anderson's Goodbye by Lucille Clifton: Henry Holt

If It Weren't for You by Charlotte Zolotow: Harper and Row

I'll Fix Anthony by Judith Viorst: Atheneum/Macmillan

Koala Lou by Mem Fox: Harcourt Brace Jovanovich

Leo the Late Bloomer by Robert Kraus: Simon and Schuster

Time To Go by Beverly & David Fiday: Harcourt Brace Jovanovich

When I Was Young in the Mountains by Cynthia Rylant: E. P. Dutton

Will I Have a Friend? by Miriam Cohen: Macmillan

Activity

Teachers:

■ Collect and read books aloud to children.

Teachers and children:

■ Discuss the emotional issue raised by the stories, e.g., sibling rivalry, grief at death, fear, moving, feared loss of love, growing up.

■ Relate the emotional response of characters in books to personal situations. Discuss.

■ Compare the responses of characters in several books.

Children:

■ Continue to discuss with classmates the emotional issues raised in varied genres of children's literature.

Key Experiences

■ Stating facts and observations in their own words

■ Recalling thoughts and observations in a purposeful context

■ Experiencing varied genres of children's literature

■ Reading and listening to others read in a purposeful context

■ Acquiring, strengthening, and extending specific reading skills:
  • Auditory discrimination
  • Letter recognition
  • Decoding—*phonetic analysis* (letter/sound associations, factors affecting sounds, syllabication; *structural analysis* (forms, prefixes, suffixes)
  • Vocabulary development

■ Expanding comprehension and fluency skills:
  • Activating prior knowledge
  • Determining purpose, considering context, making predictions
  • Developing strategies for interpreting narrative and expository text
  • Reading varied genres of children's literature

Questions to Ask

How do you think the main character in this story felt? Have you ever felt like the main character? When? What would you do if you were the main character?

Extension

1. Children use puppets to dramatize these and similar stories.

2. Children enact stories using available classroom props.

3. Children write stories deriving themes similar to those in the selected books.

4. Teachers and children add more examples of literature to the collection so children can compare and contrast the treatment of the topic among various books.

5. Teachers and children explore poetry in a similar manner.

Grades K–3

It Happened Here

Children explore the setting of a favorite book, gathering information from additional resources.

Materials

A favorite storybook with an identifiable setting, e.g.:

> *Koala Lou* by Mem Fox: Harcourt Brace Jovanovich (Australia)
>
> *Make Way for Ducklings* by Robert McCloskey: Penguin (Boston)
>
> *Charlotte's Web* by E. B. White: Harper and Row (farm, barn)

Additional, related expository texts; writing, art, and construction materials

Activity

Teachers:

- Collect and read aloud storybooks with a related setting, e.g., several books about Australia.
- Engage children in a discussion about the setting.

Teachers and children:

- Consider text and illustrations to see what elements of the setting can be identified and what characters are featured in the setting, e.g., in *Koala Lou* identify "the bush," "gum trees;" also, identify "emu," "platypus," "wombat," and "kookaburra."
- Consult other books about the topic, e.g. Australia, to learn more about land, animals, lifestyle.
- Compare storybooks with expository texts, identifying relevant information whenever possible.
- Discuss and compare real/fantasy features of a setting.
- Plan re-creation of a setting.

Children:

- Explore storybooks, other resource books, and filmstrips to compile information for the setting.

Key Experiences

- Stating facts and observations in their own words
- Recalling thoughts and observations in a purposeful context
- Experiencing varied genres of children's literature
- Reading in specific content areas
- Expanding comprehension and fluency skills:
  - Determining purpose, considering context, making predictions
  - Developing strategies for interpreting narrative and expository text
  - Reading varied genres of children's literature

- Look for other storybooks from the same setting to compare and contrast.
- Using materials appropriate to the age level, construct a setting.
- Plan dioramas in shoeboxes, clay settings on movable pieces of paneling, or make a painted background setting on cardboard.
- Share with classmates.

Questions to Ask

I wonder if you have ever been in a place like the one in this book? Do you think the pictures in this book show a real place or an imaginary place? What are the clues? How would we learn about the place where____ lived?

Extension

1. Children explore increasingly more remote locations as understanding is developed. For example, young children could do a farm setting to accompany *Rosie's Walk* by Pat Hutchins. Children with additional experiences might move on to the setting for *Tikki Tikki Tembo* by Arlene Mosel.

2. Children use multiple sources to develop a thorough setting of a time long ago, e.g., prehistoric plants and dinosaurs to accompany *The Tyrannosaurus Game* by Steven Kroll.

3. Children create imaginary settings for their own stories.

4. Children produce and stage puppet plays to enhance their presentations.

5. Teachers plan a small-group workshop about settings—their development and effect on story content.

6. Teachers develop strategies for helping children to gain a more complete understanding of expository text.

Grade 1–3
Wanted—Alive!

Children explore "Wanted!" posters, "missing person" posters, and "position wanted" advertisements. Children use these posters to guide their understanding of the characters in stories and their writings about the characters.

Materials

Storybooks; paper; writing tools: typewriters and computers

Activity

Teachers:

- Collect a variety of storybooks that have interesting, strong characters—both human and animal. Seek a balance between realism and fantasy.

- Read aloud these storybooks and encourage open-ended questions about the characters, their motivations, their adventures, and the ways they solve problems.

Teachers and children:

- Select a well-known, well-liked story to re-read, e.g., *Little Red Riding Hood.*

- Encourage discussion about Little Red Riding Hood, Grandmother, the woodcutter, and the wolf. Ask such open-ended questions as "Do you have an idea what Little Red Riding Hood's parents must have thought or done when she did not return from her trip to grandmother's house?"

- Explore local advertisements for missing persons and consider what information is presented. Explore "wanted" posters from the Police Department or Post Office and consider what information is presented. (**Note**: Appropriate judgment should be used in selecting the material to be reviewed.)

- Discuss which of these formats might be appropriate for advertising for the return of Little Red Riding Hood and which for the wolf.

- Brainstorm ideas about the information that should be included, how it should be presented, where it should be placed, etc.

Key Experiences

- Stating facts and observations in their own words

- Recalling thoughts and observations in a purposeful context

- Writing in conventional forms

- Expressing thoughts in writing

- Sharing writing in a purposeful context

- Using writing equipment (e.g., computers, typewriters)

- Expanding the forms of composition:
  - Expressive mode
  - Transactional mode— expository, argumentative, descriptive
  - Poetic mode—narrative poetry

- Publishing selected compositions

- Experiencing varied genres of children's literature

- Expanding comprehension and fluency skills:
  - Activating prior knowledge
  - Determining purpose, considering context, making predictions
  - Developing strategies for interpreting narrative and expository text
  - Reading varied genres of children's literature

- Encourage children to use their prior knowledge of the subject to fill in the information available in the text so that the poster attracts attention and is useful.

Children:

- Choose a format and develop a poster based on the character of a selected story, the detailed information that is available in the story, and additions that could be made to make the poster more realistic.
- Add an illustration and necessary details.
- Review the poster with peers to see if there is enough accurate information, if editing is needed to make the task of finding the character easier, etc.
- Try developing other literary posters based on other characters in their favorite storybooks. Use a variety of formats such as "Missing Person" or "Missing Character" posters. Use the story text to provide the details; peers guess the identity and respond by making their own "Found" posters, using information about the setting from the storybook.

Questions to Ask

What problem did (the character) face? Why was it a problem? Do you have an idea about how (the character) could have solved his/her problem? Have you read about other characters in storybooks who have had similar problems? If you were a character in (the story), how might you have gotten your job?

Extension

1. Teachers and children could develop bulletin boards featuring "Missing Person" or "Wanted!" posters. Persons reading the posters could respond in writing about where the person might be located or apprehended.

2. Teachers and children could develop story-related advertisements for the class newspaper's "Help Wanted" column, e.g., an advertisement for someone to build substantial wolf-proof houses for a family of young pigs.

3. Children could include a regular "Seeking Employment" column in their class newspaper and use literary characters and situations as the basis for the jobs and workers.

4. Teachers and children could compile either posters or advertisements into class books.

Grades 2–3
Think About It!

Teachers model aloud the thinking they do as they read, so children become aware of reasoning strategies.

Materials

Storybooks, expository texts, subject-matter texts

Activity

Teachers:

- Select, for reading aloud, passages that contain difficult material, e.g., unfamiliar phrases, unknown words, difficult concepts.

Teachers and children:

- Children read the passage silently as the teacher reads aloud.
- Teachers think—aloud—about solving the problems presented in the passage.
- Teachers select specific problems and model aloud the strategies that could be employed to work through the problems. Examples:
  - *Make predictions* about the nature of the material, e.g., "I wonder if this could be the name of a piece of equipment. . ."
  - *Describe images* about what might be logical, e..g., "I can see the stormy sea that is described—perhaps this has something to do with that storm."
  - *Link prior knowledge* about the topic to the passage, e.g., "When I was on Cape Cod I saw boats like this. . ."
  - *Verbalize troubling issues* as a way of keeping track of what is understood, e.g., "I've read this twice and I still do not quite understand what this word could be."
  - *Demonstrate fix-up strategies* by considering the contextual sense of a word if the first attempt to phonetically identify a word has resulted in incomplete understanding, e.g., "ballet."
- Encourage children to participate in the think-aloud process with different passages.

Key Experiences

- Reading and listening to others read in a purposeful context
- Reading in specific content areas
- Acquiring, strengthening, and extending specific reading skills:
  - Vocabulary development
- Expanding comprehension and fluency skills:
  - Activating prior knowledge
  - Determining purpose, considering context, making predictions
  - Developing strategies for interpreting narrative and expository text
  - Reading varied genres of children's literature

- Discuss the conditions which these strategies will be especially useful—e.g., reading in science, social studies.

Children:

- Use strategies when reading with a partner or reading independently.

Questions to Ask

What do you do if you come to a passage that you have trouble understanding? What ideas are the most helpful to you when you are "stuck"? What do you try first that might "fix-up" a mistake?

Extension

Teachers use the thinking-aloud process in other naturally occurring situations—demonstrating strategies that prove useful to adults as well as to children.

Note: Teacher modeling is effectively done with a whole-group, extended and repeated in workshops, and used to guide children's independent reading.

Grades 2–3

K-W-L

Develop a framework for improving children's understanding of expository text.

Materials

Expository texts, all subject matter textbooks

Activity

Teachers:

- Guide children in brainstorming about their prior knowledge of a selected topic featured in expository text.
- Guide children in recording what they think they **know (K)** about the topic.

Teachers and children:

- Generate questions about what they **want (W)** to learn about the topic. Record the questions.
- Read the text.

Children:

- Identify what they already **know (K)**.
- Identify the questions they **want (W)** to have answered.
- Think about what they are **learning (L)**.
- Incorporate this framework as a frequently used strategy for helping children actively focus on and comprehend expository text.

Questions to Ask

Brainstorming questions about varied topics. What do you think adults do when they are trying to understand difficult passages in books?

Key Experiences

- Reading and listening to others read in a purposeful context
- Reading in specific content areas
- Acquiring, strengthening, and extending specific reading skills:
  - Vocabulary development
- Expanding comprehension and fluency skills:
  - Activating prior knowledge
  - Determining purpose, considering context, making predictions
  - Developing strategies for interpreting narrative and expository text
  - Reading varied genres of children's literature

Extension

1. Teachers use workshops to expand this strategy.

2. Teachers expand the variety of texts considered to include less familiar topics.

3. Teachers look for ways to provide additional prior-knowledge experiences for children.

4. Children keep written records of the **K-W-L** strategy.

Grade K–3

Shop 'til You Drop!

Children use catalogs from local and national businesses to discuss, read, write, and solve problems.

Materials

Assorted catalogs, mailings available to schools, teachers, families; writing material—paper, pencils, computers

Activity

Teachers:

- Collect and display catalogs that feature products and services of interest to children.
- Introduce catalogs.

Teachers and children:

- Explore catalogs, identifying familiar items.
- Discuss products and services available; compare material in several catalogs.
- Using context and all other available cues, encourage children to read and compare the information presented in the catalogs, including cost, size, and availability.
- Encourage children to develop a list of products they would like to buy for themselves from a catalog and a list of items they would like to buy to give to family members.
- Encourage children to classify items that would be useful for completing a specific job, e.g., furnishing a bedroom, cooking dinner, dressing up for a party, dressing for school, going hunting or fishing.
- Brainstorm catalog items that fulfill a certain criterion, e.g., they are red, they are large, they are made of leather, they can be eaten, they make noise, they are toys.
- Using the information in the catalog, discuss problems that could be written up and read.

Key Experiences

- Asking and answering questions
- Stating facts and observations in their own words
- Using language to solve problems
- Writing in unconventional forms
  - Scribbles
  - Drawings
  - Letters—random or patterned, possibly including elements of names copied from the environment
  - Invented spellings—of initial sounds, syllabic sounds, concluding sounds, and intermediate sounds
- Writing in conventional forms
- Expressing thoughts in writing
- Sharing writing in a purposeful context
- Writing in specific content areas
- Reading in specific content areas
- Acquiring, strengthening, and extending specific reading skills:
  - Vocabulary development
- Expanding comprehension and fluency skills:
  - Activating prior knowledge
  - Determining purpose, considering context, making predictions

- Ask children to tell or write problems that their classmates could solve by reading the catalog. Discuss the kinds of information children would need to solve the problem and encourage them to discuss what interests them. For example:
  - See if you can find five items in this catalog that you would wear on the first day of school.
  - You need to buy new jeans and a shirt. Could you find ones that you like in your size and in your favorite colors? How much would they cost?
  - Pretend that you have $25. to spend for clothes. What would you buy? Would you have any money left for a treat?
  - On page 23 there are socks priced at 3 pair/$10.00 and on page 24 there is a special sale—socks for $3.39 a pair. Which is the better price? How much can be saved?
  - Two shirts cost $49.50; how much does one shirt cost?
  - If you were allergic to wool, which sweaters would you choose to purchase? What would the materials be?
  - Which country seems to be importing most of the fabric that is used to make winter coats? Why might this be the case?
  - On page 79 there is a fur-lined parka. What animal provided the fur? Where does that animal live? Why would its fur be suitable for lining a winter coat? Would you like the idea of a fur-lined parka? Why or why not?

Children:

- Pose or write problems for others to solve.
- Share problems with others to see if enough information is available to solve the problem and what the other persons think about the problem.
- Examine the informational details (cost, number of items etc.) and structure (mathematical operation etc.) of the problems.
- Exchange problems and attempt to solve them.
- Try different catalogs.

Questions to Ask

Why do schools and families receive catalogs? What information is provided in a catalog to help people who are reading it to purchase the products? How do the products shown in the catalog get to the people who order them? How do people pay for the products they order from catalogs? How are the catalogs put together?

Extension

1. Children develop their own catalogs of books available in the classroom, paintings or art work they have produced, or services children could provide.

2. Children assemble puzzlebooks of the problems they have developed from a particular catalog.

3. Children present more difficult problems for older students or much easier problems for younger students.

4. Children work specifically with catalogs related to a content area, e.g., nursery and plant materials for science.

Grade K–3
Adopt a Tree

The class identifies a tree in the school environment to observe, study, discuss, and read and write about during an entire school year.

Materials

A conveniently located tree; resource materials in the reading, writing, math, science, social studies, and art centers; *optional*—camera, video camera, tape recorder; storybook that features a tree either very similar to or very different from the tree to be studied, e.g., *The Giving Tree* by Shel Silverstein

Activity

Teachers:

- Read a storybook that introduces the topic of paying careful attention to a tree.

Teachers and children:

- Discuss what is known about trees in general, about trees near the school, about a particular tree.

- Discuss what is observed, once a tree is "adopted" and plans have been made to study it carefully for the entire school year.

- Speculate on changes that might be observed and predict what might be documented, measured, and recorded about these changes.

- Discuss relevant vocabulary, e.g., "deciduous," "leaf," "vein," "sapling," "seed," etc.

- Discuss methods of observing and documenting the change process.

- Consider other information that influences the growth and change of the tree, e.g., weather, ecology, habitat, seasonal change, drought.

- Discuss the various uses for trees, e.g., lumber, homes for animals, furniture, shade, beauty, log cabins, firewood, climbing.

- Brainstorm resources available for studying growth and change.

Key Experiences

- Stating facts and observations in their own words

- Recalling thoughts and observations in a purposeful context

- Acquiring, strengthening, and extending speaking and listening skills:
  - Discussing to clarify observations or to better follow directions
  - Discussing to expand speaking and listening vocabulary
  - Discussing to strengthen critical thinking and problem-solving abilities

- Writing in unconventional forms
  - Scribbles
  - Drawings
  - Letters—random or patterned, possibly including elements of names copied from the environment
  - Invented spellings—of initial sounds, syllabic sounds, concluding sounds, and intermediate sounds

- Writing in conventional forms

- Sharing writing in a purposeful context

- Writing in specific content areas

- Expanding the forms of composition:
  - Expressive mode
  - Transactional mode—expository, argumentative, descriptive
  - Poetic mode—narrative poetry

- Publishing selected compositions

- Consider materials available in the reading, math, science, and art centers that contribute to understanding the growth and change of the "adopted" tree.
- Consider how often information will be collected, how the information will be used, how the results will be presented, and what any far-reaching impacts might be.

Children:

- Observe the tree; discuss growth and change in small-group workshop sessions and independently, during the plan-do-review process.
- Write about the tree—poems, stories, essays.
- Share writing with classmates.
- Collect, edit, and publish a diary or other record relating to the tree theme.
- Share fiction and nonfiction books about trees with classmates.
- Summarize observations and findings.

Questions to Ask

What changes do you predict you will see as you watch the tree we have adopted? Is there anything about this that surprises you? How will you document the changes we observe?

Extension

1. Teachers provide photographs showing the tree at an earlier time. Consider related events and people of the earlier time (age of the school building, teachers who recall the planting of the tree.)

2. Teachers and children compile collections of cross-cut tree slices, providing opportunities to determine the age of various trees and to speculate on the reasons for variations in the growth of the trees.

3. Teachers invite scientists, builders, environmentalists, forest rangers, paper manufacturers, Christmas tree farmers, and cabinet-makers to discuss their involvement with trees.

4. Children develop hall displays, art shows, presentations for other classes—documenting what they have learned about trees.

- Reading and listening to others read in a purposeful context
- Reading in specific content areas
- Acquiring, strengthening, and extending specific reading skills:
  - Auditory discrimination
  - Letter recognition
  - Decoding—*phonetic analysis* (letter/sound associations, factors affecting sounds, syllabication; *structural analysis* (forms, prefixes, suffixes)
  - Vocabulary development
- Expanding comprehension and fluency skills:
  - Activating prior knowledge
  - Determining purpose, considering context, making predictions
  - Developing strategies for interpreting narrative and expository text
  - Reading varied genres of children's literature

Thematic Projects— Integrated Learning

Opportunities for children to relate all areas of the curriculum in learning activities that are developmental, open-ended, and designed to provide broad experiences in the language and literacy area.

Materials

Any print or nonprint resources that activate sensory experiences: *Teacher resources*—e.g.,

> Katz, L. & Chard, S. C. (1989). *Engaging children's minds: The project approach.* Norwood, NJ: Ablex Publishing Corp.

> Gamber, R., Kwak, W., Hutchings, M. & Altheim, J., with Edwards, G. (1988). *Learning and loving it.* Portsmouth, NH: Heinemann Educational Books, Inc.

Activity

Teachers:

- Become familiar with the "project" or "thematic" approach.
- Consider working with other teachers, either at grade level or at adjoining grade levels.
- Brainstorm projects or possible themes that reflect both the interests and age levels of children, in particular, their interests in geography and current events. Consider community resources, applicability to district or state objectives.
- Brainstorm topics appropriate for the project or theme.
- Brainstorm curriculum topics that can be integrated; consider especially the ways that the learning experiences can be linked and made more understandable and comprehensive.
- Use High/Scope's key experiences to develop age-appropriate skill activities.
- Brainstorm resource possibilities, e.g., print materials, materials with sensory appeal,

Key Experiences

- Speaking their own language or dialect
- Asking and answering questions
- Stating facts and observations in their own words
- Using language to solve problems
- Participating in singing, storytelling, poetic and dramatic activities
- Making and using recordings
- Recalling thoughts and observations in a purposeful context
- Acquiring, strengthening, and extending speaking and listening skills:
  - Discussing to clarify observations or to better follow directions
  - Discussing to expand speaking and listening vocabulary
  - Discussing to strengthen critical thinking and problem-solving abilities
- Observing the connections between spoken and written language
- Writing in unconventional forms:
  - Scribbles
  - Drawings
  - Letters—random or patterned, possibly including elements of names copied from the environment
  - Invented spellings—of initial sounds, syllabic sounds, concluding sounds, and intermediate sounds

community—related resources, field-trip experiences and materials.

■ Plan introductory activities for engaging children in projects or themes, e.g., storybooks, newspaper articles, videos, materials children bring into the classroom.

Teachers and children:

■ Discuss what is known about the topic, what might be of further interest, what might be learned.

■ Brainstorm additional activities, resources, and experiences that might link the areas of math, science, social studies, music, art, and movement with the areas of speaking, listening, writing, and reading.

■ Discuss the amount of time such a project or theme might take, e.g., two weeks, a month, the entire school year, and the extent of the involvement, e.g., one class, all classes at a grade level, all classes in the primary division, the entire school, or all of the elementary schools within a school district.

■ Brainstorm activities for initiating the project.

■ Discuss activities that will occur in workshops and the extent to which project and theme materials will be added to the math, reading, writing, science, social studies centers.

Children:

■ Add project-related materials to the centers.

■ Discuss the project or theme at home to see if there are family resources that might be shared with the group in school.

■ Explore project or theme topics in centers, in independent research, and in the community.

■ Learn and love it!

Questions to Ask

Broad, open-ended questions designed to elicit children's interests and to demonstrate the interconnectedness of the broad areas of learning, i.e., math, science, language and literacy, art, movement, music, etc.

■ Writing in conventional forms

■ Expressing thoughts in writing

■ Sharing writing in a purposeful context

■ Using writing equipment (e.g., computers, typewriters)

■ Writing in specific content areas

■ Acquiring, strengthening, and extending writing skills:
  • Letter formation
  • Sentence and paragraph formation
  • Capitalization, punctuation, and grammatical usage
  • Spelling
  • Editing and proofreading for mechanics, content, and style

■ Expanding the forms of composition:
  • Expressive mode
  • Transactional mode—expository, argumentative, descriptive
  • Poetic mode—narrative poetry

■ Publishing selected compositions

■ Experiencing varied genres of children's literature

■ Reading own compositions

■ Reading and listening to others read in a purposeful context

■ Using audio/or video recordings in reading experiences

■ Reading in specific content areas

■ Acquiring, strengthening, and extending specific reading skills:
  • Auditory discrimination
  • Letter recognition

Extension

1. The possibilities are endless! Consider broad, general topics, such as the following brief list:

- *Animals*—Circus animals, farm animals, mammals, African animals, marsupials, kangaroos, dogs, insects, bees, animals that develop from eggs, fish, amphibians, birds, reptiles, etc.
- *The world*—Earth, sky, weather, mountains, lakes, oceans, rivers, ecology, the environment, the seasons, the solar system, etc.
- *Imagination*—Dragons, monsters, giants, etc.
- *Food*—Fruits, vegetables, growing conditions, pasta, etc.
- *People*—In history, around the world, family, friends, birth, death, abilities and interests, etc.
- *Genres of literature*—Folklore, fables, myths, poetry, nonfiction, etc.

2. Once a topic is chosen, explore it across the following broad content areas:

- *Literature*: Provide topic-related books at reading level, at all interest levels, of varied genres, for reading aloud
- *Writing*: Give children opportunities to express their knowledge in symbolic form, to acquire and extend their writing skills, to write in all forms and in varied genres
- *Math*: Give children opportunities for incorporating collections of objects, performing operations on number, relating geometry and space concepts, measuring, recording or graphing attributes or features
- *Science*: Encourage children to make collections, design and build structures, analyze and test, make surveys, solve problems
- *Music*: Provide recordings, introduce historical or cultural interpretations, encourage children's self-expression, encourage children to play instruments
- *Art*: Employ all media so that children can explore color, line, shape, form, texture, representation; encourage children's self-expression.
- *Social studies*: Discuss historical and cultural events, human responses, family beliefs, geographical conditions, etc.

Note: See the "Adopt a Tree" activity (page 161) for a discussion of a possible long-term thematic project.

- Decoding—*phonetic analysis* (letter/sound associations, factors affecting sounds, syllabication; *structural analysis* (forms, prefixes, suffixes)
- Vocabulary development

■ Expanding comprehension and fluency skills:
- Activating prior knowledge
- Determining purpose, considering context, making predictions
- Developing strategies for interpreting narrative and expository text
- Reading varied genres of children's literature

9
▼

Assessment— Looking Back & Looking Forward

We began this guide by suggesting that helping children become literate is like taking a journey. We talked about planning a destination, deciding which route to take, and checking up on our progress. We speculated about enjoying the trip along the way, and we looked forward to arriving at our final destination: conventional and fluent reading and writing for children.

In this chapter we consider the matter of assessing children's progress along the literacy continuum. We propose a process for gathering multiple forms or strands of evidence together to take a "snapshot" look at the progress children have made along the literacy route. We also consider another purpose for assessment—relating the assembled evidence to the High/Scope K–3 Curriculum and using it to plan future instruction.

This process of looking back and looking forward requires a conscious determination to use diverse forms of information sensitively, wisely, and appropriately. We know, for example, that in gauging literacy progress we should employ varied methods to ensure that children have opportunities to work in ways that are comfortable for them. We should be certain that occasions for collecting such information are frequent; indeed this process should be virtually continuous. We must also be alert to the quality of the assessment occasions themselves. The interest level of young children in learning tasks and the length of time they can remain attentive are important factors in determining how best to assess their progress.

... "Listen to me!" They had never heard their teacher sound like that.

"The test doesn't tell everything. It doesn't tell all the things you can do!

"You can build things! You can read books!

"You can make pictures! You have good ideas!

"And another thing, the test doesn't tell you if you are a kind person who helps your friend.

"Those are important things."

— In *First Grade Takes a Test* by Miriam Cohen

Children frequently sustain interest in stories and play activities for 20 to 30 minutes, so a playful assessment activity will most likely engage them for an equal length of time. Young children are usually not able to be as attentive during longer, more formal testing.

Since the ability to understand instructions and read directions varies from child to child, the assessment process must take these individual differences into account. Group tasks that demand following instructions in timed situations should be avoided. Teachers should assess students either on a one-to-one basis or in a manner that uses natural observation and performance sampling methodology.

Well-planned and carefully implemented assessment is necessary for several reasons. First, appropriate assessment *documents the effectiveness of school programs and curriculum approaches.* Second, *it provides specific information about progress* children are making in acquiring understanding about oral and written language. Third, assessment *identifies the skills children are acquiring* in all forms of oral and written language and offers evidence about the nature of children's interests. And finally, assessment *furnishes teachers with valuable information for planning future instruction.*

Appropriate assessment helps teachers decide *what* to teach and *how* to teach it most effectively. This **formative assessment** documents the strategies and experiences that best articulate the curriculum's focus, and thus teachers can use it to shape and to improve classroom practices. Information afforded by this sampling of children's performance and progress informs the decisions teachers make about curriculum and instruction.

As William Teale (1988) views it, assessment is "a process of gathering information to fulfill diverse evaluative needs," drawing upon "a variety of instruments and measurement strategies" (p. 175) In recent years, however, assessment has too often failed to rely on varied or multiple strategies and instruments. Instead, it has too often come to mean just *testing*, and too many schools have relied on this single method for obtaining all evaluative information. When testing is mistakenly viewed as the *sole* means of assessing children's performance and progress it becomes the "driving force" for instruction. When this happens the original purposes of assessment are compromised.

Relying on a single evaluative method—testing—not only offers limited resources for assessing children's progress but also has additional repercussions for evaluating teacher competency and documenting program accountability. With so much "riding" on the tests, programs have even altered the nature of reading instruction itself to stress those specific skills likely to be measured on standardized reading tests. And at that, the limited range and focus of tests of children's language and literacy skills, offers quantifiable data but little additional information teachers can use to improve or refine instruction.

Adding to the seriousness of this misuse of assessment is the fact that the minimum competency evaluation and program accountability has placed a heavy burden on assessment as a way of evaluating staff and educational programs. Testing of language and literacy skills has limited range and focus, offering quantifiable data but little additional information about ways to improve or refine instruction. Indeed, many programs have altered the nature of reading instruction itself to stress those specific skills likely to be measured on standardized reading tests.

Measuring specific skills is easier than measuring generalized proficiency; thus, many tests assess a child's reading ability exclusively in terms of narrow, discrete skill measurement, e.g., knowledge of letters and letter-sound correspondence. Similarly, measuring reading comprehension in terms of its separate components, such as "main idea" and "word meaning," is easier than measuring how fully children have captured meaning in continuous text. Frequently, tests measure comprehension solely through short answers and multiple-choice items, using brief pieces of unrelated text.

Not surprisingly, to compete favorably in such an evaluative atmosphere, teachers and specialists frequently emphasize activities that generate high scores in those discrete literacy skill areas that are likely to be tested, and they also proportion instructional time accordingly.

With the goal of documenting the attention given to discrete skill instruction, researcher Elfrieda Hiebert (1988) surveyed kindergarten and readiness books from four reading series. She reported that approximately half the activities in student books dealt solely with discrete skills of auditory and visual discrimination; the remaining pages were allocated to discrete skill activities for listening comprehension and for color, number, and shape recognition. Hiebert summarized, "Little attention was devoted to reading words and none to reading stories" (p. 166).

Durkin (1987) reached similar conclusions when she observed teachers and children in 42 kindergarten classrooms; she reported that 71 percent of the time allotted to reading and reading-related activities was devoted to learning letter names and sounds.

The Commission for the Study of Reading (Anderson et al., 1985) looked at how instructional time was spent, and they concluded that many basal reading programs provided little time for children to build up the "difficult-to-assess" background knowledge that is crucial for deriving meaning from text. The report also called attention to the limited opportunities provided by basal reading systems for practicing strategies for comprehending different genres of text. These drawbacks of basal systems, the Commission found, resulted in increased instructional emphasis on those subordinate elements likely to be tested and decreased instructional emphasis on broad but crucial meaning outcomes. The pressures accompanying standardized reading tests inadvertently led to inadequate topic coverage.

Ironically, the wealth of information produced by standardized reading tests rarely serves the best interests of teachers. The tests quantify *products*, e.g., words read, but shed little light on which *strategies* children employ as they read or attempt to read the words, and whether the strategies are appropriate. Teachers typically do not return to standardized reading tests to decide how to help children learn more words or to improve instruction in a general way. Instead, teachers look to their own observations of children's writing and reading and to samples of children's progress to refine instructional methodology.

To accent the appropriate focus of assessment and to avoid "assessment-driven instruction," **High/Scope views assessment as a resource for improving instruction**. The High/Scope approach, as reflected in the K–3 Curriculum and the instructional activities suggested in it, emphasizes

■ Collecting information about the *characteristics* of children as they learn to read and write

■ Collecting information about the *progress* of children as they learn to read and write

- Using this information to *plan instruction* in reading and writing

We suggest three approaches for gathering the information necessary for fulfilling these assessment purposes:

- **Performance sampling**—through criterion-referenced measures, observation, and documentation

- **Portfolios** or samples of children's work

- **Summarization** through progress reports

Performance Sampling

The term **performance sampling** describes a method of gathering samples of literacy-related behaviors from children over a period of time. These samples of children's performance can include *criterion-referenced measures*, such as *key experience checklists* and *inventories*, or other such instruments that are useful for describing the extent or frequency of specific behavior.

Teachers in High/Scope classrooms employ a variety of checklists and inventories as they observe children in natural work settings. At the *kindergarten level* inventories assess early strategies children use for reading before they read conventionally. Others document strategies children use when composing and rereading their writing. In *first*, *second*, and *third grade*, teachers use inventories or checklists to assess skills approaching conventional literacy levels and to evaluate reading and writing skills that are already conventional and expanding.

In each instance, when teachers collect samples several times a year, the measurement focuses on specific criteria (awareness of letters, letter-sound correspondence, sentence structure, punctuation) and gauges children's *longitudinal progress* rather than comparing their performance with that of other children. Comparisons of performance are of interest to teachers only insofar as they indicate whether performance falls within an expected broad range of typical age-level expectation. The primary interest and focus of assessment centers on whether the sampled performance is appropriate for a specific child

Eliza's Progress Reports

The following narrative entries from three progress reports, during second and third grade, document Eliza's performance. Note how the teachers incorporate specific information, anecdotes, and comments to provide insights about Eliza's progress and growth over time.

...This year Eliza has read *Princess Gorilla and a New Kind of Water*, *The Blue Moose*, and *Trouble River*, and has begun *Roly the Railroad Mouse*. *Trouble River* was a very challenging book both in vocabulary and length, but Eliza sustained her concentration well and increased her skill in decoding unfamiliar words. Eliza has responded to the literature in a variety of ways, such as drawing and answering written study questions and including some questions that she and her classmates wrote themselves.

...Eliza follows written directions well and her written work is generally thoughtful and thorough.

Teachers note what children choose to do during work time and which materials they choose to use.

Eliza Rides a Horse—and Lives to Write About It!

The teachers incorporated information about an experience that had special meaning for Eliza.

...Eliza wrote a nice description of her own 'challenging adventure'—her first ride on a horse. She used words well to convey how large that horse seemed! Eliza writes with considerable variety in her journal, and increasingly her entries (which she fortunately shares often with the class) have a real 'voice.'

Eliza approaches writing with diligence and persistence, and she completed and published her epic *Mrs. Color* in mid-October. While the length of this story represented a real milestone in her writing development, she discovered that editing such a lengthy work can be quite daunting! She has more recently completed a delightful story called *Kitty and Me*; we are encouraging her to complete its final editing and copying to prepare it to be published.

and whether this performance represents growth and progress. (See Appendix C for High/Scope's Key Experience Checklist as well as other reading/writing checklists and related information).

Teachers **document and collect anecdotal evidence** when they observe children working in informal classroom situations. In this way teachers attend to the strategies or techniques children employ when they are writing and reading. Teachers gain insight into the level of awareness children have about the processes they use to figure out unknown words or to compose a story. Such continuous monitoring of children's strategies is an effective indicator of each child's developmental level, extent of self-awareness, change or progress evident in the strategies employed, and appropriateness of teaching methods.

Teachers find these observations good prompts for their memories. Some teachers carry small notebooks or

"Post-It™" notes so they can jot down a brief incident—"Courtney...list of animals 2/11/90." Other teachers keep clipboards at the reading or writing center to make similar abbreviated entries. At the end of the day teachers enter these comments into an ongoing file or Child Observational Record; at that time, teachers often expand the comments. Over time, a collection of entries points to developing patterns and illustrates growth and change.

The High/Scope classroom offers many sources and occasions for these observational records during language workshop activities, during the plan-do-review sequence, and during other whole-class experiences. Teachers observe children speaking, listening, reading, and writing, and they note the extent to which children are able to use language to solve problems in naturally occurring play situations or when acting out stories. Teachers observe children reading, whether in emergent fashion or in an extended form, when children share their reading with other children. Teachers observe older children as they self-correct while reading and figure out unknown words or unclear meaning; this often occurs when children play games that require following printed directions or reading in other content areas. *Teachers do not have to schedule specific time to collect these samples—the samples are already there, they need only be "captured" and recorded.*

Another way teachers can gather anecdotal evidence is through conversations with children about reading and writing. These observations are more systematic than merely noting that a child is reading books, but less formal than assigning written questions to be answered. For example, teachers find that language workshop discussions about characters, setting, and events in the plots of the stories are good indications of how well children understand what they have read.

The gathering of evidence is actually a natural outgrowth of the task itself. When teachers encourage children to extend their involvement with a reading task—for example, by dramatizing a story or developing a diorama to illustrate it—they gain additional anecdotal information. The teacher discovers how extensively a child understands the reading material or learns why this understanding might be incomplete—e.g., the child had insufficient existing knowledge about the topic and could not make any inferences or rely on contextual cues.

Throughout the process of focusing on specifics of children's performance and sampling or documenting it

Eliza Loves to Read

The teachers have observed closely the process Eliza employs as she decodes words.

...Since January Eliza has read *Roly the Railroad Mouse, Tucker's Countryside,* and *Be a Perfect Person in Just Three Days.* She also read and participated in a choral reading of Longfellow's "Hiawatha." Eliza's reading fluency has grown considerably in the last few months, and she is now reading well above grade level. She is very often able to decode unfamiliar words, working silently in her head until she gets it. She has also laughed a couple of times after making a mistake—another real achievement for her!

Eliza has both written and answered some challenging study questions; she enjoys this written work, if anything more than the actual reading! She continues to do thoughtful, careful work, and recently we have been encouraging her to increase the length and fullness of her responses as she approaches third grade.

Teachers collect samples of children's work to document their performance and progress.

The teachers compiled ongoing samples of Eliza's work.

...Eliza has worked hard on her spelling during the last few weeks. She has the memory to become a good speller and seems to enjoy the structure and predictability of this activity.

In writing, Eliza has continued to generate fine journal entries. Her recently published stories, *Oona's Trip to the Zoo*, and *The Wondrous Spaceship*, represent real development in her story-telling abilities. *Oona's Trip to the Zoo* approached her first book of the year (*Mrs. Color*) in length, but showed far more complexity and structure in its story line; it also showed some real humor. *The Wondrous Spaceship* builds further on her storywriting skills including more descriptive and experiential material.

Eliza deserves to be proud of her accomplishments this year—the ending of *The Wondrous Spaceship* suggests that indeed she does feel both pleasure and pride in her accomplishments.

through various means, *teachers direct their attention to the student as an individual.* While anecdotal observations can be purely that—observation—they can also help teachers to closely monitor each child's work as they collect and compile evidence of performance.

Portfolios or Work Samples

Portfolios or work samples are collections of products and experiences that demonstrate, over time, the typical work of individual children. *Teachers and students choose and collect work for a variety of reasons: the child and/or teacher think the work is well done, the child and/or teacher think the work is challenging and represents a newly acquired skill or understanding, or the child and/or teacher think the work is innovative.*

Many teachers find **writing folders** useful for compiling samples of children's work. The specific features of writing folders vary as children mature in their abilities to write conventionally and to express themselves in expanding forms of composition. In general, teachers and students jointly select and include many of the following in the folders:

- Writing in any form—dated to include emergent and unconventional examples of scribble, drawing, random letter strings, and invented spellings, as well as examples of conventional composition

- Writing that is especially descriptive, elicits positive comments from peers, or explains feelings and emotions

- Explanations about why work is valued, what is learned in producing the writing, or why the writing was difficult to do

- Work completed on the computer, the typewriter, or in some other format

- Drafts, revisions, and edited final versions of work completed over a period of time

In much the same way, teachers and students collect naturally occurring **reading work samples**. As children acquire and extend their skills with genres of literature and ways of interpreting them, they encounter additional opportunities for collecting samples of their work. The following examples, however, are easily collected at any grade level:

- Print copies of text—dated to indicate when the text was read and an indication of whether the text was familiar or unfamiliar

- Oral reading tapes of familiar text recorded at several points during the year—demonstrating not only skill level and complexity of text but also the capacity for self-correction and interpretation

- Videotapes of dramatic enactments

- Explanations about why selections of text are included—giving insight into the interests of children, the skills being acquired, and the problems being solved

- Books and poetry written by students themselves—read and shared with others

- Book lists—identifying favorite read-aloud and independent reading favorites, pinpointing interests of children and documenting the extent of challenge sought by young readers

Eliza Takes Some Risks

The teachers noted information that explains why the samples are valued.

...Eliza is an active participant in class discussions of *The Island of the Blue Dolphins*. She has done a nice job of following the complex plot and empathizing with the central character. This is particularly evident in her class-journal entries where she writes from the point of view of Karana.

I sense that Eliza is taking more risks; often she volunteers to predict a future event or to infer meaning in a part of the text. Eliza comes to class prepared and completes her homework in a thorough manner. I am delighted to have her with us.

Progress Reports

Teachers in High/Scope classrooms find that the focus on children afforded by collecting multiple forms of evidence prepares them for readily summarizing or analyzing information. These summaries are offered on **progress reports, report cards**, or in **parent conferences** four or more times each year. Specific school requirements dictate the format of report forms or parent conferences, but High/Scope teachers use diverse forms of information to provide documentary evidence of individual progress.

In most cases teachers find summarizing children's performance and progress with letter grades or using systems that report "satisfactory" or "unsatisfactory," to be inadequate. An "A" or "satisfactory" in *Reading* may be an accurate indicator of a child's reading performance at a given time, but it offers little information about whether this level of performance represents progress and growth. Further, letter grades or "satisfactory" statements do not provide information about observed or predicted skill development. Teachers find it more valuable to be specific about skills: Which skills are presently developed? Which skills are likely to emerge on the basis of what is presently observed in the child's work? Which skills appear to be delayed? Which skills are not expected to develop until a later time?

In High/Scope classrooms teachers use the **Key Experience Checklist for Language and Literacy** (see Appendix C) to document each child's progress and to analyze information gathered from multiple sources, so it can be shared and used. This permutation of the key experiences provides teachers with accurate information about each child's developmental milestones and offers a continuous display of the child's skill development.

Finally, **narrative comments,** as seen in the excerpts from Eliza's progress reports provided, offer yet another form of insight gained by teachers in High/Scope classrooms. Narrative comments provide supplementary information that adds "color" to the "snapshot" of the individual learner.

Eliza Finds the Right Words

The teachers noted the progress made in acquiring literacy skills.

...Eliza's writing is imaginative; she makes good use of descriptive language and uses a varied vocabulary to illustrate her ideas and feelings. Eliza's quiet sense of humor is evident in her writing. She demonstrates an accurate use of simple spelling rules but has difficulty with more complex words. Her sentence construction and use of punctuation conventions is excellent for her age and stage.

...Eliza forms her letters neatly and carefully in cursive handwriting. She has mastered both the formation of and connections between all of the lower-case alphabet.

Planning Instruction

High/Scope teachers regularly refer to the Key Experience Checklist when planning instruction. As noted, this checklist also serves as a useful framework for keeping track of each child's progress over time—documenting typical milestones within a child's development in speaking, listening, writing, and reading.

The interrelated quality of the components of literacy, along with the natural language capacities of children, underscores the need for this checklist to be viewed as a *continuum* of skills development. The skills are not segmented into prescribed kindergarten, grade 1, 2, or 3 domains because children do not fit neatly into such arbitrary divisions. First graders have general developmental characteristics—they are likely to understand letter-sound correspondence, they are likely to be able to produce some conventional print, they are emerging readers and writers—but it is not possible to totally separate their expected performance from that of kindergartners or second graders.

In a study of literacy development in whole language kindergartens, JoBeth Allen (1988) observed that a cumulative pattern of literacy skill development exists: children continue to use several categories of writing, e.g., scribbling, drawing, and phonemic forms, even while moving toward more conventional approaches. To assess progress according to preconceived notions of "first grade" or "third grade" flies in the face of the theoretical foundations of language and literacy skill development. Children often move toward conventional and more complex forms of writing and reading while retaining earlier forms to accomplish some tasks. Because children exhibit writing and reading behaviors consistent with their cognitive abilities, their prior experiences, the richness of their home literacy background, the instructional environment, and a host of other variables, assessment must reflect their progress without stratifying children unnecessarily.

The Key Experience Checklist clearly demonstrates that skills in speaking, listening, writing, and reading develop in relationship to other skills. Such *concurrent* rather than *sequential* skill development means that teachers weave multiple domains together; they seek ways to integrate learning and plan additional experiences that permit continued exposure to new ideas while making certain that children have adequate opportunities to

Eliza Explores the World of Science

The teachers specifically addressed the topic of science in this report.

...Eliza has learned how water and nutrients circulate through a tree, how to determine a tree's age, and how trees are susceptible to injury and disease. She also enjoyed our trip to the Arboretum to observe the maple sugaring process and later the chance to enjoy real maple syrup on pancakes at school!

Early in March we began our study of birds, and Eliza has learned to identify several birds by sight and/or their calls. She has also explored some specific adaptations of birds, such as how placement of their eyes is influenced by whether they are predator or prey, and how the size and shape of the beak relates to their diet. She has been introduced to the concept of migration and has studied birds' nests by taking one apart and building one of her own.

Eliza was fascinated by the incubation of our chicks and delighted in the triumph of each hatching! Eliza's written work in science shows clearly her fine grasp of the material we have covered. Her recent field journal entries, in particular, demonstrate not only her good skills in observation and memory but also her understanding of underlying concepts; she is beginning to do some fine thinking in science. Her writing also occasionally includes some expressions of delight in what she has seen and done. In sum, Eliza is the kind of student who delights a science teacher!

practice what is known. Teachers often draw upon experiences that encourage several layers of skills to emerge and at the same time use the procedure itself to provide a "window" on the process children are employing. The following examples of problem-solving activities for children offer opportunities to observe the results of the problem-solving process:

- **Cloze procedure**—Children complete "gaps" in printed text, demonstrating their understanding of the flow of language and their ability to use multiple semantic, syntactic, or phonic cues in recognizing words.

- **Think-aloud strategies**—Children talk through the procedures they employ while attempting to construct meaning from text, demonstrating the processes they have at their disposal and the extent to which they are able to generalize and make use of information.

- **Retelling**—Children relate what they have read, demonstrating their degree of awareness of the structure of the text, the elements of the text, and the meaning the text has for them.

- **Self-correction**—Children actively explore the correctness of forms while they read, demonstrating which cues they use first, which generalizations they make, and which strategies they employ when there is confusion.

- **Miscue analysis**—Teachers analyze children's miscues, noting the types of errors and whether children were able to correct them.

To sum up, in this chapter we briefly reviewed the process by which children become literate, and we identified some procedures for assessing the development and progress children make along the way to attaining independence and fluency. We addressed the need for teachers to assess children's language and literacy efforts in *natural* ways, mirroring as much as possible the naturally occurring, functional language and literacy activities that children enjoy. We suggested that sampling the performance of children continuously—or as continuously as possible—provides the best evidence of what children are learning and also indicates whether the observed learning represents growth and progress in acquiring and expanding skills. We pointed out that collecting samples of children's ongoing work of varying kinds informs the teacher's interpretation of their performance by adding information about the processes that are developing. We suggested

Eliza Enjoys Active Learning Experiences

From the progress report excerpts presented here and throughout this chapter, we can see how the teachers thoroughly observed, documented, and summarized the performance and progress of one child over a period of two years.

...This year Eliza has listened to many forest-related fairy tales and, through small-group work and whole-group discussion, participated in the creation of a retrieval chart. Its purpose is to highlight recurring themes and structural elements of fairy tales.

Early on, a visit by LIttle Red Riding Hood and the Wolf encouraged the class to begin turning our room into a forest. This project combines science and themes because we are creating specific 'real' trees and vines. Eliza enjoys the painting, cutting, and papier-mâché involved in this project.

As a response to our earlier reading and to attending a live performance of *Hansel and Gretel,* our final activity before vacation was making gingerbread houses. Eliza seems to be enjoying our theme this year. She is an active participant in both craft and thinking activities, and we have come to count on her leadership!

that teachers who observe children regularly as they go about their work gain valuable insight into the strategies children employ as they actively construct new and more complex hypotheses about how to read and write.

And, with all of that, we pointed out that such a focus on children's language and literacy *growth* enables teachers to plan appropriate instruction and sets the stage for additional growth and learning opportunities.

Afterword

In much of his seminal work Donald Graves (1983) encourages teachers to replace predetermined curricula with daily interaction around what each child is doing. He describes this as "drawing curriculum from each child." In much the same vein this guide is offered as a "watch children do it" or "support them as they are doing it" resource rather than the typical "how to do it" teacher's manual.

By producing this curriculum guide, we set out to offer some assistance to High/Scope teachers who are embarking on the literacy journey with K–3 children. We have recounted the different interpretations that educators have brought to the literacy enterprise during the past two hundred years, and we have recalled the ways that learning to read and write have been presented during that time. We have noted, sometimes with amazement, just how differently the process of becoming literate has been viewed in the brief years between editions of the same textbook.

But our real purpose is to encourage teachers and children to set off on the journey to literacy with confidence and enthusiasm. We approach literacy with a determination to view language in its characteristic wholeness and with a commitment to trust young children to initiate their own learning and construct their own complete understanding. This guide urges teachers to use oral and written language as a *dynamic* process that does not rely solely on one's ability to identify and master discrete skills. Instead the learning process should be one that enables natural, motivated growth and awareness.

We harbor the hope that each child's journey to becoming a motivated, fluent speaker, writer, and reader will always involve a sense of magic!

There is a place where the sidewalk ends
And before the street begins,
And there the grass grows soft and white,
And there the sun burns crimson bright,
And there the moon-bird rests from his flight
To cool in the peppermint wind.

Let us leave this place where the smoke blows black
And the dark street winds and bends.
Past the pits where the asphalt flowers grow
We shall walk with a walk that is measured and slow.
And watch where the chalk-white arrows go
To the place where the sidewalk ends.

Yes we'll walk with a walk that is measured and slow,
And we'll go where the chalk-white arrows go,
For the children, they mark, and the children, they know
The place where the sidewalk ends.

— Where the Sidewalk Ends
by Shel Silverstein; reprinted
with permission.

Bibliography

Books

Adams, A. H., Johnson, M. S., & Connors, J. M. (1980). *Success in kindergarten reading and writing: The readiness concept of the future.* Santa Monica, CA: Goodyear Publishing Company, Inc.

Adams, M. J., (1990). *Beginning to read: Thinking and learning about print.* Champaign, IL: Center for the Study of Reading, The Reading Research and Education Center.

Anderson, R. C., Hiebert, E., Scott, J., & Wilkinson, I. (1985). *Becoming a nation of readers: The report of the commission on reading.* Washington, DC: National Institute of Education.

Applebee, A. N. (1987). *The child's concept of story.* Chicago: University of Chicago Press.

Atwell, N. (Ed.). (1989). *Workshop by and for teachers: Writing and literature.* Portsmouth, NH: Heinemann Educational Books, Inc.

Atwell, N. (Ed.). (1990). *Workshop by and for teachers: Beyond the basal.* Portsmouth, NH: Heinemann Educational Books, Inc.

Bean, W., & Bouffler, C. (1987). *Spell by writing.* Portsmouth, NH: Heinemann Educational Books, Inc.

Bissex, G. L. (1980). *GYNS AT WRK: A child learns to write and read.* Cambridge, MA: Harvard University Press.

Bredekamp, S. (Ed.). (1987). *Developmentally appropriate practice in early childhood programs serving children from birth through age 8.* Washington, DC: National Association for the Education of Young Children.

Brown, H., & Cambourne, B. (1987). *Read and retell.* Portsmouth, NH: Heinemann Educational Books, Inc.

Butler, D. & Clay, M. (1987). *Reading begins at home.* Portsmouth, NH: Heinemann Educational Books, Inc.

Calkins, L. M. (1986). *The art of teaching writing.* Portsmouth, NH: Heinemann Educational Books, Inc.

Carr, T. H. (1985). *The development of reading skills.* San Francisco: Jossey-Bass Inc.

Chall, J. S. (1967). *Learning to read: The great debate.* New York: McGraw-Hill.

Clay, M. M. (1972). *Sand: The concepts about print test.* Auckland: Heinemann Educational books, Inc.

Clay, M. M. (1975). *What did I write?* Portsmouth, NH: Heinemann Educational Books, Inc.

Clay, M. M. (1979). *The early detection of reading difficulties.* Portsmouth, NH: Heinemann Educational Books, Inc.

Clay, M. M. (1979). *Stones: The concepts about print test.* Auckland: Heinemann Eductional Books, Inc.

Clay, M. M. (1988). *Writing begins at home.* Portsmouth, NH: Heinemann Educational Books, Inc.

Danish, B. (1981). *Writing as a second language.* New York: Teachers & Writers.

De Vries, R. H., & Kohlberg, L. (1987). *Programs of early education: The constructivist view.* New York: Longmans.

Durkin, D. (1966). *Children who read early.* New York: Teacher's College Press.

Durkin, D. (1972). *Teaching young children to read.* Boston: Allyn and Bacon, Inc.

Dyson, A. H. (1989). *Multiple worlds of child writers: Friends learning to write.* New York: Teachers College Press.

Fields, M. Y., & Lee, D. (1987). *Let's begin reading right.* Columbus, OH: Merrill Publishing Co.

Flesch, R. (1955). *Why Johnny can't read.* New York: Harper & Row.

Gamberg, R., Kwak, W., Hutchings, M., & Altheim, J. (1988). *Learning and loving it.* Portsmouth, NH: Heinemann Educational Books, Inc.

Gibson, L. (1989). *Literacy learning in the early years: Through children's eyes.* New York: Teachers College Press.

Goodman, K. (1986). *What's whole in whole language?* Portsmouth, NH: Heinemann Educational Books, Inc.

Goodman, K., Goodman, Y., & Hood, W. (1989). *The whole language evaluation book.* Portsmouth, NH: Heinemann Educational Books, Inc.

Goodman, K., Shannon, P., Freeman, Y. S., & Murphy, S. (1987). *Report card on basal readers.* Katonah, NY: Richard C. Owen Publishers.

Gordon, N. (Ed.). (1984). *Classroom experiences: The writing process in action.* Portsmouth, NH: Heinemann Educational Books, Inc.

Graves, D. L. (1983). *Writing: Teachers & children at work.* Portsmouth, NH: Heinemann Educational Books, Inc.

Graves, D. L. (1984). *A researcher learns to write.* Portsmouth, NH: Heinemann Educational Books, Inc.

Hall, N. (1987). *The emergence of literacy.* Portsmouth, NH: Heinemann Educational Books, Inc.

Hancock, J., & Hill, S. (Eds.). (1987). *Literature-based reading programs at work.* Portsmouth, NH: Heinemann Educational Books, Inc.

Hansen, J. (1987). *When writers read.* Portsmouth, NH: Heinemann Educational Books, Inc.

Harste, J., Short, K., & Burke, C. (1988). *Creating classrooms for authors.* Portsmouth, NH: Heinemann Educational Books, Inc.

Hohmann, M., Banet, B., & Weikart, D. (1979). *Young children in action.* Ypsilanti, MI: The High/Scope Press.

Holdaway, D. (1979). *The foundations of literacy.* Sydney: Ashton Scholastic.

Johnson, T. D., & Louis, D. R. (1987). *Literacy through literature.* Portsmouth, NH: Heinemann Educational Books, Inc.

Katz, L. (Ed.). (1982). *Current topics in early childhood education* (Vol. IV). Norwood, NJ: Ablex.

Katz, L., & Chard, S. (1989). *Engaging children's minds: The project approach.* Norwood, NJ: Ablex.

Katz, L., Evangelou, D., & Hartman, J. (1990). *The case for mixed-age grouping in early education.* Washington, DC: National Association for the Education of Young Children.

Lloyd-Jones, R., & Lunsford, A. (Eds.). (1989). *The English coalition conference: Democracy through language.* Urbana, IL: National Council of Teachers of English.

Lloyd, P. (1987). *How writers write.* Portsmouth, NH: Heinemann Educational Books, Inc.

Mandel, B. J. (Ed.). (1980). *Three language-arts curriculum models: Pre-kindergarten through college.* Urbana, IL: National Council of Teachers of English.

Manning, M., Manning, G., Long, R., & Wolfson, B. (1987). *Reading and writing in the primary grades.* Washington, DC: National Education Association.

Marzollo, J. (1987). *The new kindergarten: Full-day, child-centered, academic.* New York: Harper & Row.

McCracken, R. A., & McCracken, M. J. (1972). *Reading is only the tiger's tail.* San Rafael, CA: Leswing Press.

Michigan State Board of Education, Reading Curriculum Review Committee. (1988). *The state of reading: Reading professional development leadership series.*

Newkirk, T. (1989). *More than stories: The range of children's writing.* Portsmouth, NH: Heinemann Educational Books, Inc.

National Commission on Excellence in Education. (1983). *A nation at risk: The imperative for educational reform.* Washington, DC: U.S. Dept. of Education.

Nathan, R., Temple, F., Juntunen, K., & Temple, C. (1989). *Classroom strategies that work: An elementary teacher's guide to process writing.* Portsmouth, NH: Heinemann Educational Books, Inc.

Newmann, J. (1985). *Whole language theory in use.* Portsmouth, NH: Heinemann Educational Books, Inc.

Pflaum, S. (1986). *The development of language and literacy in young children.* Columbus, OH: Charles E. Merrill.

Pinnell, G. S., & Matlin, M. L. (Eds.). (1989). *Teachers and research: Language learning in the classroom*. Newark, DE: International Reading Association.

Samuels, S. J., & Pearson, P. D. (1988). *Changing school reading programs*. Newark, NJ: International Reading Association.

Schickedanz, J. A. (1986). *More than the ABCs: The early stages of reading and writing*. Washington, DC: National Association for the Education of Young Children.

Smith, F. (1971). *Understanding reading*. New York: Holt, Rinehart and Winston.

Smith, F. (1982). *Writing and the writer*. London: Heinemann Educational Books, Inc.

Smith, F. (1986). *Insult to intelligence: The bureaucratic invasion of our classrooms*. Portsmouth, NH: Heinemann Educational Books, Inc.

Stewig, J. W., & Sebesta, S. L. (1978). *Using literature in the elementary classroom*. Urbana, IL: National Council of Teachers of English.

Strickland, D. S., & Morrow, L. (Eds.). (1989). *Emerging literacy: Young children learn to read and write*. Newark, DE: International Reading Association.

Teale, W. H., & Sulzby, E. (Eds.). (1986). *Emergent literacy: Writing and reading*. Norwood, NJ: Ablex.

Temple, C., Nathan, R., Burris, N., & Temple, F. (1988). *The beginnings of writing*. Boston: Allyn and Bacon, Inc.

Tiedt, I. (1983). *Teaching writing in K–8 classrooms: The time has come*. Englewood Cliffs, NJ: Prentice-Hall, Inc.

Watson, D. J. (Ed.). (1987). *Ideas and insights: Language arts in the elementary school*. Urbana, IL: National Council Teachers of English.

Wuertenberg, J. (1980). *Helping children become writers*. Tulsa: Educational Progress.

Journal Articles and Chapters in Edited Books

Afflerbach, P. (1988). Preservice teachers use think-aloud protocols to study writing. *Language Arts, 65*, 693–701.

Allen, J. (1988). *Literacy development in whole language kindergartens* (Report No. 436). Champaign, IL: Reading Research and Education Center.

Allington, R. L., & McGill-Franzen, A. (1989). School response to reading failure: Instruction for chapter 1 and special education students in grades two, four, and eight. *Elementary School Journal, 89*, 529–542.

Carbo, M. (1987). Reading styles research: 'What works' isn't always phonics. *Phi Delta Kappan, 68*, 431–435.

Carbo, M. (1988). Debunking the great phonics myth. *Phi Delta Kappan, 70*, 226–240.

Carbo, M. (1990). Igniting the literacy revolution through reading styles. *Educational Leadership, 48*, 26–29.

Cadenhead, K. (1987). Reading level: A metaphor that shapes practice. *Phi Delta Kappan, 68*, 436–441.

Cariello, M. (1990). "The path to a good poem, that lasts forever": Children writing poetry. *Language Arts, 67*, 832–838.

Carroll, J. B. (1987). The national assessments in reading: Are we misreading the findings? *Phi Delta Kappan, 68*, 424–430.

Chall, J. S. (1989). Learning to read: The great debate 20 years later—A response to 'Debunking the great phonics myth.' *Phi Delta Kappan, 70*, 521–538.

Chittenden, E., & Courtney, R. (1989). Assessment of young children's reading: Documentation as an alternative to testing. In D. S. Strickland & L. Morrow (Eds.), *Emerging literacy: Young children learn to read and write*. Newark, DE: International Reading Association.

D'Alessandro, M. (1990). Accommodating emotionally handicapped children through a literature-based reading program. *The Reading Teacher, 44*, 288–293.

Diorio, F. L. (1991). Adapting and utilizing a primary holistic scoring rubric to identify developmental levels in process writing by six-, seven-, and eight-year-olds. Unpublished Dissertation.

Dobson, L. (1988). *Connection in learning to write and read: A study of children's development through kindergarten and grade one* (Report No. 418). Champaign, IL: Reading Research and Education Center.

Dolch, E. L. (1954). Unsolved problems in reading. *Elementary English, 31*, 325–338.

Durkin, D. (1988). *A classroom observation study of reading instruction in kindergarten* (Report No. 422). Champaign, IL: Reading Research and Education Center.

Durkin, D. (1989). *Curriculum reform: Teaching reading in kindergarten* (Report No. 465). Champaign, IL: Reading Research and Education Center.

Durkin, D. (1989). *New kindergarten basal reader materials: What's a teacher supposed to do with all this?* (Report No. 475). Champaign, IL: Reading Research and Education Center.

Durkin, D. (1990). *Phonics instruction in new basal reader programs* (Report No. 496). Champaign, IL: Reading Research and Education Center.

Dyson, A. H. (1990). Weaving possibilities: Rethinking metaphors for early literacy development. *The Reading Teacher, 44*, 202–213.

Egawa, K. (1990). Harnessing the power of language: First graders' literature engagement with *Owl Moon. Language arts, 67*, 582–588.

Ehri, L. & Wilce, L., (1987). Does learning to spell help beginners learn to read words? *Reading Research Quarterly, XXII(i)*, 48–63.

Evans, P. L. (1988). The corporate kindergarten: Writing to read. *Educational Horizons, 66*, 160–163.

Fisher, C. W., & Hiebert, E. (1990). Characteristics of tasks in two approaches to literacy instruction. *The Elementary School Journal, 91*, 3–18.

Genishi, C. (1988). Children's language: Learning words from experience. *Young Children, 44*, 16–23.

Genishi, C. (1988). Kindergartners and computers: A case study of six children. *The Elementary School Journal, 89*, 185–201.

Gersie, T. (1990). Finding the healing tale. *Storytelling, 2*, 18–19.

Glazer, J. I., & Lamme, L. L. (1990). Poem picture books and their uses in the classroom. *The Reading Teacher, 44*, 102–109.

Goldenburg, C. N. (1989). Parents' effects on academic grouping for reading: Three case studies. *American Educational Research Journal, 26*, 329–352.

Hall, W. S. (1989). Reading comprehension. *American Psychologist, 44*, 157–161.

Harste, J. C., & Woodward, V. A. (1989). Fostering needed change in early literacy programs. In D. S. Strickland & L. Morrow, (Eds.), *Emerging literacy: Young children learn to read and write*. Newark, DE: International Reading Association.

Hatch, J. A., & Freeman, E. B. (1988). Who's pushing whom? Stress and kindergarten. *Phi Delta Kappan, 70*, 145–147.

Hiebert, E. H. (1988). The role of literacy experiences in early childhood programs. *The Elementary School Journal, 89*, 161–171.

Hiebert, E. H. (1990). Research directions: Starting with oral language. *Language Arts, 67*, 502–506.

Juliebo, M., & Edwards, J. (1989). Encouraging meaning making in young writers. *Young Children, 44*, 22–27.

Kawakami-Arakaki, A. J., Oshior, M. E., & Farran, D. C. (1988). *Research to practice: Integrating reading and writing in a kindergarten curriculum* (Report No. 415). Champaign, IL: Reading Research and Education Center.

Kontos, S. (1986). What preschool children know about reading and how they learn it. *Young Children, 42*, 58–66.

Langer, J. (1990). Understanding literature. *Language Arts, 67, 812–816*.

Le, T. (1989). Computers as partners in writing: A linguistic perspective. *Journal of Reading, 32*, 606–610.

Lee, S., Ichikawa, V., & Stevenson, H. W. (1987). Beliefs and achievement in mathematics and reading: A cross-national study of Chinese, Japanese, and American children and their mothers. In M. L. Maehr & D. A. Kielber (Eds.), *Advances in motivation and achievement: Enhancing motivation* (Vol. 5). Greenwich, CT: JAI Press, Inc.

McGinley, W., & Madigan, D. (1990). The research "story": A forum for integrating reading, writing, and learning. *Language Arts, 67*, 474–483.

McKenna, M., & Kear, D. (1990). Measuring attitude toward reading: A new tool for teachers. *The Reading Teacher, 43*, 626–639.

McLean, L. D., & Goldstein, H. (1988). The U.S. national assessments in reading: Reading too much into the findings. *Phi Delta Kappan, 69*, 369–372.

Maehr, J. (1989). Right! Young children can write! *High/Scope Extensions*, 4(3).

Manning, M., Manning, G., & Kamii, C. (1988). Early phonics instruction: Its effect on literacy development. *Young Children, 44*, 4–7.

Mason, J. M., Peterman, C. L., & Kerr, B. M. (1989). Reading to kindergarten children. In D. S. Strickland & L. Morrow, (Eds). *Emerging Literacy: Young children learn to read and write*. Newark, DE: International Reading Association.

Mitchell, F. (1990). Introducing art history through children's literature. *Language Arts, 67*, 839–846.

Nessel, D. (1987). Reading comprehension: Asking the right questions. *Phi Delta Kappan, 68*, 442–444.

Newman, J. M., & Church, S. M. (1990). Commentary: Myths of whole language. *The Reading Teacher, 44*, 20–26.

Norton, D. E. (1990). Teaching multicultural literature in the reading curriculum. *The Reading Teacher, 44*, 28–40.

Palincsar, A. S., & Brown, A. L. (1989). Instruction for self-regulated reading. In L. B. Resnick & L. E. Klopfer, (Eds.). *Toward the thinking curriculum: Current cognitive research*. 1989 Yearbook. Association for Supervision and Curriculum Development.

Parks, D. (1988). Direct instruction and the disadvantaged. *Negro Education Review, XXXVIV*, 28–32.

Phillips, L. M. (1989). *Using children's literature to foster written language development* (Report No. 446). Champaign, IL: Reading Research and Education Center.

Pikulski, J. (1990). Informal Reading Inventories. *The Reading Teacher, 43*, 514–516.

Purcell-Gates, V. (1989). What oral written language differences can tell us about beginning instruction. *The Reading Teacher, 43*, 290–294.

Shepard, L. A., & Smith, M. L. (1988). Escalating academic demand in kindergarten: Counterproductive policies. *The Elementary School Journal, 89*, 135–144.

Schickedanz, J. A. (1989). The place of specific skills in preschool and kindergarten. In D. S. Strickland & L. M. Morrow, (Eds.), *Emerging literacy: Young children learn to read and write*. Newark, DE: International Reading Association.

Smith, F. (1989). Overselling literacy. *Phi Delta Kappan, 70*, 352–359.

Spodek, B. (1988). Conceptualizing today's kindergarten curriculum. *The Elementary School Journal, 89*, 203–211.

Sulzby, E. (1981). *Kindergartners as writers and readers* (Revision of final report). Urbana, IL: National Council of Teachers of English.

Sulzby, E. (1982). Oral and written language mode adaptations in stories by kindergarten children. *Journal of Reading Behavior, 14*(1), 51–59.

Sulzby, E. (1984, Summer). Helping children learn to read and write. *Northwestern Educator.*

Sulzby, E. (1985). Children's emergent reading of favorite storybooks: A developmental study. *Reading Research Quarterly, 20*, 458–481.

Sulzby, E. (1986, October). Forms of writing and rereading from writing: A preliminary report (Conference paper). Center for the Study of Writing and Reading.

Sulzby, E. (1987). Children's development of prosodic distinction in telling and dictation modes. In A. Matsuhashi (Ed.), *Writing in real time: Modelling production processes.* Norwood, NJ: Ablex.

Sulzby, E. (1990). *Writing and reading instruction and assessment for young children: Issues and implications.* Paper commissioned by Forum on the Future of Children and Families. National Academy of Sciences and the National Association of State Boards of Education.

Sulzby, E., & Barnhart, J. (1990). The developing kindergartner: All our children emerge as writers and readers. In J. S. McKee (Ed.), *The developing kindergarten: Programs, children, and teachers.* Ann Arbor: MiAEYC.

Sulzby, E., Teale, W. H., & Kamberelis, G. (1989). Emergent writing in the classroom: Home and school connections. In D. S. Strickland & L. Morrow (Eds.), *Emerging literacy: Young children learn to read and write.* Newark, DE: International Reading Association.

Teale, W. H. (1988). Developmentally appropriate assessment of reading and writing in the early childhood classroom. *The Elementary School Journal, 89*, 173–184.

Teale, W. H., & Martinez, M. G. (1988). Getting on the right road to reading: Bringing books and young children together in the classroom. *Young Children, 44*, 10–15.

Trachtenburg, P. (1990, May). Using children's literature to enhance phonics instruction. *The Reading Teacher,* 648–654.

Weaver, C. (1988). How does language mean, and why does it matter in the teaching of reading? In *Reading process and practice.* Portsmouth, NH: Heinemann Educational Books, Inc.

Wells, M. (1988). The roots of literacy. *Psychology Today, 22*, 20–22.

Winn, D. D. (1988). Develop listening skills as a part of the curriculum. *The Reading Teacher, 42*, 144–146.

▼

Appendix A:

Children's Literature Resource Lists*

Read-Aloud Books

Primary Students

Aardema, Verna. *Why Mosquitoes Buzz in People's Ears: A West African Tale.* Dial Books, 1978.

Alexander, Martha. *Three Magic Flip Books (The Magic Hat; The Magic Picture; The Magic Box).* Dial Books, 1984.

Allard, Harry. *Miss Nelson Is Missing.* Scholastic, 1978.

_____. *The Stupids Step Out.* Houghton Mifflin, 1974.

Barrett, Ron. *Hi-Yo Fido!* Crown, 1984.

Birrer, Cynthia, and William Birrer. *The Shoemaker and the Elves.* Lothrop, Lee and Shepard, 1983.

Collodi, Carlo. *The Adventures of Pinocchio: Tale of a Puppet.* Trans. by M. L. Rosenthal. Lothrop, Lee and Shepard, 1983.

de Paola, Tomie. *Strega Nona.* Prentice-Hall, 1975.

Domanska, Janina. *If All the Seas Were One Sea.* Macmillan. 1971.

Fisher, Robert, ed. *Ghosts Galore: Haunting Verse.* Faber and Faber, 1986.

Ga'g, Wanda. *Millions of Cats.* Coward, McCann and Geoghegan/Putnam, 1977.

Heide, Florence Parry. *The Shrinking of Treehorn.* Holiday House, 1971.

Hoban, Russell. *Bedtime for Frances.* Harper and Row, 1976.

*This extensive bibliography of children's literature and resources involved with children's literature appeared in the following publication: Watson, Dorothy J. (Ed.). (1987). *Ideas and insights: Language arts in the elementary school.* Urbana, IL: NCTE. Copyright 1987 by the National Council of Teachers of English. Reprinted with permission.

Hogrogian, Nonny. *One Fine Day*. Macmillan, 1971.

Kellogg, Steven. *The Island of the Skog*. Dial Books, 1976.

_____. *Pinkerton, Behave!* Dial Books, 1982.

_____. *A Rose for Pinkerton*. Dial Books, 1984.

Kennedy, Richard. *The Contests at Cowlick*. Little, Brown, 1975.

Larrick, Nancy, comp. *When the Dark Comes Dancing: A Bedtime Poetry Book*. Philomel/Putnam, 1983.

Lobel, Arnold. *Frog and Toad Are Friends*. Harper and Row, 1985. (See also other books in the series.)

Lowry, Lois. *The One Hundredth Thing about Caroline*. Dell, 1985.

Lunn, Janet. *The Root Cellar*. Penguin, 1985.

McCloskey, Robert. *Make Way For Ducklings*. Penguin, 1976.

Michels, Barbara, and Bettye White. *Apples on a Stick: The Folklore of Black Children*. Coward, McCann and Geoghegan/Putnam, 1983. (Poetry)

Mosel, Arlene. *The Funny Little Woman*. Dutton, 1972.

_____. *Tikki Tikki Tembo*. Scholastic, 1984.

Ness, Evaline. *Sam, Bangs, and Moonshine*. Henry Holt, 1966.

Parish, Peggy. *Amelia Bedelia*. Harper and Row, 1983. (See also other books in the series.)

Pinkwater, Jill. *The Cloud Horse*. Lothrop, Lee and Shepard, 1983.

Potter, Beatrix. *The Tale of Peter Rabbit*.

Robison, Deborah. *Bye-Bye, Old Buddy*. Houghton Mifflin, 1983.

Ross, Tony. *I'm Coming to Get You!* Dial Books, 1984.

Sadler, Marilyn. *Alistair in Outer Space*. Prentice-Hall, 1984.

Sendak, Maurice. *Where the Wild Things Are*. Harper and Row, 1984.

Steig, William. *Amos and Boris*. Penguin, 1977.

_____. *Doctor De Soto*. Scholastic, 1984.

_____. *Sylvester and the Magic Pebble*. Simon and Schuster, 1969.

Thomson, Pat. *Rhymes around the Day*. Lothrop, Lee and Shepard, 1983.

Viorst, Judith. *Alexander and the Terrible, Horrible, No Good, Very Bad Day*. Atheneum/Macmillan, 1976.

_____. *Alexander Who Used to Be Rich Last Sunday*. Atheneum/Macmillan, 1980.

_____. *The Tenth Good Thing about Barney*. Atheneum/Macmillan, 1975.

Waber, Bernard. *The House on East 88th Street*. Houghton Mifflin, 1975.

_____. *Ira Sleeps Over*. Houghton Mifflin, 1975.

Williams, Margery. *The Velveteen Rabbit.*

Zemach, Harve. *The Judge: An Untrue Tale.* Farrar, Straus and Giroux, 1969.

Zemach, Margot. *The Little Red Hen: An Old Story.* Farrar, Straus and Giroux, 1983.

Middle Elementary Students

Babbit, Natalie. *The Devil's Storybook.* Farrar, Straus and Giroux, 1974.

Blume, Judy. *Freckle Juice.* Dell, 1986.

Bulla, Clyde Robert. *Dexter.* Crowell, 1973.

Cleary, Beverly. *Ramona the Pest.* Dell, 1982.

Dahl, Roald. *Danny: The Champion of the World.* Bantam, 1978.

_____. *The Magic Finger.* Harper and Row, 1966.

Erickson, Russell. *A Toad for Tuesday.* Lothrop, Lee and Shepard, 1974. (See also other books in the series.)

Fleischman, Paul. *The Half-a-Moon Inn.* Harper and Row, 1980.

Grahame, Kenneth. *The Reluctant Dragon.* Henry Holt, 1983.

Hicks, Clifford. *Peter Potts.* Avon, 1979.

Kennedy, Richard. *Inside my Feet: The Story of a Giant.* Harper and Row, 1979.

Miles, Miska. *Annie and the Old One.* Little, Brown, 1971.

Peterson, John. *The Littles.* Scholastic, 1986. (See also other books in the series.)

Richler, Mordecai. *Jacob Two-Two Meets the Hooded Fang.* Bantam, 1977.

Robinson, Barbara. *The Best Christmas Pageant Ever.* Avon, 1986.

Smith, Doris B. *A Taste of Blackberries.* Scholastic, 1976.

Smith, Robert Kimmel. *Chocolate Fever.* Dell, 1978.

Van Allsburg, Chris. *Jumanji.* Houghton Mifflin, 1981.

Upper Elementary Students

Aesop. *Aesop's Fables.*

Alcott, Louisa May. *Little Women.*

Andersen, Hans Christian. *The Fir Tree.*

Arbuthnot, May Hill, ed. *Time for Fairy Tales, Old and New.* Scott, Foresman, 1952.

Armstrong, William H. *Sounder.* Harper and Row, 1972.

Babbit, Natalie. *The Search for Delicious.* Avon, 1974.

_____. *Tuck Everlasting.* Farrar, Straus and Giroux, 1975.

Bellairs, John. *The House with a Clock in Its Walls.* Dell, 1974.

Brink, Carol Ryrie. *Caddie Woodlawn*, rev. ed. Macmillan, 1970.

Burnett, Frances Hodgson. *The Secret Garden.*

Burnford, Shelia. *The Incredible Journey.* Bantam, 1967.

Byars, Betsy. *The 18th Emergency.* Penguin, 1981.

_____. *The Midnight Fox.* Penguin, 1981.

Carroll, Lewis, *Alice's Adventures in Wonderland.*

——. *Through the Looking Glass.*

Cleary, Beverly. *Dear Mr. Henshaw.* Dell, 1984.

Dahl, Roald. *Charlie and the Chocolate Factory.* Bantam, 1986.

_____. *Charlie and the Great Glass Elevator.* Bantam, 1977.

_____. *James and the Giant Peach.* Penguin, 1983.

Dickens, Charles. *A Christmas Carol.*

Dodge, Mary Mapes. *Hans Brinker; Or, The Silver Skates.*

Faber, Doris. *Robert Frost, America's Poet.* Prentice-Hall, 1964.

Fitzgerald, John D. *The Great Brain.* Dell, 1971.

Gates, Doris. *Blue Willow.* Penguin, 1976.

George, Jean. *My Side of the Mountain.* Dutton, 1975.

Gipson, Fred. *Old Yeller.* Harper and Row, 1956.

Grahame, Kenneth. *The Wind in the Willows.*

Hague, Kathleen, and Michael Hague, retold by. *East of the Sun and West of the Moon.* Harper and Row, 1980.

Holling, Holling C. *Paddle-to-the-Sea.* Houghton Mifflin, 1941.

Hunt, Irene. *Across Five Aprils.* Ace, 1984.

Juster, Norton. *The Phantom Tollbooth.* Random House, 1961.

Knight, Eric. *Lassie, Come Home.*

Konigsburg, E. L. *Jennifer, Hecate, Macbeth, William McKinley and Me, Elizabeth.* Dell, 1986.

Langton, Jane. *The Fledgling.* Harper and Row, 1981.

Lawson, Robert. *Ben and Me.* Dell, 1973.

_____. *Rabbit Hill.* Penguin, 1977.

L'Engle, Madeline. *A Wrinkle in Time.* Dell, 1986.

Lewis, C. S. *The Lion, the Witch, and the Wardrobe.* Macmillan, 1986.

Lindgren, Astrid. *Pippi Longstocking.*

Martin, Bill, Jr. *Sounds Jubilee.* N.d.

_____. *Sounds of a Distant Drummer.* N.d.

_____. *Sounds of a Hunter.* N.d.

_____. *Sounds of Mystery.* N.d.

Norton, Mary. *The Borrowers.* Harcourt Brace Jovanovich, 1986.

O'Brien, Robert C. *Mrs. Frisby and the Rats of Nimh*. Macmillan, 1986.

O'Dell, Scott. *Island of the Blue Dolphins*. Dell, 1987.

_____. *Sing Down the Moon*. Houghton Mifflin, 1970.

Paterson, Katherine. *Bridge to Terabithia*. Avon, 1979.

Peck, Robert Newton. *Soup in the Saddle*. Knopf, 1983.

Pene du Bois, William. *The Twenty-One Balloons*. Viking, 1947.

Rawls, Wilson. *Summer of the Monkeys*. Doubleday, 1977.

_____. *Where the Red Fern Grows*. Doubleday, 1961.

Saint-Exupery, Antoine de. *The Little Prince*. Harcourt Brace Jovanovich, 1982.

Selden, George. *The Cricket in Times Square*. Dell, 1970.

Silverstein, Shel. *The Giving Tree*. Harper and Row, 1964.

_____. *Lafcadio: The Lion Who Shot Back*. Harper and Row, 1963.

_____. *A Light in the Attic*. Harper and Row, 1981.

_____. *Where the Sidewalk Ends*. Harper and Row, 1974.

Singer, Isaac Bashevis. *Zlateh the Goat and Other Stories*. Harper and Row, 1984.

Spyri, Johanna. *Heidi*.

Steig, William. *Abel's Island*. Farrar, Straus and Giroux, 1976.

Stevenson, Robert Lewis. *Treasure Island*.

Taylor, Theodore. *The Trouble with Tuck*. Avon, 1983.

Twain, Mark. *The Adventures of Tom Sawyer*.

Voight, Cynthia. *The Callender Papers*. Atheneum/Macmillan, 1983.

_____. *Dicey's Song*. Atheneum/Macmillan, 1982.

White, E. B. *Charlotte's Web*. Harper and Row, 1952.

_____. *Stuart Little*. Harper and Row, 1945.

Wilder, Laura Ingalls. *Little House on the Prairie*. (Also see other books in the series.).

Poetry

Cassedy, Sylvia. *Behind the Attic Wall*. Avon, 1985.

Cole, William, ed. *Beastly Boys and Ghastly Girls*. Collins-World, 1964.

Covernton, Jane, and Craig Smith. *Putrid Poems*. Omnibus Books, n.d.

de Regniers, Beatrice Shenk. *Poems Children Will Sit Still For*. Scholastic, 1979.

Downie, Mary Alice, and Barbara Robertson. *The New Wind Has Wings: Poems from Canada*. Oxford University Press, 1984.

Fleischman, Paul. *Path of the Pale Horse.* Harper and Row, 1983.

Hoban, Russell. *Egg Thoughts and Other Frances Songs.* Harper and Row, 1972.

Hopkins, Lee Bennett, ed. *Moments: Poems about the Seasons.* Harcourt Brace Jovanovich, 1980.

_____. *Potato Chips and a Slice of Moon.* Scholastic, 1976.

_____. *Time to Shout: Poems for You.* Scholastic, 1973.

Hopkins, Lee Bennett, and Misha Arenstein. *Faces and Places: Poems for You.* Scholastic, 1971.

Hughes, Monica. *The Isis Pedlar.* Atheneum/Macmillan, 1983.

Kuskin, Karla. *Dogs and Dragons, Trees and Dreams: A Collection of Poems.* Harper and Row, 1980.

Lee, Dennis. *Alligator Pie.* Houghton Mifflin, 1975.

_____. *Garbage Delight.* Houghton Mifflin, 1978.

McGovern, Ann. *The Arrow Book of Poetry.* Scholastic, 1965.

Mason, Anne. *The Dancing Meteorite.* Harper and Row, 1984.

Merriam, Eve. *Out Loud.* Atheneum, 1973.

O'Neill, Mary. *Hailstones and Halibut Bones.* Doubleday, 1961.

Payne, Bernal C., Jr. *It's about Time.* Macmillan, 1984.

Prelutsky, Jack. *Nightmares: Poems to Trouble Your Sleep.* Greenwillow, 1976.

_____. *Rainy Rainy Saturday.* Greenwillow, 1980.

_____. *Rolling Harvey down the Hill.* Greenwillow, 1980.

Silverstein, Shel. *A Light in the Attic.* Harper and Row, 1981.

_____. *Where the Sidewalk Ends.* Harper and Row, 1974.

Sleator, William. *Interstellar Pig.* Bantam, 1986.

Spinelli, Jerry. *Who Put That Hair in My Toothbrush?* Dell, 1986.

Viorst, Judith. *If I Were in Charge of the World and Other Worries.* Atheneum/Macmillan, 1981.

Wilner, Isabel. *The Poetry Troupe: Poems to Read Aloud.* Scribner, 1977.

(Compiled by Kay Clapp, Northeast Missouri State University, Kirksville, and Donna L. Fisher, Columbia, Missouri.)

Wordless Books

Alexander, Martha. *Bobo's Dream.* Dial Books, 1970.

_____. *Out, Out, Out.* Dial Books, 1968.

Amoss, Berthe. *By the Sea.* Parents Magazine Press, 1969.

Anderson, Laurie. *The Package.* Bobbs-Merrill, 1971.

Angel, Marie. *The Ark.* Harper and Row, 1973.

Anno, Mitsumasa. *Anno's Animals.* Philomel, 1979.

_____. *Anno's Britain.* Philomel, 1982.

_____. *Anno's Counting Book.* Harper and Row, 1986.

_____. *Anno's Italy.* Philomel, 1984.

_____. *Anno's Journey.* Philomel, 1981.

_____. *Dr. Anno's Magical Midnight Circus.* Weatherhill, 1972.

_____. *Topsy-Turvies: Pictures to Stretch the Imagination.* Weatherhill, 1970.

Ardizzone, Edward. *The Wrong Side of the Bed.* Doubleday, 1970.

Arnosky, Jim. *Mouse Numbers and Letters.* Harcourt Brace Jovanovich, 1982.

_____. *Mudtime and More: Nathaniel Stories.* Addison-Wesley, 1979.

Aruego, Jose. *Look What I Can Do.* Scribner, 1971.

Asch, Frank. *The Blue Balloon.* McGraw-Hill, 1971.

_____. *In the Eye of the Teddy.* Harper and Row, 1973.

Bakken, Harald. *The Special String.* Prentice-Hall, 1982.

Bang, Molly. *The Grey Lady and the Strawberry Snatcher.* Four Winds/Macmillan, 1980.

Barner, Bob. *The Elephant's Visit.* Atlantic Monthly/Little, Brown, 1975.

Barton, Byron. *Elephant.* Houghton Mifflin, 1971.

_____. *Where's Al?* Houghton Mifflin, 1972.

Baum, Willi. *Birds of a Feather.* Addison-Wesley, 1969.

Bollinger-Savelli, Antonella. *The Knitted Cat.* Macmillan, 1972.

Briggs, Raymond. *The Snowman.* Random House, 1986.

Brinckloe, Julie. *The Spider Web.* Doubleday, 1974.

Bruna, Dick. *Miffy's Dream.* Price, Stern, Sloan, 1984.

Burton, Marilee R. *The Elephant's Nest: Four Wordless Stories.* Harper and Row, 1979.

Carle, Eric. *Do You Want to Be My Friend?* Harper and Row, 1987.

_____. *I See a Song.* Crowell, 1973.

_____. *My Very First Book of Colors.* Crowell, 1985.

_____. *My Very First Book of Shapes.* Crowell, 1985.

_____. *1 2 3 to the Zoo.* World, 1968.

_____. *A Very Long Tail: A Folding Book.* Crowell, 1972.

_____. *A Very Long Train: A Folding Book.* Crowell, 1977.

Carrick, Donald. *Drip Drop.* Macmillan, 1973.

Carroll, Ruth. *The Chimp and the Clown.* Walck, 1968.

_____. *The Dolphin and the Mermaid.* Walck, 1974.

_____. *Rolling Downhill.* Walck, 1973.

_____. *What Whiskers Did.* Walck, 1965.

_____. *The Witch Kitten.* Walck, 1973.

Carroll, Ruth, and Latrobe Carroll. *The Christmas Kitten.* Walck, 1973.

Charlip, Remy, and Jerry Joyner. *Thirteen.* Four Winds, 1985.

Crews, Donald. *Truck.* Penguin, 1985.

Cristini, Ermanno, and Luigi Puricelli. *In My Garden.* Picture Book Studio USA, 1985.

de Groat, Diane. *Alligator's Toothache.* Crown, 1977.

de Paola, Tomie. *Flicks.* Harcourt Brace Jovanovich, 1979.

_____. *The Hunter and the Animals.* Holiday House, 1981.

_____. *Pancakes for Breakfast.* Harcourt Brace Jovanovich, 1978.

Eastman, Philip D. *Go, Dog, Go.* Beginner Books, 1961.

Elzbieta. *Little Mops and the Butterfly.* Doubleday, 1974.

_____. *Little Mops and the Moon.* Doubleday, 1974.

_____. *Little Mops at the Seashore.* Doubleday, 1974.

Emberley, Ed. *A Birthday Wish.* Little, Brown, 1977.

Ets, Marie Hall. *Talking without Words.* Viking, 1968.

Fromm, Lilo. *Muffel and Plums.* Macmillan, 1973.

Fuchs, Erich. *Journey to the Moon.* Delacorte, 1970.

Gilbert, Elliott. *A Cat Story, Told in Pictures.* Henry Holt, 1963.

Goodall, John S. *The Adventures of Paddy Pork.* Harcourt Brace Jovanovich, 1968.

_____. *The Ballooning Adventures of Paddy Pork.* Harcourt Brace Jovanovich, 1969.

_____. *Creepy Castle.* Atheneum, 1975.

_____. *An Edwardian Christmas.* Atheneum/Macmillan, 1978.

_____. *An Edwardian Summer.* Atheneum, 1976.

_____. *Jacko.* Harcourt Brace Jovanovich, 1984.

_____. *The Midnight Adventures of Kelly, Dot, and Esmeralda.* Atheneum/Macmillan, 1973.

_____. *Naughty Nancy.* Atheneum/Macmillan, 1975.

_____. *Paddy Pork—Odd Jobs.* Atheneum/Macmillan, 1983.

_____. *Paddy Pork's Holiday.* Atheneum/Macmillan, 1976.

_____. *Paddy's Evening Out.* Atheneum/Macmillan, 1973.

_____. *Paddy's New Hat.* Atheneum, 1980.

_____. *Shrewbettina's Birthday.* Harcourt Brace Jovanovich, 1983.

_____. *The Story of an English Village.* Atheneum/Macmillan, 1979.

_____. *The Surprise Picnic.* Atheneum, 1977.

Hamberger, John. *The Lazy Dog.* Scholastic, 1973.

Hartelius, Margaret A. *A Sleepless Day.* Scholastic, 1975.

_____. *The Birthday Trombone.* Doubleday, 1977.

_____. *The Chicken's Child.* Scholastic, 1977.

Heller, Linda. *Lily at the Table.* Macmillan, 1979.

Hoban, Tana. *Big Ones, Little Ones.* Greenwillow, 1976.

_____. *Circles, Triangles and Squares.* Macmillan, 1974.

_____. *Count and See.* Macmillan, 1972.

_____. *Dig, Drill, Dump, Fill.* Greenwillow, 1975.

_____. *Look Again!* Macmillan, 1971.

_____. *Over, Under and Through and Other Spatial Concepts.* Macmillan, 1973.

_____. *Push Pull, Empty Full: A Book of Opposites.* Macmillan, 1972.

_____. *Shapes and Things.* Macmillan, 1970.

Hoest, William. *A Taste of Carrot.* Atheneum, 1974.

Hogrogian, Nonny. *Apples.* Macmillan, 1972.

Hughes, Shirley. *Up and Up.* Lothrop, Lee and Shepard, 1986.

Hutchins, Pat. *Changes, Changes.* Macmillan, 1971.

_____. *Rosie's Walk.* Macmillan, 1968.

Keats, Ezra Jack. *Kitten for a Day.* Four Winds/Macmillan, 1974.

_____. *Pssst! Doggie.* Watts, 1973.

_____. *Skates.* Watts, 1973.

Kent, Jack. *The Egg Book.* Macmillan, 1975.

Kilbourne, Frances. *Overnight Adventure.* Women's Writing Press, 1977.

Knobler, Susan. *The Tadpole and the Frog.* Harvey House, 1974.

Kojima, Naomi. *The Flying Grandmother.* Harper and Row, 1981.

Krahn, Fernando. *April Fools.* Dutton, 1974.

_____. *Arthur's Adventure in the Abandoned House.* Dutton, 1981.

_____. *The Biggest Christmas Tree on Earth.* Atlantic Monthly, 1978.

_____. *Catch the Cat!* Dutton, 1978.

_____. *The Creepy Thing.* Paradox, 1982.

_____. *A Flying Saucer Full of Spaghetti.* Dutton, 1970.

_____. *A Funny Friend from Heaven.* Lippincott, 1977.

_____. *The Great Ape.* Viking, 1978.

_____. *Here Comes Alex Pumpernickel.* Atlantic Monthly/Little, Brown, 1981.

_____. *How Santa Claus Had a Long and Difficult Journey Delivering His Presents.* Delacorte, 1977.

_____. *Little Love Story.* Lippincott, 1976.

_____. *The Mystery of the Giant's Footprints.* Dutton, 1977.

_____. *Robot-Bot-Bot.* Dutton, 1979.

_____. *Sebastian and the Mushroom.* Delacorte, 1976.

_____. *The Secret in the Dungeon.* Houghton Mifflin, 1983.

_____. *The Self-Made Snowman.* Lippincott, 1974.

_____. *Sleep Tight, Alex Pumpernickel.* Atlantic Monthly/Little, Brown, 1982.

_____. *Who's Seen the Scissors?* Dutton, 1975.

Lisker, Sonia O. *The Attic Witch.* Four Winds, 1973.

_____. *Lost.* Harcourt Brace Jovanovich, 1975.

Lustig, Loretta. *The Pop-Up Book of Trucks.* Random House, 1974.

McCully, Emily Arnold. *Picnic.* Harper and Row, 1984.

McPhail, David M. *Oh No Go.* Atlantic Monthly/Little, Brown, 1973.

McTrusty, Ron. *Dandelion Year.* Harvey House, 1974.

Mari, Iela. *Eat and Be Eaten.* Barrons, n.d.

Mari, Iela, and Enzo Mari. *The Apple and the Moth.* Pantheon, 1970.

_____. *The Chicken and the Egg.* Pantheon, 1970.

Mayer, Mercer. *A Boy, a Dog, and a Frog.* Dial Books, 1967.

_____. *Ah-Choo.* Dial Books, 1976.

_____. *Bubble Bubble.* Four Winds/Macmillan, 1980.

_____. *Frog Goes to Dinner.* Dial Books, 1977.

_____. *Frog on His Own.* Dial Books, 1980.

_____. *Frog, Where Are You?* Dial Books, 1980.

_____. *The Great Cat Chase.* Four Winds/Scholastic, 1974.

_____. *Hiccup.* Dial Books, 1978.

_____. *Oops.* Dial Books, 1978.

_____. *Two Moral Tales.* Four Winds/Scholastic, 1974.

_____. *Two More Moral Tales.* Four Winds/Scholastic, 1974.

Meyer, Renate. *Hide-and-Seek.* Bradbury, 1972.

Mordillo, Guillermo. *The Damp and Daffy Doings of a Daring Pirate Ship.* Quist, 1971.

Morris, Terry Neil. *Good Night, Dear Monster!* Knopf, 1980.

_____. *Lucky Puppy, Lucky Boy.* Knopf, 1980.

Oakley, Graham. *Graham Oakley's Magical Changes.* Atheneum/Macmillan, 1980.

Olschewski, Alfred. *Winterbird*. Houghton Mifflin, 1969.

Ormerod, Jan. *Moonlight*. Penguin, 1984.

_____. *Sunshine*. Penguin, 1984.

Remington, Barbara. *Boat*. Doubleday, 1975.

Richter, Mischa. *Quack?* Harper and Row, 1978.

Ringi, Kjell. *The Magic Stick*. Harper and Row, 1968.

_____. *The Winner*. Harper and Row, 1969.

Rockwell, Anne F. *Albert B. Cub and Zebra: An Alphabet Story-book*. Crowell, 1977.

Ross, Pat. *Hi Fly*. Crown, 1974.

Schneider, Herman, and Nina Schneider. *Science Fun for You in a Minute or Two: Quick Science Experiments You Can Do*. McGraw-Hill, 1975.

Scott, Foresman Reading Systems. *The Baby Monkey*. Scott, Foresman, n.d. (Reading Unlimited Program, Level Three)

_____. *The Man and the Donkey*. Scott, Foresman, n.d. (Reading Unlimited Program, Level Five)

Shimin, Symeon. *A Special Birthday*. McGraw-Hill, 1976.

Simmons, Ellie. *Family*. McKay, 1970.

Spier, Peter. *Noah's Ark*. Doubleday, 1981.

_____. *Peter Spier's Rain*. Doubleday, 1982.

Turkle, Brinton. *Deep in the Forest*. Dutton, 1976.

Ueno, Noriko. *Elephant Buttons*. Harper and Row, 1973.

Wagner, Justin. *The Bus Ride*. Scott, Foresman, 1976. (Reading Unlimited Program, Level Two)

Ward, Lynd Kendall. *The Silver Pony: A Story in Pictures*. Houghton Mifflin, 1973.

Wezel, Peter. *The Good Bird*. Harper and Row, 1966.

Winter, Paula. *The Bear and the Fly*. Crown, 1976.

_____. *Sir Andrew*. Crown, 1980.

(Compiled by Kay Clapp, Northeast Missouri State University, Kirksville, and Donna L. Fisher, Columbia, Missouri.)

Extending Literature: Reading Leading to Writing

Alain. *One, Two, Three, Going to Sea*. Scholastic, 1969.

Alexander, Martha. *Nobody Asked Me If I Wanted a Baby Sister*. Dial Books, 1977.

_____. *When the New Baby Comes, I'm Moving Out*. Dial Books, 1981.

Aliki. *Go Tell Aunt Rhody*. Macmillan, 1986.

_____. *Hush Little Baby.* Prentice-Hall, 1968.

_____. *My Five Senses.* Crowell, 1962.

Allinson, Beverly. *Mitzi's Magic Garden.* Garrard, 1971.

Asbjornsen, Peter C., and Jorgen Moe; ed. by Marcia Brown. *The Three Billy Goats Gruff.* Harcourt, Brace and World, 1957.

Asch, Frank. *Monkey Face.* Parents Magazine Press, 1977.

_____. *Turtle Tale.* Dial Books, 1980.

Balian, Lorna. *The Animal.* Abingdon, 1972.

_____. *Where in the World Is Henry?* Bradbury, 1972.

Banchek, Linda. *Snake In, Snake Out.* Crowell, 1978.

Barchas, Sarah. *I Was Walking down the Road.* Scholastic, 1976.

_____. *Janie and the Giant.* Scholastic, 1978.

Barrett, Judith. *Animals Should Definitely Not Wear Clothing.* Atheneum/Macmillan, 1980.

Barton, Byron. *Buzz, Buzz, Buzz.* Penguin, 1979.

Baum, Arline, and Joseph Baum. *One Bright Monday Morning.* Random House, 1962.

Becker, John. *Seven Little Rabbits.* Scholastic, 1985.

Beckman, Per, and Kaj Beckman. *Lisa Cannot Sleep.* Watts, 1969.

Bellah, Melanie. *A First Book of Sounds.* Golden Press, 1963.

Benchley, Nathaniel. *The Strange Disappearance of Arthur Cluck.* Harper and Row, 1979.

_____. *Red Fox and His Canoe.* Harper and Row, 1985.

Berenstain, Stan, and Jan Berenstain. *The Berenstain Bears and the Spooky Old Tree.* Random House, 1978.

Bishop, Claire H. *The Five Chinese Brothers.* Coward/Putnam, 1938.

_____. *Twenty-Two Bears.* Viking, 1964.

Blance, Ellen, et al. *Monster Books,* Sets I and II. Bowmar, Noble, 1973.

Blegvad, Eric. *The Three Little Pigs.* Atheneum, 1980.

Brand, Oscar. *When I First Came to This Land.* Putnam, 1974.

Brandenberg, Franz. *I Once Knew a Man.* Macmillan, 1970.

_____. *Nice New Neighbors.* Greenwillow, 1977.

_____. *What Can You Make of It?* Greenwillow, 1977.

Bridwell, Norman. *Clifford, The Big Red Dog.* Scholastic, 1985. (See also other books in the series.)

_____. *Crazy Zoo.* Scholastic, 1972.

_____. *Kangaroo Stew.* Scholastic, 1979.

_____. *A Tiny Family.* Scholastic, 1968.

Brooke, Leslie. *Johnny Crow's Garden*. Warne, 1986.

Brown, Margaret Wise. *The Dead Bird*. Addison-Wesley, 1958.

_____. *Four Fur Feet*. Addison-Wesley, 1961.

_____. *Goodnight, Moon*. Harper and Row, 1977.

_____. *Home for a Bunny*. Western, 1983.

_____. *The Important Book*. Harper and Row, 1949.

_____. *The Runaway Bunny*. Harper and Row, 1977.

_____. *Where Have You Been?* Hastings, 1963.

Burningham, John. *Avocado Baby*. Crowell, 1982.

_____. *Mr. Gumpy's Motor Car*. Penguin, 1983.

Byars, Betsy. *Go and Hush the Baby*. Penguin, 1982.

Carle, Eric. *The Grouchy Ladybug*. Harper and Row, 1986.

_____. *The Mixed-Up Chameleon*. Crowell, 1984.

_____. *The Very Hungry Caterpillar*. Philomel/Putnam, 1981.

Cauley, Lorinda B., illus. *The Story of the Three Little Pigs*. Putnam, 1980. (Words by Joseph Jacobs)

Charlip, Remy. *Fortunately*. Four Winds/Macmillan, 1985.

_____. *What Good Luck, What Bad Luck*. Scholastic, 1964.

Cohen, Miriam. *Will I Have a Friend?* Macmillan, 1971.

Cook, Ann, and Herb Mack. *Robot and the Flea Market*. Dell, 1982. (See also other books in the series.)

Cook, Bernadine. *The Little Fish That Got Away*. Scholastic, 1962.

de Paola, Tomie. *Bill and Pete*. Putnam, 1978.

_____. *Oliver Button Is a Sissy*. Harcourt Brace Jovanovich, 1979.

de Regniers, Beatrice. *Catch a Little Fox*. Seabury, 1970.

_____. *How Joe the Bear and Sam the Mouse Got Together*. Scholastic, 1983.

_____. *The Little Book*. Walck, 1961.

_____. *May I Bring a Friend?* Atheneum/Macmillan, 1974.

_____. *Willy O'Dwyer Jumped in the Fire*. Atheneum, 1968.

de Regniers, Beatrice S., and Nonny Hogrogian. *The Day Everybody Cried*. Viking, 1967.

De Rico, Ul. *The Rainbow Goblins*. Thames and Hudson, 1978.

Domanska, Janina. *If All the Seas Were One Sea*. Macmillan, 1971.

Domjan, Joseph. *I Went to the Market*. Holt, Rinehart and Winston, 1970.

Duff, Maggie. *Jonny and His Drum*. Walck, 1972.

_____. *Rum Pum Pum*. Macmillan, 1978.

Elkin, Benjamin. *Six Foolish Fishermen*. Scholastic, n.d.

Elting, Mary, and Michael Folsom. *Q Is for Duck.* Houghton Mifflin, 1980.

Emberley, Barbara. *Drummer Hoff.* Prentice-Hall, 1967.

_____. *Simon's Song.* Prentice-Hall, 1969.

Emberley, Ed. *Klippity Klop.* Little, Brown, 1974.

Ernst, Kathryn F. *Danny and His Thumb.* Prentice-Hall, 1975.

Ets, Marie Hall. *Elephant in a Well.* Viking, 1972.

_____. *Play with Me.* Penguin, 1976.

Flack, Marjorie. *Ask Mr. Bear.* Macmillan, 1986.

Freeman, Don. *Corduroy.* Penguin, 1976.

_____. *Dandelion.* Penguin, 1977.

Friskey, Margaret. *Indian Two Feet and His Horse.* Childrens Press, 1959.

Gage, Wilson. *Squash Pie.* Dell, 1980.

Galdone, Paul. *The House That Jack Built.* McGraw-Hill, 1961.

_____. *The Little Red Hen.* Houghton Mifflin, 1985.

_____. *The Three Billy Goats Gruff.* Houghton Mifflin, 1981.

_____. *The Three Little Pigs.* Houghton Mifflin, 1984.

Ginsburg, Mirra. *The Chick and the Duckling.* Macmillan, 1972.

Graham, John. *I Love You, Mouse.* Harcourt Brace Jovanovich, 1978.

Greenberg, Polly. *Oh Lord, I Wish I Was a Buzzard.* Macmillan, 1968.

Hargreaves, Roger. *Mr. Men Mealtime.* Price, Stern, Sloan, 1983. (See also other books in the series.)

Hazen, Barbara Shook. *The Gorilla Did It.* Atheneum/Macmillan, 1978.

_____. *Tight Times.* Penguin, 1983.

Heilbroner, Joan. *This Is the House Where Jack Lives.* Harper and Row, 1962.

Hoban, Lillian. *Arthur's Honey Bear.* Harper and Row, 1982.

Hoban, Russell. *A Baby Sister for Frances.* Harper and Row, 1976.

_____. *Bedtime for Frances.* Harper and Row, 1976.

Hoff, Syd. *Danny and the Dinosaur.* Harper and Row, 1978.

Hoffman, Hilde. *The Green Grass Grows All Around.* Macmillan, 1968.

Hogrogrian, Nonny. *One Fine Day.* Macmillan, 1971.

Hunt, Bernice Kohn. *Your Aunt Is a Which: Fun with Homophones.* Harcourt Brace Jovanovich, 1976.

Hurd, Edith Thacher. *Come and Have Fun.* Harper and Row, 1962.

Hutchins, Pat. *Don't Forget the Bacon!* Greenwillow, 1976.

_____. *Good-Night Owl.* Macmillan, 1972.

_____. *Rosie's Walk.* Macmillan, 1971.

_____. *Titch.* Macmillan, 1971.

Johnson, Crockett. *Harold and the Purple Crayon.* Harper and Row, 1981. (See also other books in the series.)

Keats, Ezra Jack. *Louie.* Greenwillow, 1983.

_____. *The Snowy Day.* Penguin, 1976.

_____. *Whistle for Willie.* Penguin, 1977.

_____. illus. *Over in the Meadow.* Scholastic, 1985. (Words by Olive A. Wadsworth)

Kellogg, Steven. *Can I Keep Him?* Dial Books, 1976.

Kent, Jack. *The Fat Cat.* Scholastic, 1972.

_____. *There's No Such Thing as a Dragon.* Western, 1975.

Klein, Leonore. *Brave Daniel.* Scholastic, 1969.

_____. *Silly Sam.* Scholastic, 1971.

Krasilovsky, Phyllis. *The Man Who Didn't Wash His Dishes.* Doubleday, 1950.

Kraus, Robert. *Leo the Late Bloomer.* Crowell, 1971.

_____. *Whose Mouse Are You?* Macmillan, 1972.

Krauss, Ruth. *The Carrot Seed.* Harper and Row, 1945.

Kroll, Steven. *The Tyrannosaurus Game.* Holiday, 1976.

Langstaff, John. *Frog Went A-Courtin'.* Harcourt Brace Jovanovich, 1972.

_____. *Gather My Gold Together: Accumulative Songs for Four Seasons.* Doubleday, 1971.

_____. *Oh, A-Hunting We Will Go.* Antheneum, 1974.

_____. *Over in the Meadow.* Harcourt Brace Jovanovich, 1973.

Laurence, Ester H. *We're Off to Catch a Dragon.* Abingdon, 1969.

Lear, Edward. *The Jumblies.* Silver Burdett, 1986.

Lexau, Joan M. *Crocodile and Hen.* Harper and Row, 1969.

_____. *That's Good, That's Bad.* Dial Press, 1963.

Littledale, Freya. *The Boy Who Cried Wolf.* Scholastic, 1977.

Lobel, Anita. *King Rooster, Queen Hen.* Greenwillow, 1975.

Lobel, Arnold. *Frog and Toad Are Friends.* Harper and Row, 1985. (See also other books in the series.)

_____. *Mouse Soup.* Harper and Row, 1983.

_____. *Mouse Tales.* Harper and Row, 1978.

_____. *Owl at Home.* Harper and Row, 1982.

_____. *A Treeful of Pigs.* Greenwillow, 1979.

Logan, Dick. *Thunder Goes for a Walk.* Creative Education, 1977.

Lopshire, Robert. *Put Me in the Zoo.* Beginner Books, 1960.

McGovern, Ann. *Too Much Noise.* Houghton Mifflin, 1967.

Mack, Stan. *10 Bears in My Bed: A Goodnight Countdown.* Pantheon Books, 1974.

Margolis, Richard J. *Big Bear, Spare That Tree.* Greenwillow, 1980.

Marshall, James. *George and Martha.* Houghton Mifflin, 1972. (See also other books in the series.)

Martin, Bill. *Brown Bear, Brown Bear, What Do You See?* Holt, Rinehart and Winston, 1983.

_____. *Fire! Fire! Said Mrs. McGuire.* Holt, Rinehart and Winston, 1982.

_____. *The Haunted House.* Holt, Rinehart and Winston, n.d.

_____. *Monday, Monday, I Like Monday.* Holt, Rinehart and Winston, 1983.

_____. *My Days Are Made of Butterflies.* Holt, Rinehart and Winston, n.d.

_____. *A Spooky Story.* Holt, Rinehart and Winston, n.d.

_____. *Tatty Mae and Catty Mae.* Holt, Rinehart and Winston, n.d.

_____. *When It Rains, It Rains.* Holt, Rinehart and Winston, n.d.

_____. *Whistle, Mary, Whistle.* Holt, Rinehart and Winston, n.d.

Mayer, Mercer. *If I Had . . . .* Dial Books, 1977.

_____. *Just for You.* Western, 1975.

_____. *Just Me and My Dad.* Western, 1977.

_____. *There's a Nightmare in My Closet.* Dial Books, 1976.

Memling, Carl. *Ten Little Animals.* Western, 1961.

Mendoza, George. *A Wart Snake in a Fig Tree.* Dial Press, 1976.

Mills, Alan, and Rose Bonne. *I Know an Old Lady.* Rand McNally, 1961.

Minarik, Else Holmelund. *Father Bear Comes Home.* Harper and Row, 1978.

_____. *Little Bear's Visit.* Harper and Row, 1984.

Moffett, Martha. *A Flower Pot Is Not a Hat.* Dutton, 1972.

Mosel, Arlene. *Tikki Tikki Tembo.* Scholastic, 1984.

Noodles. *How to Catch a Ghost.* Holt, Rinehart and Winston, 1983.

Palmer, Helen. *Why I Built the Boogle House.* Beginner Books, 1964.

Parish, Peggy. *Too Many Rabbits.* Scholastic, 1976.

Peppe, Rodney. *The House That Jack Built.* Delacorte, 1985.

_____. *Odd One Out.* Penguin, 1975.

Pinkwater, D. Manus. *The Hoboken Chicken Emergency.* Prentice-Hall, 1984.

Piper, Watty. *The Little Engine That Could.*

Polushkin, Maria. *Mother, Mother, I Want Another.* Crown, 1986.

Preston, Edna Mitchell. *The Sad Story of the Little Bluebird and the Hungry Cat.* Scholastic, 1975.

_____. *Where Did My Mother Go?* Scholastic, 1978.

Quackenbush, Robert. *She'll Be Comin' 'Round the Mountain.* Lippincott, 1973.

_____. *Skip to My Lou.* Harper and Row, 1975.

_____. *Too Many Lollipops.* Parents Magazine Press, 1975.

Raskin, Ellen. *Who, Said Sue, Said Whoo?* Atheneum, 1976.

Rey, Margaret. *Pretzel.* Harper and Row, 1984.

Rice, Eve. *Ebbie.* Greenwillow, 1975.

_____. *Goodnight, Goodnight.* Penguin, 1983.

_____. *New Blue Shoes.* Penguin, 1979.

_____. *Oh, Lewis!* Penguin, 1979.

_____. *Sam Who Never Forgets.* Penguin, 1980.

Robison, Deborah. *Anthony's Hat.* Scholastic, 1977.

_____. *No Elephants Allowed.* Houghton Mifflin, 1981.

Rockwell, Anne. *Poor Goose.* Crowell, 1976.

Rockwell, Harlow. *My Kitchen.* Greenwillow, 1980.

Rokoff, Sandra. *Here Is a Cat.* Hallmark Children's Editions, n.d.

Rose, Gerald. *Trouble in the Ark.* Merrimack Publishers Circle, 1985.

Scheer, Jullian. *Rain Makes Applesauce.* Holiday House, 1964.

Sendak, Maurice. *Alligators All Around.* Harper and Row, 1962.

_____. *Chicken Soup with Rice.* Scholastic, 1986.

_____. *One Was Johnny.* Harper and Row, 1962.

_____. *Pierre.* Harper and Row, 1962.

_____. *Where the Wild Things Are.* Harper and Row, 1984.

Seuss, Dr. *Green Eggs and Ham.* Beginner Books, 1960.

_____. *Hop on Pop.* Beginner Books, 1963.

_____. *One Fish Two Fish Red Fish Blue Fish.* Beginner Books, 1960.

Sharmat, Marjorie Weinman. *I Don't Care.* Macmillan, 1977.

Shaw, Charles G. *It Looked like Spilt Milk.* Harper and Row, 1947.

Shulevitz, Uri. *One Monday Morning.* Scribner, 1967.

Sivulich, Sandra Stroner. *I'm Going on a Bear Hunt.* Dutton, 1973.

Skaar, Grace. *What Do the Animals Say?* Scholastic, 1973.

Sonneborn, Ruth A. *Someone Is Eating the Sun.* Random House, 1974.

Spier, Peter. *The Fox Went Out on a Chilly Night.* Doubleday, 1961.

Stevens, Carla. *Hooray for Pig.* Houghton Mifflin, 1974.

Stevenson, James. *Could Be Worse!* Penguin, 1979.

Stover, Jo Ann. *If Everybody Did.* McKay, 1960.

Sullivan, Joan. *Round Is a Pancake.* Holt, Rinehart and Winston, 1963.

Sutton, Eve. *My Cat Likes to Hide in Boxes.* Parents Magazine Press, 1974.

Testa, Fulvio, and Anthony Burgess. *The Land Where the Ice Cream Grows.* n.d.

Thaler, Mike. *A Hippopotamus Ate the Teacher.* Avon, 1981.

_____. *There's a Hippopotamus Under My Bed.* Avon, 1978.

Tolstoy, Alexei. *The Great Big Enormous Turnip.* Watts, 1969.

Ungerer, Tomi. *Crictor.* Harper and Row, 1983.

Van Leeuwen, Jean. *Tales of Oliver Pig.* Dial Books, 1979.

Viorst, Judith. *Alexander and the Terrible, Horrible, No Good, Very Bad Day.* Atheneum/Macmillan, 1976.

_____. *I'll Fix Anthony.* Atheneum/Macmillan, 1983.

_____. *The Little Boy Who Loved Dirt and Almost Became a Super-slob.* Atheneum, 1975.

_____. *My Mama Says There Aren't Any Zombies, Ghosts, Vampires, Creatures, Demons, Monsters, Fiends, Goblins, or Things.* Atheneum/Macmillan, 1977.

Vogel, Ilse-Margret. *The Don't Be Scared Book: Scares, Remedies, and Pictures.* Atheneum/Macmillan, 1972.

Waber, Bernard. *A Firefly Named Torchy.* Houghton Mifflin, 1970.

_____. *Ira Sleeps Over.* Houghton Mifflin, 1975.

Wahl, Jan. *Grandmother Told Me.* Little, Brown, 1972.

Watson, Clyde. *Catch Me and Kiss Me and Say It Again.* Philomel/Putnam, 1983.

Weiss, Leatie. *Heather's Features.* Avon, 1978.

Welber, Robert. *Goodbye, Hello.* Pantheon Books, 1974.

Wildsmith, Brian. *Brian Wildsmith's "The Twelve Days of Christmas."* Watts, 1972.

Williams, Barbara. *Someday, Said Mitchell.* Dutton, 1976.

Williams, Jay. *Everybody Knows What a Dragon Looks Like.* Four Winds/Macmillan, 1976.

Wolkstein, Diane. *The Visit.* Knopf, 1977.

Wondriska, William. *All the Animals Were Angry.* Holt, Rinehart and Winston, 1970.

Wright, H. R. *A Maker of Boxes.* Holt, Rinehart and Winston, 1964.

Yolen, Jane. *An Invitation to the Butterfly Ball: A Counting Rhyme.* Philomel/Putnam, 1983.

Zaid, Barry. *Chicken Little.* Random House, n.d.

Zemach, Harve. *The Judge: An Untrue Tale.* Farrar, Straus and Giroux, 1969.

Zemach, Margot. *Hush, Little Baby.* Dutton, 1975.

_____. *The Little, Tiny Woman.* Bobbs-Merrill, 1965.

Zion, Gene. *Harry the Dirty Dog.* Harper and Row, 1976.

Zolotow, Charlotte. *Do You Know What I'll Do?* Harper and Row, 1958.

_____. *If It Weren't for You.* Harper and Row, 1966.

_____. *Mr. Rabbit and the Lovely Present.* Harper and Row, 1977.

_____. *Some Things Go Together.* Harper and Row, 1987.

_____. *Summer Is . . . .* Crowell, 1983.

(Compiled by Barbara Flores, Phoenix, Arizona; Susan Lehr, Skidmore College, Saratoga Springs, New York; Lynn K. Rhodes, University of Colorado at Denver; Regie Routman, Shaker Heights City School District, Ohio.)

Predictable Language

Repetition

Aliki. *Use Your Head, Dear.* Greenwillow, 1983.

Argent, Kerry, and Rod Trinca. *One Woolly Wombat.* Kane-Miller, 1985.

Arno, Ed. *The Gingerbread Man.* Scholastic, 1973.

Asch, Frank. *Just Like Daddy.* Prentice-Hall, 1984.

Baum, Arline, and Joseph Baum. *One Bright Monday Morning.* Random House, 1962.

Bayer, Jane. *A My Name is Alice.* Dial Books, 1984.

Becker, John. *Seven Little Rabbits.* Scholastic, 1985.

Bond, Felicia. *Four Valentines in a Rainstorm.* Crowell, 1983.

Brandenberg, Franz. *I Wish I Was Sick, Too!* Penguin, 1978.

Brown, Margaret Wise. *The Runaway Bunny.* Harper and Row, 1977.

_____. *Where Have You Been?* Hastings, 1963.

Carle, Eric. *The Very Hungry Caterpillar.* Philomel/Putnam, 1981.

Cowley, Joy. *Meanies*. Auckland, N.Z.: Shorthand Publications, 1983. (Distributed by the Wright Group)

de Regniers, Beatrice Schenk. *Going for a Walk*. Harper and Row, 1982.

Ets, Marie Hall. *Just Me*. Penguin, 1978.

Flack, Marjorie. *Ask Mr. Bear*. Macmillan, 1986.

Ga'g, Wanda. *Millions of Cats*. Coward, McCann and Geoghegan/Putnam, 1977.

Galdone, Paul. *Henny Penny*. Houghton Mifflin, 1984.

_____. *The House That Jack Built*. McGraw-Hill, 1961.

_____. *The Little Red Hen*. Houghton Mifflin, 1985.

_____. *The Three Bears*. Ticknor and Fields, 1985.

_____. *The Three Billy Goats Gruff*. Houghton Mifflin, 1981.

Graboff, Abner. *Old MacDonald Had a Farm*. Scholastic, 1970.

Guilfoile, Elizabeth. *Nobody Listens to Andrew*. Modern Curriculum Press, 1957.

Heide, Florence Parry, and Sylvia Van Clief. *That's What Friends Are For*. Scholastic, 1971.

Hutchins, Pat. *Don't Forget the Bacon*. Greenwillow, 1976.

Kesselman, Wendy. *There's a Train Going by My Window*. Doubleday, 1982.

Klein, Leonore. *Silly Sam*. Scholastic, 1971.

Koide, Tan. *May We Sleep Here Tonight?* Atheneum/Macmillan, 1983.

Krauss, Ruth. *The Carrot Seed*. Harper and Row, 1945.

_____. *The Happy Egg*. Scholastic, 1972.

Kwitz, Mary DeBall. *Little Chick's Story*. Harper and Row, 1978.

Langstaff, John. *Oh, A-Hunting We Will Go*. Atheneum, 1974.

Lexau, Joan. *That's Good, That's Bad*. Dial Press, 1963.

Littledale, Freda. *The Magic Fish: Easy to Read Folktales*. Scholastic, 1986.

Lobel, Arnold. *A Treeful of Pigs*. Greenwillow, 1979.

McGovern, Ann. *Stone Soup*. Scholastic, 1986.

_____. *Too Much Noise*. Houghton Mifflin, 1967.

Martin, Bill, Jr. *Brown Bear, Brown Bear, What Do You See?* Holt, Rinehart and Winston, 1983.

_____. *Fire! Fire! Said Mrs. McGuire*. Holt, Rinehart and Winston, 1982.

_____. *Monday, Monday, I Like Monday*. Holt, Rinehart and Winston, 1983.

Mayer, Mercer. *If I Had . . . .* Dial Books, 1977.

Melser, June, and Joy Cowley. *The Big Toe*. Auckland, N. Z.: Shorthand Publications, 1982. (Distributed by the Wright Group)

_____. *In a Dark Dark Wood*. Auckland, N.Z.: Shorthand Publications, 1982. (Distributed by the Wright Group)

_____. *Lazy Mary*. Auckland, N.Z.: Shorthand Publications, 1982. (Distributed by the Wright Group)

_____. *One Cold Wet Night*. Auckland, N.Z.: Shorthand Publications, 1982. (Distributed by the Wright Group)

_____. *Sing a Song*. Auckland, N.Z.: Shorthand Publications, 1982. (Distributed by the Wright Group)

_____. *Yes Ma'am*. Auckland, N.Z.: Shorthand Publications, 1981. (Distributed by the Wright Group)

Mills, Alan, and Rose Bonne. *I Know an Old Lady*. Rand McNally, 1961.

Minarik, Else Holmelund. *Little Bear*. Harper and Row, 1978.

Morris, William Barrett. *The Longest Journey in the World*. Holt, Rinehart and Winston, 1982.

Peppe, Rodney. *The Kettleship Pirates*. Lothrop, Lee and Shepard, 1983.

Pienkowski, Jan. *Dinnertime*. Price, Stern, Sloan, 1981.

Pomerantz, Charlotte. *One Duck, Another Duck*. Greenwillow, 1984.

Preston, Edna M., and Rainey Bennett. *The Temper Tantrum Book*. Penguin, 1976.

Rose, Anne. *Akimba and the Magic Cow*. Four Winds/Scholastic, 1979.

Ruwe, Mike. *Ten Little Bears*. Scott, Foresman, 1976. (Reading Unlimited Program)

Seuling, Barbara. *The Teeny Tiny Woman: An Old English Ghost Tale*. Penguin, 1978.

Shulevitz, Uri. *One Monday Morning*. Atheneum/Macmillan, 1986.

Slobodkina, Esphyr. *Caps for Sale*. Scholastic, 1984.

Sonneborn, Ruth A. *Someone Is Eating the Sun*. Random House, 1974.

Stevenson, James. *Grandpa's Great City Tour: An Alphabet Book*. Greenwillow, 1983.

Szeghy, Joe. *The Lion's Tail*. Scott, Foresman, 1976. (Reading Unlimited Program)

Vigna, Judith. *Gregory's Stitches*. Whitman, 1974.

Viorst, Judith. *Alexander and the Terrible, Horrible, No Good, Very Bad Day*. Atheneum/Macmillan, 1976.

_____. *The Little Boy Who Loved Dirt and Almost Became a Superslob*. Atheneum, 1975.

_____. *The Tenth Good Thing about Barney*. Atheneum/Macmillan, 1975.

Wagner, Justin. *The Bus Ride*. Scott, Foresman, 1976. (Reading Unlimited Program, Level Two)

Williams, Barbara. *Someday, Said Mitchell*. Dutton, 1976.

Wood, Audrey. *The Napping House*. Harcourt Brace Jovanovich, 1984.

_____. *Quick as a Cricket*. Child's Play/Playspaces, 1982.

Zemach, Margot. *Hush, Little Baby*. Dutton, 1975.

Zolotow, Charlotte. *Some Things Go Together*. Harper and Row, 1987.

Rhyme

Aardema, Verna. *Bringing the Rain to Kapiti Plain*. Dial Books, 1983.

Aliki. *Hush Little Baby*. Prentice-Hall, 1968.

Ahlberg, Allan. *Cops and Robbers*. Greenwillow, 1979.

Ahlberg, Janet, and Allan Ahlberg. *Each Peach Pear Plum*. Scholastic, 1985.

Baer, Edith. *Words Are Like Faces. Pantheon, 1980.*

Barchas, Sarah. *I Was Walking down the Road*. Scholastic, 1976.

Berenstain, Stan, and Janice Berenstain. *Bear Detectives*. Beginner Books, 1975.

_____. *The Berenstain Bears and the Missing Dinosaur Bone*. Beginner Books, 1980.

Boynton, Sandra. *Hippos Go Berserk*. Little, Brown, 1986.

Brown, Marc. *Witches Four*. Parents Magazine Press, 1980.

Brown, Margaret Wise. *Goodnight, Moon*. Harper and Row, 1977.

_____. *Yesterday I Climbed a Mountain*. Putnam, 1977.

Cameron, Polly. *I Can't Said the Ant*. Coward/Putnam, 1961.

Charles, Donald. *Time to Rhyme with Calico Cat*. Childrens Press, 1978.

Clifton, Lucille. *Everett Anderson's 1-2-3*. Holt, Rinehart and Winston, 1977.

_____. *Everett Anderson's Nine Month Long*. Holt, Rinehart and Winston, 1978.

Cole, William. *What's Good for a 5-Year-Old?* Holt, Rinehart and Winston, 1971.

Cowley, Joy. *Mrs. Wishy-Washy*. Auckland, N.Z.: Shorthand Publications, 1982. (Distributed by the Wright Group)

Craft, Ruth. *Carrie Hepple's Garden*. Atheneum/Macmillan, 1979.

_____. *The Winter Bear*. Atheneum/Macmillan, 1979.

Crowley, Arthur. *The Boogey Man.* Houghton Mifflin, 1978.

de Regniers, Beatrice Schenk. *May I Bring a Friend?* Atheneum/Macmillan, 1974.

_____. *Red Riding Hood.* Atheneum/Macmillan, 1977.

Edelman, Elaine. *Boom-De-Boom.* Pantheon, 1980.

Eichenberg, Fritz. *Ape in a Cape: An Alphabet of Odd Animals.* Harcourt Brace Jovanovich, 1973.

Elkin, Benjamin. *The King Who Could Not Sleep.* Parents Magazine Press, 1975.

Farber, Norma. *There Once Was a Woman Who Married a Man.* Addison-Wesley, 1978.

Farber, Norma, and Arnold Lobel. *As I Was Crossing Boston Common.* Creative Arts, 1982.

Fisher, Aileen. *Anybody Home?* Crowell, 1980.

_____. *Once We Went on a Picnic.* Harper and Row, 1975.

Ga'g, Wanda. *The ABC Bunny.* Coward, McCann, and Geoghegan/Putnam, 1978.

Gage, Wilson. *Down in the Boondocks.* Greenwillow, 1977.

Gelman, Rita Golden. *The Biggest Sandwich Ever.* Scholastic, 1980.

_____. *Hey Kid!* Avon, 1978.

_____. *More Spaghetti I Say.* Scholastic, 1977.

_____. *Mortimer K. Saves the Day.* Scholastic, 1982.

_____. *Why Can't I Fly?* Scholastic, 1977.

Ginsburg, Mirra. *The Sun's Asleep behind the Hill.* Greenwillow, 1982.

Hall, Katy. *Nothing But Soup.* Follett, 1976.

Harrison, David L. *Detective Bob and the Great Ape Escape.* Parents Magazine Press, 1981.

Hillert, Margaret. *What Is It?* Modern Curriculum Press, 1978.

Hoban, Tana. *One Little Kitten.* Greenwillow, 1979.

Hoberman, Mary Ann. *A House Is a House for Me.* Penguin, 1982.

Holl, Adelaide. *The Parade.* Watts, 1975.

Hutchins, Pat. *Don't Forget the Bacon.* Greenwillow, 1976.

Ipcar, Dahlov. *Hard Scrabble Harvest.* Doubleday, 1976.

Jensen, Virginia A. *Sara and the Door.* Addison-Wesley, 1977.

Kahl, Virginia. *Gunhilde and the Halloween Spell.* Scribner, 1975.

_____. *How Many Dragons Are behind the Door?* Scribner, 1977.

Kalan, Robert. *Jump, Frog, Jump!* Greenwillow, 1981.

Knab, Linda Z. *The Day Is Waiting.* Viking, 1980.

Kraus, Robert. *Ladybug, Ladybug!* Dutton, 1977.

_____. *Whose Mouse Are You?* Macmillan, 1972.

Kuskin, Karla. *A Boy Had a Mother Who Bought Him a Hat.* Houghton Mifflin, 1976.

_____. *Herbert Hated Being Small.* Houghton Mifflin, 1979.

Langstaff, John. *Over in the Meadow.* Harcourt Brace Jovanovich, 1973.

Livermore, Elaine. *Three Little Kittens.* Houghton Mifflin, 1979.

Lobel, Arnold. *On Market Street.* Scholastic, 1985.

Martin, Bill, Jr. *Fire! Fire! Said Mrs. McGuire.* Holt, Rinehart and Winston, 1982.

_____. *The Happy Hippopotami.* Holt, Rinehart and Winston, 1983.

Marzollo, Jean. *Uproar on Hollercat Hill.* Dial Press, 1982.

Melser, June, and Joy Cowley. *Boo-Hoo.* Auckland, N.Z.: Shorthand Publications, 1982. (Distributed by the Wright Group)

_____. *Grandpa Grandpa.* Auckland, N.Z.: Shorthand Publications, 1983. (Distributed by the Wright Group)

_____. *Hairy Bear.* Auckland, N.Z.: Shorthand Publications, 1981. (Distributed by the Wright Group)

_____. *Obadiah.* Auckland, N.Z.: Shorthand Publications, 1982. (Distributed by the Wright Group)

_____. *Poor Old Polly.* Auckland, N.Z.: Shorthand Publications, 1982. (Distributed by the Wright Group)

_____. *Whoosh!* Auckland, N.Z.: Shorthand Publications, 1982. (Distributed by the Wright Group)

Moncure, Jane B. *About Me.* Child's World, 1976.

_____. *Magic Monsters Count to Ten.* Child's World, 1979.

Noodles. *Super Midnight Menu.* Holt, Rinehart and Winston, n.d.

Orbach, Ruth. *Apple Pigs.* Philomel/Putnam, 1981.

Paterson, A. B. *Mulga Bill's Bicycle.* Parents Magazine Press, 1975.

Patrick, Gloria. *A Bug in a Jug and Other Funny Poems.* Scholastic, 1973.

Pavey, Peter, illus. *One Dragon's Dream.* Bradbury, 1979.

Peck, Robert N. *Hamilton.* Little, Brown, 1976.

Peet, Bill. *The Luckiest One of All.* Houghton Mifflin, 1985.

Peterson, Jeanne W. *While the Moon Shines Bright: A Bedtime Chant.* Harper and Row, 1981.

Petie, Haris. *The Seed the Squirrel Dropped.* Prentice-Hall, 1976.

Polhamus, Jean B. *Doctor Dinosaur.* Prentice-Hall, 1975.

Pomerantz, Charlotte. *Ballad of the Long-Tailed Rat.* Macmillan, 1975.

Prelutsky, Jack. *The Mean Old Mean Hyena.* Greenwillow, 1978.

Rand, Paul, and Ann Rand. *I Know a Lot of Things.* Harcourt Brace Jovanovich, 1973.

Schwartz, Stephen. *The Perfect Peach.* Little, Brown, 1977.

Sendak, Maurice. *Chicken Soup with Rice.* Scholastic, 1986.

_____. *Seven Little Monsters.* Harper and Row, 1977.

Seuss, Dr. *I Can Read with My Eyes Shut!* Beginner Books, 1978.

_____. *In a People House.* Random House, 1972.

_____. *Tooth Book.* Random House, 1981.

Shore, Wilma. *Who in the Zoo?* Lippincott, 1976.

Silverstein, Shel. *Giraffe and a Half.* Harper and Row, 1964.

Skorpen, Liesel M. *Plenty for Three.* Coward, 1971.

Slepian, Jan, and Ann Seidler. *The Hungry Thing.* Scholastic, 1972.

Sundgaard, Arnold. *Jethro's Difficult Dinosaur.* Pantheon, 1977.

Thomas, Patricia. *There Are Rocks in My Socks! Said the Ox to the Fox.* Lothrop, Lee and Shepard, 1979.

Watson, Clyde. *Midnight Moon.* Philomel, 1979.

Wells, Rosemary. *Don't Spill It Again, James.* Dial Books, 1977.

_____. *Noisy Nora.* Dial Books, 1980.

Willard, Nancy. *All on a May Morning.* Putnam, 1975.

Yolen, Jane. *All in the Woodland Early: An ABC Book.* Philomel/Putnam, 1983.

Zolotow, Charlotte. *The Hating Book.* Harper and Row, 1969.

(Compiled by Lynn K. Rhodes, University of Colorado at Denver, and Regie Routman, Shaker Heights City School District, Ohio.)

Sing-Along Books

Abisch, Roz, and Boche Kaplan. *Sweet Betsy from Pike.* Dutton, 1970.

Adams, Adrienne, illus. *Bring a Torch, Jeannette Isabella.* Scribner, 1963.

Adams, Pam, illus. *There Was an Old Lady Who Swallowed a Fly.* Child's Play/Playspaces, 1973.

_____. *This Old Man.* Child's Play/Playspaces, n.d.

Aliki. *Go Tell Aunt Rhody.* Macmillan, 1986.

_____. *Hush Little Baby.* Prentice-Hall, 1968.

Bangs, Edward. *Yankee Doodle.* Scholastic, 1980.

Brand, Oscar. *When I First Came to This Land.* Putnam, 1974.

Broomfield, Robert, illus. *The Twelve Days of Christmas: A Picture Book.* McGraw-Hill, 1965.

Bryan, Ashley. *I'm Going to Sing: Black American Spirituals, vol. 2.* Atheneum/Macmillan, 1982.

Chase, Richard. *Billy Boy.* Golden Gate, 1966.

Child, Lydia M. *Over the River and through the Wood.* Scholastic, 1975.

Conover, Chris. *Six Little Ducks.* Crowell, 1976.

Crane, Walter. *The Baby's Opera.* Windmill Books, 1981.

de Paola, Tomie. *The Friendly Beasts: An Old English Christmas Carol.* Putnam, 1981.

de Regniers, Beatrice Schenk. *Catch a Little Fox.* Houghton Mifflin, 1970.

Emberley, Barbara. *Simon's Song.* Prentice-Hall, 1969.

Emberley, Barbara, and Ed Emberley. *One Wide River to Cross.* Scholastic, 1970.

Emberley, Ed. *London Bridge Is Falling Down.* Little, Brown, 1967.

Freschet, Berniece. *The Ants Go Marching.* Scribner, 1973.

Galdone, Paul, illus. *The Star Spangled Banner.* Crowell, 1966. (Words by Francis Scott Key)

Gauch, Patricia L. *On to Widecombe Fair.* Putnam, 1978.

Ginsburg, Mirra. *The Sun's Asleep behind the Hill.* Greenwillow, 1982.

Goudge, Eileen. *I Saw Three Ships.* Coward, McCann and Geoghegan, 1969.

Graboff, Abner. *Old MacDonald Had a Farm.* Scholastic, 1970.

Hart, Jane, ed. *Singing Bee! A Collection of Favorite Children's Songs.* Lothrop, Lee and Shepard, 1982.

Hazen, Barbara. *Frere Jacques.* Lippincott, 1973.

Hurd, Thacher. *Mama Don't Allow.* Harper and Row, 1985.

Ipcar, Dahlov. *The Cat Came Back.* Knopf, 1971.

Jeffers, Susan. *All the Pretty Horses.* Scholastic, 1985.

Johnson, James W., and J. R. Johnson. *Lift Every Voice and Sing.* Hawthorn, 1970.

Karasz, Ilonka. *The Twelve Days of Christmas.* Harper and Row, 1949.

Keats, Ezra Jack, illus. *Over in the Meadow.* Scholastic Books, 1985. (Words by Olive A. Wadsworth)

_____. *The Little Drummer Boy.* Macmillan, 1972. (Words and music by K. Davis, H. Onorati, and H. Simeone)

Kellogg, Steven. *There Was an Old Woman.* Four Winds/Scholastic, 1980.

Kennedy, Jimmy. *The Teddy Bears' Picnic.* Green Tiger Press, 1983.

Kent, Jack. *Jack Kent's Twelve Days of Christmas*. Parents Magazine Press, 1973.

Langstaff, John. *Hot Cross Buns and Other Old Street Cries*. Atheneum, 1978.

Langstaff, John, ed. *Oh, A-Hunting We Will Go*. Atheneum/Macmillan, 1974.

Langstaff, John, et al. *The Swapping Boy*. Harcourt Brace Jovanovich, 1960.

Langstaff, John, and David Gentleman. *The Golden Vanity*. Harcourt Brace Jovanovich, 1972.

Langstaff, John, and Joe Krush. *Ol' Dan Tucker*. Harcourt Brace Jovanovich, 1963.

Langstaff, John, and Feodor Rojankovsky. *Frog Went A-Courtin'*. Harcourt Brace Jovanovich, 1955.

_____. *Over in the Meadow*. Harcourt Brace Jovanovich, 1973.

Mills, Alan, and Rose Bonne. *I Know an Old Lady*. Rand McNally, 1961.

Nic Leodhas, Sorche. *Always Room for One More*. Holt, Rinehart and Winston, 1965.

_____. *Kellyburn Braes*. Holt, Rinehart and Winston, 1968.

Paterson, A. B., illus. *Waltzing Matilda*. Holt, Rinehart and Winston, 1972.

Price, Christine. *Widdecombe Fair*. Warne, 1968.

Quackenbush, Robert. *Clementine*. Lippincott, 1974.

_____. *Go Tell Aunt Rhody*. Lippincott, 1973.

_____. *The Man on the Flying Trapeze: The Circus Life of Emmett Kelly Sr. Told with Pictures and Song!* Lippincott, 1975.

_____. *Old MacDonald Had a Farm*. Lippincott, 1972.

_____. *Pop! Goes the Weasel and Yankee Doodle: New York in 1776 and Today, with Songs and Pictures*. Lippincott, 1976.

_____. *She'll be Comin' 'Round the Mountain*. Lippincott, 1973.

_____. *Skip to My Lou*. Harper and Row, 1975.

_____. *There'll Be a Hot Time in the Old Town Tonight*. Lippincott, 1974.

Rounds, Glenn, illus. *Casey Jones: The Story of a Brave Engineer*. Golden Gate/Childrens Press, 1968.

_____. *The Strawberry Roan*. Golden Gate/Childrens Press, 1970.

_____. *Sweet Betsy from Pike*. Golden Gate/Childrens Press, 1973.

Rourke, Constance. *Davy Crockett*. Harcourt Brace Jovanovich, 1955.

Sawyer, Ruth. *Joy to the World*. Little, Brown, 1966.

Seeger, Pete, and Charles Seeger. *The Foolish Frog*. Macmillan, 1973.

Schackburg, Richard. *Yankee Doodle.* Prentice-Hall, 1965.

Spier, Peter. *The Erie Canal.* Doubleday, 1970.

_____. *The Fox Went Out on a Chilly Night.* Doubleday, 1961.

_____. *London Bridge Is Falling Down.* Doubleday, 1985.

_____. *The Star-Spangled Banner.* Doubleday, 1986.

Watson, Clyde. *Father Fox's Feast of Songs.* Philomel/Putnam, 1983.

_____. *Fisherman Lullabies.* World, 1968.

Westcott, Nadine Bernard. *I Know an Old Lady Who Swallowed a Fly.* Atlantic Monthly/Little, Brown, 1980.

Yulya. *Bears Are Sleeping.* Scribner, 1967.

Zemach, Harve. *Mommy, Buy Me a China Doll.* Farrar, Straus and Giroux, 1975.

Zemach, Margot, illus. *Hush Little Baby.* Dutton, 1975.

Zuromskis, Diane, illus. *The Farmer in the Dell.* Little, Brown, 1978.

(Compiled by Yetta M. Goodman, University of Arizona, Tucson, and Ann Marek, Department of Human Resources, Sparks, Nevada.)

Children's Magazines

Boy's Life. Age range: 8–18. Boys, especially those involved in scouting. Address: Boy Scouts of America, 1325 Walnut Hill Lane, Irving, TX 75038-3096.

Canada. Address: Scholastic-TAB Publications Ltd., 123 Newkirk Road, Richmond Hill, Ontario, Canada L4C 3G5.

Chickadee. Age range: 4–8. The environment. Address: The Young Naturalist Foundation, Box 11314, Des Moines, IA 50347.

Child Life. Age range: 8–11. Health, safety, and nutrition. Address: P.O. Box 10681, Des Moines, IA 50381.

Children's Playmate. Age range: 5–8. Health, safety, and nutrition. Address: P.O. Box 10242, Des Moines, IA 50381.

Cobblestone: The History Magazine for Young People. Age range: 8–14. American History. Address: 20 Grove Street, Peterborough, NH 03458.

Cricket: The Magazine for Children. Age range: 6–12. Literary magazine for young people. Address: Box 2672, Boulder, CO 80321.

Current Events, Read, and *Know Your World.* Current events. Address: Subscription Department, *Weekly Reader, Secondary Periodicals, P.O. Box 16686, Columbus, OH 43216.*

The Electric Company. Age range: 6–10. General interest reading. Address: P.O. Box 2896, Boulder, CO 80322.

Family Computing. Age range: Entire family. Families who own or are about to own their first computer. Address: Neodata Services, P.O. Box 2511, Boulder, CO 80322.

Highlights for Children. Age range: 2–12. General interest. Address: P.O. Box 269, Columbus, OH 43272-0002.

Humpty Dumpty's Magazine. Age range: 4–6. Health, safety, and nutrition. Address: P.O. Box 10225, Des Moines, IA 50381.

Jack and Jill. Age range: 7–10. Health, safety, nutrition. Address: P.O. Box 10222, Des Moines, IA 50381.

Muppet Magazine. Age range: 7–13. Contemporary humor magazine. Address: 300 Madison Avenue, New York, NY 10017.

National Geographic World. Age range: 8–13. Nonfiction of general interest. Address: Box 2330, Washington, DC 20013.

Peanut Butter. Age range: 5–7. Nature, news, and activities. Address: 730 Broadway, New York, NY 10003.

Penny Power. Age range: 8–14. Consumer education. Address: P.O. Box 2859, Boulder, CO 80321.

Pennywhistle Press. Age range: 4–12. General interest. Weekly feature available through purchase of subscribing newspaper. Syndication information: Box 500-P, Washington, DC 20044.

Ranger Rick. Age range: 6–12. Nature study, Ranger Rick's Nature Club Members. Address: Ranger Rick's Nature Magazine, The National Wildlife Federation, 1412 16th Street NW, Washington, DC 20036.

Scienceland. Age range: 5–8. Nurtures scientific thinking. Address: 501 Fifth Avenue, Suite 2102, New York, NY 10017-6165.

Seedling Series Short Story. Age range: 10–12. Short stories from all over the world. Address: P.O. Box 405, Great Neck, NY 11022.

Sesame Street. Age range: 2–6. Preschool prereading. Address: P.O. Box 2896, Boulder, CO 80322.

Stickers and Stuff Magazine (formerly *Stickers!*). Age range: 6–14. Sticker enthusiasts. Address: Ira Friedman Inc., 10 Columbus Circle, Suite 1300, New York, NY 10019.

Stone Soup. Age range: 6–13. Literary magazine. Address: P.O. Box 83, Santa Cruz, CA 95063.

3-2-1 Contact. Age range: 8–14. Science. Address: Box 2896, Boulder, CO 80322.

Turtle Magazine for Preschool Kids. Age range: 2–5. Preschool health, safety, and nutrition. Address: P.O. Box 10222, Des Moines, IA 50381.

Your Big Backyard. Age range: 3–5. Nature. Address: The National Wildlife Federation, 1412 16th Street, NW, Washington, DC 20036.

*(Compiled by Educational Press Association of America;
Nancy Wiseman Seminoff, Winona State University,
Minnesota.)*

Publishers of Children's Writing

Young and Unpublished Authors

Lacuna, Lacuna Press, Box 10957, St. Louis, MO 63135. Editor:
Beth Ivie.

3-2-1 Contact, Children's Television Workshop, One Lincoln
Plaza, New York, NY 10023. Editor: Jonathan Rosenbloom.

Piedmont Literary Review, Piedmont Literary Society, Box 3656,
Danville, VA 24541. Editor: David Craig.

Jump River Review, Jump River Press, Inc., P.O. Box 1151, Me-
dina, OH 44256. Editor: Mark Bruner.

The Denver Quarterly. University of Denver, Denver, CO 80208.
Editor: David Milofsky.

▼

Appendix B

Selected Computer Software for Language & Literacy Development

Alice in Wonderland
    Queue, Inc.
    Remembering a sequence of events

Animal Alphabet and Other Things
    McGraw-Hill Media
    Letter recognition, alphabetical order

Bald-Headed Chicken, The
    D. C. Heath & Company
    Language experience

Bank Street Writer III
    The Scholastic Software, Inc.
    Word processing

Brand New View, A
    D. C. Heath & Company
    Language experience

Children's Writing & Publishing Center
    The Learning Company
    Creative writing, creating printed material

Clue in on Phonics
    Gamco Industries, Inc.
    Practice with letter sounds

Color 'n' Canvas
    Wings for Learning
    Visual art, drawing, painting, symmetry

Color Me
    Mindscape, Inc.
    Drawing, creating

Dr. Peet's Talk/Writer
    Hartley Courseware, Inc.
    Language exploration and skills

Early Childhood Program
    Tapestry Learning
    Language Independence, prediction, etc.

Emerging Literacy Program
    Tapestry Learning
    Language, independence, prediction, etc.

ESL Writer
    Scholastic Software, Inc.
    Word processing

First Letter Fun
    MECC
    Letter recognition

Fun From A to Z
    MECC
    Alphabet skills practice

Grammar Toy Shop
    MECC
    Nouns, verbs, adjectives

Great Leap, A
    D. C. Heath & Company
    Language experience

I Love You in the Sky
    Butterfly Tapestry Learning
    Language experience, thematic material

Jack and the Beanstalk
    Tom Snyder Productions, Inc.
    Letter and word recognition, reading stories

Just Around the Block
    D. C. Heath & Company
    Language experience

KidsTime
    Great Wave Software
    Letters, numbers, matching, writing, music

KidTalk
    First Byte, Inc.
    Language experience

Magic Slate
    Sunburst Communications, Inc.
    Word processing

Mickey's Magic
    Reader Sunburst Communications, Inc.
    Reading for enjoyment

Milliken Storyteller
    The Milliken Publishing Co.
    Early reading skills

Muppet Slate
    Sunburst Communications, Inc.
    Language experiences

Muppet Word Book
Sunburst Communications, Inc.:
Letters and words

My Words
Hartley Courseware, Inc.
Language experience

Not Too Messy, Not Too Neat
D. C. Heath & Company
Language experience

Paint With Words
MECC
Word recognition

Phonics Plus
Stone & Associates
Letter/word relationships

Phonics Prime Time: Initials
MECC
Initial consonant, phonic skills

Playroom, The
Broderbund Software
Letters, numbers, and time

Primary Editor Plus
IBM Educational Systems
Word processing, drawing,
making banners

Princess and the Pea, The
William K. Bradford Publishing
Creative writing

Print Shop
Broderbund
Making cards, posters,
banners

Reader Rabbit
The Learning Company
Basic reading skills/compre-
hension

Reading and Me
Davidson and Associates, Inc.
Matching, classifying, recogniz-
ing letters & word

Reading Comprehension: Level 1
Houghton Mifflin Co.
Reading comprehension skills

Rosie the Counting Rabbit
D. C. Heath & Company
Language experience

Sesame Street First Writer
Hi Tech Expressions
Writing and printing words,
sentences, and stories

Sleepy Brown Cow, The
D. C. Heath & Company
Language experience

Sound Ideas: Consonants
Houghton Mifflin Co.
Consonant sounds

Sound Ideas: Vowels
Houghton Mifflin Co.
Five vowel sounds (long,
short) and y

Sound Ideas: Word Attack
Houghton Mifflin Co.
Consonant blends, clusters
and digraphs

Spelling Puzzles and Tests
MECC
Practice spelling

Stickybear Parts of Speech
Optimum Resource, Inc.
Parts of speech

Stickybear Reading
Optimum Resource, Inc.
Word and sentence fun

Stone Soup
William K. Bradford Publishing
Creative writing

Storybook Weaver
MECC
Create, design stories

Talking Textwriter
Scholastic Software, Inc.
Exploration of written language

Three Little Pigs, The
William K. Bradford Publishing
Creative writing

Tiger's Tales
Sunburst Communications, Inc.
Reading vocabulary & compre-
hension

Touch & Write
Sunburst Communications, Inc.
Printing practice

What Makes a Dinosaur Sore?
D. C. Heath & Company
Language experience

Where Did My Toothbrush Go?
D. C. Heath & Company
Language experience

Word Munchers
MECC
Vowel-sound discrimination

Write On: Primary Level
Humanities Software
Writing

Note: Detailed information on these
and many other software programs
can be found in the *High/Scope Survey of Early Childhood Software*, an
annual compilation of the latest programs rated as to their developmental appropriateness for children
aged 3 to 8. Over 400 programs are
rated each year. The *Survey* can be
purchased from the High/Scope
Press, 600 N. River St., Ypsilanti, MI
48198, 313/485-2000
FAX 313/485-0704.

▼

Appendix C:

Writing/Reading Checklists & Inventories

Teachers have a wide array of instruments to choose from when gathering information about the characteristics of children and the progress they are making in developing language and literacy proficiency. Some of these are presented in this appendix.

A Checklist

The High/Scope **Key Experience Checklist**, presented on the next three pages, covers major language and literacy milestones and is useful for documenting children's progress over time. It also is a valuable guide for teachers to use in planning instruction. In addition, High/Scope's **K–3 Observation Card** suggests a framework for recording information about language and literacy and other main content areas. It also draws attention to the need to record observations about children's social relationships in the classroom and the extent to which children demonstrate initiative and are motivated to learn. The **Student Progress Report**, also presented in this appendix, provides a practical system for summarizing checklist milestones and classroom observations.

High/Scope Language and Literacy Key Experience Checklist

Speaking & Listening	**Dates Observed**

☐ Speaks own language or dialect

☐ Asks and answers questions

☐ States facts and observations in own words

☐ Uses language to solve problems

☐ Participates in singing, storytelling, poetic and dramatic activities

☐ Makes and uses recordings

☐ Recalls thoughts and observations in a purposeful context

☐ Acquires, strengthens, and extends speaking and listening skills:

  ☐ Discusses to clarify observations or to better follow directions

  ☐ Discusses to expand speaking and listening vocabulary

  ☐ Discusses to strengthen critical thinking and problem-solving abilities

High/Scope Language and Literacy Key Experience Checklist

Writing	**Dates Observed**

☐ Observes the connections between spoken and written language

☐ Writes in unconventional forms:

- ◻ Scribbles

- ◻ Drawings

- ◻ Letters—random or patterned, possibly including elements of names copied from the environment

- ◻ Invented spellings—of initial sounds, syllabic sounds, concluding sounds, and intermediate sounds

☐ Writes in conventional forms

☐ Expresses thoughts in writing

☐ Shares writing in a purposeful context

☐ Uses writing equipment (e.g., computers, typewriters)

☐ Writes in specific content areas

☐ Acquires, strengthens, and extends writing skills:

- ◻ Letter formation

- ◻ Sentence and paragraph formation

- ◻ Capitalization, punctuation, and grammatical usage

- ◻ Spelling

- ◻ Editing and proofreading for mechanics, content, and style

☐ Expands the forms of composition:

- ◻ Expressive mode

- ◻ Transactional mode—expository, argumentative, descriptive

- ◻ Poetic mode—narrative poetry

☐ Publishes selected compositions

High/Scope Language and Literacy Key Experience Checklist

Reading	Dates Observed

☐ Experiences varied genres of children's literature

☐ Reads own compositions

☐ Reads and listens to others read in a purposeful context

☐ Uses audio and/or video recordings in reading experiences

☐ Reads in specific content areas

☐ Acquires, strengthens, and extends specific reading skills:

    ▫ Auditory discrimination

    ▫ Letter recognition

    ▫ Decoding—phonetic analysis (letter/sound associations, factors affecting sounds, syllabication); structural analysis (forms, prefixes, suffixes)

    ▫ Vocabulary development

☐ Expands comprehension and fluency skills:

    ▫ Activating prior knowledge

    ▫ Determining purpose, considering context, making predictions

    ▫ Developing strategies for interpreting narrative and expository text

    ▫ Reading varied genres of children's literature

An Observation Form

Teachers use multiple formats to **record** their **observations** of children's performance and progress in classrooms. The **K–3 Observation Card** offers one possibility:

Teacher's Name:	Child's Name:	
LANGUAGE AND LITERACY	**MATHEMATICS AND SCIENCE**	**THE ARTS**
K-3 Observation Card		**© 1990 High/Scope Foundation**

Front of High/Scope's K–3 Observation Card

Teacher's Name:	Child's Name:	
MOTIVATION AND INITIATIVE	**SOCIAL RELATIONS**	**MOVEMENT**
K-3 Observation Card		**© 1990 High/Scope Foundation**

Back of High/Scope's K–3 Observation Card

A Progress Report

Teachers **summarize** the information gathered in check-lists, performance samples, anecdotal observations, and portfolios and communicate the analysis to parents. The **High/Scope Student Progress Report**, presented on this and the following page, offers such a summary:

High/Scope Student Progress Report

Dear Parent:

This report summarizes my observations of the behavior and products of your child, _____ during the period from __/__/__ to __/__/__. Included with it are:

- my daily observations of events and products representing your child's behavior pertaining to the topics listed

- checklists on your child's behavior that I have completed

- products made by your child, such as pages of writing and computation, pictures made and photographs taken, audiotapes, and videotapes.

This information will give you an idea of your child's developmental status and daily achievements. For a time, we have become partners in teaching your child. I trust that you will communicate with me about your child freely and often.

Sincerely,

_____

LANGUAGE AND LITERACY (speaking, listening, reading, writing, interest in reading and writing)

```

```

MATHEMATICS AND SCIENCE (classifying, comparing, counting, adding, subtracting, measuring, using time concepts, graphing, interpreting data)

```

```

Front of the High/Scope Student Progress Report

THE ARTS (drawing, painting, making, building, pretending, role playing)

```

```

MOTIVATION AND INITIATIVE (interest in learning, making decisions, planning, organizing activities, reviewing activities, following classroom rules)

```

```

SOCIAL RELATIONS (getting along with adults and classmates, having classmate friends, interpersonal problem solving, expressing feelings acceptably)

```

```

MOVEMENT (following movement directions, moving the body, moving with objects, moving creatively, expressing beat, moving with others to a beat)

```

```

OTHER (specify any other curriculum topic that has received attention)

```

```

Back of the High/Scope Student Progress Report

Inventories

Standardized tests have become a staple in measuring
children's skill acquisition, but they also have come under
frequent attack because they primarily measure conventional reading and writing. This type of assessment often
ignores actual classroom activities. It ignores early literacy progress children make before they read and write
conventionally, and the resulting information offers
little practical assistance to teachers in planning further
instruction.

Chittendon's and Courtney's *Observation Forms—
Assessment of Young Children's Reading* (Chittendon &
Courtney, 1989); Schickedanz's *Word Creation Strategies
Record Sheet* (Schickendanz, 1989); and Sulzby's *Simpli-
fied Version of a Classification Scheme for Children's
Emergent Reading of Favorite Storybooks* (Sulzby, 1985)
offer useful alternatives.

As teachers focus attention on children by using these
forms of assessment, they are guided to plan additional
appropriate literacy events and activities that extend and
strengthen the children's skills.

As illustrated by the observation forms* presented on
the next two pages, Edward Chittendon and Rosalea
Courtney advocate the *documentation* of children's literacy
development through an analysis of children's interest in
classroom situations or settings.

Observation Forms

Description of child's work and behavior for each context
(cite specific indications of skills or knowledge)

Settings and Activities	Examples of Child's Activities
Story Time: Teacher reads to class (responses to story line; child's comments, questions, elaborations)	
Independent Reading: Book Time (nature of books child chooses or brings in; process of selecting; quiet or social reading)	
Writing (journal stories, alphabet, dictation)	
Reading Group/Individual (oral reading strategies: discussion of text, responses to instruction)	
Reading Related Activities Tasks (responses to assignments or discussion focusing on word letter properties, word games/ experience charts)	
Informal Settings (use of language in play, jokes, story-telling, conversation)	
Books and Print as Resource (use of books for projects; attention to signs, labels, names; locating information)	
Other	

Description of children's activities in classroom settings: Chittendon's and Courtney's Observation Forms—Assessment of Young Children's Reading*

*Reprinted with permission of Edward Chittenden and the International Reading Association. Appears in Chittenden, E., & Courtney, R. (1989). Assessment of young children's reading: Documentation as an alternative to testing (Figure 1, Chapter 9). In Dorothy S. Strickland & Lesley M. Morrow (Eds.), *Emerging literacy: Young children learn to read and write* (pp. 110–111). Newark, DE: International Reading Association.

Observation Forms

Child _____ Grade _____ Teacher _____ Date _____

Ratings of child's interest/investment in different classroom contexts
(based on observations over a period of several weeks)

Settings and Activities	Degree of Interest/Investment		
	Very Interested, Intense	Moderately Interested	Uninterested, Attention Is Elsewhere
Story Time: Teacher reads to class (responses to story line; child's comments, questions, elaborations)	____ ____	____ ____	____ ____
Independent Reading: Book Time (nature of books child chooses or brings in, process of selecting, quiet or social reading)	____ ____	____ ____	____
Writing (journal, stories, alphabet, dictation)	____ ____	____ ____	____ ____
Reading Group/Individual (oral reading strategies: discussion of text, responses to instruction)	____ ____	____ ____	____ ____
Reading Related Activities Tasks (responses to assignments or discussions focusing on word letter properties, word games/ experience charts)	____ ____	____ ____	____
Informal Settings (use of language in play, jokes, story-telling, conversation)	____ ____	____ ____	____ ____
Books and Print as Resource (use of books for projects; attention to signs, labels, names; locating information)	____	____	____
Other	____	____	____

Ratings of children's interest in classroom activities: Observation Forms—Assessment of Young Children's Reading*

*Reprinted with permission of Edward Chittenden and the International Reading Association. Appears in Chittenden, E., & Courtney, R. (1989). Assessment of young children's reading: Documentation as an alternative to testing (Figure 1, Chapter 9). In Dorothy S. Strickland & Lesley M. Morrow (Eds.), *Emerging literacy: Young children learn to read and write* (pp. 110–111). Newark, DE: International Reading Association.

In her record sheet and accompanying instructions*, presented on this and the following page, Judith Schickendanz records information about the strategies preschool and kindergarten children employ as they acquire skills in creating words.

Word Creation Strategies Record Sheet*

Strategy Used	Description of Incident	Date
Physical Relationship		
Visual Design		
Syllabic Hypothesis		
Letter Strings (visual rules)		
Authority Based (asking for or copying spellings)		
Early Phonemic (invented spellings)		
Transitional Phonemic		

*Boston University Early Childhood Learning Laboratory

Schickedanz's Word Creation Strategies Record Sheet*

---

*Reprinted with permission of Judith A. Schickedanz and the International Reading Association. Appears in Schickedanz, Judith A. (1989). The place of specific skills in preschool and kindergarten. In Dorothy S. Strickland & Lesley M. Morrow (Eds.), *Emerging literacy: Young children learn to read and write* (pp. 102–103). Newark, DE: International Reading Association.

Key to Word Creation Strategies Record Sheet

Physical Relationship. Child tries to relate the number or the appearance of marks to some physical aspect of the object or person represented. The child might use three marks, for example, to write her name if she is three years old.

Visual Design. Child accepts the arbitrary nature of words—that they do not resemble their referents physically. The child tries to recreate some designs. The first design attempted is often the child's name. Placeholders—other letters, circles, solid dots, or vertical lines—often are used in the place of those letters that the child cannot form.

Syllabic Hypothesis. Child realizes there is a relationship between the oral and written versions of words and also that spoken words can be segmented into "beats" or syllables. The child codes words syllabically, using one mark for each of a word's syllables.

Letter Strings (visual rules). Children create words by stringing letters together so that they look like words. They use several rules. (1) Don't use too many letters. (2) Don't use too few letters. (3) Use a variety of letters, with not more than two of the same letter in succession. (4) Rearrange the same letters to make different words. Children also ask, "What word is this?"

Authority Based. This strategy often follows on the heels of the letter string strategy, apparently because children decide that it is more efficient to ask for spellings, since so many of their letter strings yield nonwords. Children ask for spellings of whole words, or they copy known words from environmental print or books.

Early Phonemic. Children begin to generate their own words by coding sounds they hear—an idea they might get as adults provide spellings and make letter-sound associations explicit when giving spellings during the time that children are using an Authority Based strategy. Independent spelling may be delayed in children who receive complex answers to their spelling questions during the early part of this stage. No known disadvantage is associated with a delay of this kind.

Transitional Phonemic. Children begin to realize that their sound based spellings do not look quite like words they see in the environment and that specific spellings they generate are not always identical to ones they see elsewhere. Children often become dissatisfied with their own spellings and begin again to ask for whole word spellings, or they generate a spelling on their own and ask, "Is that right?" This strategy is not common among preschoolers, although children who read early often use it, presumably because they have more visual information about words than do typical preschoolers.

Note. The order of use for the strategies typically follows the order of this list, although different environments provide different information to children, which can result in variations in children's word creation strategy development.

Schickedanz's Key to the Word Creation Strategies Record Sheet *

*Reprinted with permission of Judith A. Schickedanz and the International Reading Association. Appears in Schickendanz, Judith A. (1989). The place of specific skills in preschool and kindergarten. In Dorothy S. Strickland & Lesley M. Morrow (Eds.), *Emerging literacy: Young children learn to read and write* (pp. 102–103). Newark, DE: International Reading Association.

Elizabeth Sulzby's *Simplified Version of a Classification Scheme for Children's Emergent Reading of Favorite Storybooks**, presented on this and the following page, assesses the emergent reading of preschool and kindergarten students.

Simplified Version of Sulzby's (1985) Classification Scheme for Children's Emergent Reading of Favorite Storybooks: Record Form for Classroom Teachers

This record form accompanies the Category Summaries for emergent reading of favorite storybooks. It may be used by classroom teachers to assess children's reading attempts.

Be certain that the child has selected a "favorite storybook" (one that he or she likes a lot and one that has been read repeatedly to the child).

Ask the child, "Read me your book." Listen attentively and note where the child is looking. Judge which of the five categories of speech the child's emergent reading attempt fits into and check the appropriate box. (Tape recording may help when you first try this.) List the book's title and any other comments you want to remember.

Sulzby's simplified record form

---

*Elizabeth Sulzby, Copyright 1986. Reprinted with permission of the author. Appears in Sulzby, E., & Barnhart, J. (1990). The developing kindergartner: All our children emerge as writers and readers. In J. S. McKee (Ed.), *The developing kindergarten: Programs, children, and teachers* (pp. 201–224). Ann Arbor, MI: MiAEYC.

Broad Categories	Brief Explanation of Categories
1. Attending to Pictures, Not Forming Stories	The child is "reading" by looking at the storybook's pictures. The child's speech is *just* about the picture in view: the child is not "weaving a story" across the pages. (Subcategories are "labelling and commenting" and "following the action.")
2. Attending to Pictures, Forming *ORAL* Stories	The child is "reading by looking at the storybook's pictures. The child's speech weaves a story across the pages but the wording and the intonation are like that of someone telling a story, either like a conversation about the pictures or like a fully recited story, in which the listener can see the pictures (and often *must* see them to understand the child's story). (Subcategories are "dialogic storytelling" and "monologic storytelling.")
3. Attending to Pictures, Reading and Storytelling mixed	This category for the simplified version was originally the first subcategory of (4). It fits between (2) and (4) and is easier to understand if it is treated separately. The child is "reading" by looking at the storybook's pictures. The child's speech fluctuates between sounding like a storyteller, with oral intonation, and sounding like a reader, with reading intonation. To fit this category, the majority of the reading attempt must show fluctuations between storytelling and reading.
4. Attending to Pictures, Forming *WRITTEN* Stories	The child is "reading" by looking at the storybook's pictures. The child's speech sounds as if the child is reading, both in the wording and intonation. The listener does not need to look at the pictures (or rarely does) in order to understand the story. If the listener closes his/her eyes, most of the time he or she would think the child is reading from print. (Subcategories are "reading similar-to-original story," and "reading verbatim-like story.")
5. Attending to Print	There are four subcategories of attending to print. Only the *final* one is what is typically called "real reading.;" In the others the child is exploring the print by such strategies as refusing to read based on print-related reasons, or using only some of the aspects of print. (Subcategories are "refusing to read based on print awareness," "reading aspectually," "reading with strategies imbalanced," and "reading independently" or "conventional reading.")

Brief explanation of categories in Sulzby's Simplified Classification Scheme for Children's Emergent Reading of Favorite Storybooks

Note from Elizabeth Sulzby: To use this Scheme, always use storybooks that children have had read to them repeatedly, especially the ones that they request themselves or pick up voluntarily. (It has been used with other kinds of books; sometimes it works and sometimes it does not.) The Simplified Scheme is based upon an 11-point Classification Scheme, and the subcategories mentioned above are part of the 11-point Scheme. The Sulzby Classification Scheme was published first in E. Sulzby (1985). Children's emergent reading of favorite storybooks: A developmental study. *Reading Research Quarterly, 20,* 458–481. That Scheme, along with examples from children aged 2–4, also appears in E. Sulzby (1988). A study of children's early reading development. In A. D. Pellegrini (Ed.), *Psychological bases for early education* (pp. 39–75). Chichester, England: Wiley. The Simplified Scheme is particularly useful until the point when the child begins to attend fairly consistently to the print. At that time, teachers need to consult the 11-point scheme for the finer detail of the transition to conventional literacy.

Related Materials

Teachers might consider using informal reading inventories such as Mary Wood's and Alden Moe's **Analytic Reading Inventory**, fourth edition; Jerry Johns's **Basic Reading Inventory**, fourth edition; Nicholas Silvarali's **Classroom Reading Inventory**, sixth edition; and Paul Burns's and Betty Roe's **Informal Reading Inventory**, third edition. Information about these and other inventories for assessing the conventional literacy development of young children is available in John Pikulski's discussion of informal reading inventories in the March 1990 issue of *The Reading Teacher*.

Teachers also may find the work of Marie Clay valuable in observing children's reading behavior and individual progress. Clay's "concepts about print" tests are entitled **Sand** (Clay, 1972) and **Stones** (Clay, 1979) and offer a valuable guide for teachers about changes in children's skills during early instruction.

About the Author

With an enduring commitment to understanding the dynamic process inherent in young children's language and literacy development, Jane Maehr joined the High/Scope Foundation as a curriculum consultant after nearly 20 years of classroom experience in public, private, and overseas schools. She has taught children in kindergarten and in grades one through four.

Jane M. Maehr

Ms. Maehr also has extensive experience in preservice teacher training and program development. She conducts inservice training workshops across the country on High/Scope's K–3 curriculum approach. She also conducts training workshops for staff at various National Follow Through sites using High/Scope's K–3 Curriculum.

Her other notable achievements include writing for children, developing an annotated bibliography of Middle Eastern literature for children, and writing about emergent literacy and early elementary issues for various teacher education publications.

Ms. Maehr holds a graduate degree in Elementary and Early Childhood Education from the University of Illinois and is a certified elementary teacher.